MORE ADVANCE PRA

THE BUSINESS OF COUNTERTERRORISM

"While public-private partnerships (PPPs) are certainly on the forefront of U.S. achievements in the domestic response to the terrorist threat, much writing on them doesn't present the complete picture. Unlike its predecessors, *The Business of Counterterrorism* provides a comprehensive and direct view of the growing importance of PPPs to homeland security. An outstanding contribution by Busch and Givens."

—General Norton Schwartz, United States Air Force (retired);
President and CEO, Business Executives for National Security (BENS)

"Busch and Givens present a prolific view of counterterrorism in the context of public and private partnerships. In this unique analysis, the authors leverage historical events (both positive and tragic) to establish a foundation for sustaining and improving our nation's security. Much can be learned from reading this work; may it be read by many and spawn further thought and discussion!"

—Jeffrey D. Wassmer, CEO and Chairman of the Board, Spectrum;
Chairman of the Virginia Port Authority

"For those of us who were in the trenches in the beginning, I wish we would have had this common sense book to read."

—From the Foreword, Admiral James M. Loy, Acting Secretary,
Department of Homeland Security, 2005;
Deputy Secretary of Homeland Security, 2003–2005;
Administrator, Transportation Security Administration, 2002–2003;
Commandant, United States Coast Guard, 1998–2002

THE BUSINESS OF
COUNTERTERRORISM

TERRORISM STUDIES

Lori J. Underwood
General Editor

Vol. 4

This book is part of the Peter Lang academic list.
Every volume is peer reviewed and meets
the highest quality standards for content and production.

PETER LANG
New York • Washington, D.C./Baltimore • Bern
Frankfurt • Berlin • Brussels • Vienna • Oxford

Nathan E. Busch & Austen D. Givens

THE BUSINESS OF COUNTERTERRORISM

Public-Private Partnerships in Homeland Security

PETER LANG
New York • Washington, D.C./Baltimore • Bern
Frankfurt • Berlin • Brussels • Vienna • Oxford

Library of Congress Cataloging-in-Publication Data

Busch, Nathan E.
The business of counterterrorism: public-private partnerships
in homeland security / Nathan E. Busch, Austen D. Givens.
pages cm. — (Terrorism studies; 4)
Includes bibliographical references and index.
1. Terrorism—Prevention—United States. 2. Public-private sector
cooperation—United States. 3. National security—
United States. I. Givens, Austen D. II. Title.
HV6432.B874   363.325'170973—dc 3   2013046986
ISBN 978-1-4331-1955-2 (hardcover)
ISBN 978-1-4331-1954-5 (paperback)
ISBN 978-1-4539-1294-2 (e-book)
ISSN 2167-8545

Bibliographic information published by **Die Deutsche Nationalbibliothek**.
Die Deutsche Nationalbibliothek lists this publication in the "Deutsche
Nationalbibliografie"; detailed bibliographic data is available
on the Internet at http://dnb.d-nb.de/.

Cover design by Amy Lois Mayberry
Cover photo by John Franco

The paper in this book meets the guidelines for permanence and durability
of the Committee on Production Guidelines for Book Longevity
of the Council of Library Resources.

Printed in the United States of America

For Elizabeth and Rachel

Contents

Foreword

When I encountered audiences in the first year or so after the tragedy of September 11th, 2001, the question I was most often asked was: "When are we going to get back to 'normal'?" By "normal," the questioner was referring to the life we knew before 9/11. The answer to the question was self-evident: NEVER! Instead, there was a "new normal," and our challenge was first to understand it and then to do the learning necessary to secure our homeland in the face of this "new normal."

Long before PPP was a recognizable acronym for public-private partnerships, it became clear to many leaders in the stand-up process of the Department of Homeland Security (DHS) that we could accomplish more—and do so more swiftly, efficiently, and effectively—if we reached out to the private sector for assistance. Authors Nathan Busch and Austen Givens have now inventoried and documented for the first time many of the elements that comprise one of the key pathways to what I believe will be a critical tool in securing our homeland.

Over this first decade in the "new normal" we have learned many lessons. Busch and Givens document many of them—especially those learned in the aftermath of natural catastrophes such as Hurricane Katrina or man-made failures such as the Strategic Border Initiative (SBInet). Dozens of commissions and lessons learned studies have helped to shape our understanding of and design efforts toward solving the challenges of the "new normal."

One of these lessons learned *and* a harbinger of things to come is that PPPs have evolved and will continue to evolve in the years ahead. For example, when we were challenged to stand up the new

Transportation Security Administration (TSA), Congress outlined 36 specific steps to be taken with hard deadlines provided for each step. I am convinced that we would still be working on steps #8 or #9 of this process if I had not reached out to industry. Dozens of companies, including large system integrators, airlines, trade associations, and leading edge research and development firms leaned forward and made priceless contributions in standing up the TSA. We met every deadline. Busch and Givens provide the framework for not only recognizing the first decade's collaboration but the value of sustaining that collaboration into the future.

We are now attempting to learn and understand how to lead and manage in a dynamic environment. We must be focused on producing the professionals who will work in and lead the homeland security enterprise for the next several decades. Those professionals must be agile and adaptable. But most importantly, they must be skilled collaborators. Successful local government officials must be able to coordinate their efforts with state, federal and international partners. These players will recognize that in order to be successful agents of change, they will have to be able to examine the structure, processes, capacity for idea vetting, and skill levels of the people present in all elements of the homeland security enterprise. Such a review will determine what needs to be done for those elements to remain a part of the solution for the challenges of the "new normal." I am convinced that PPPs will be a huge part of such reviews.

That framework and its reasoning are presented here for the reader. This book is a great start down the path of both our requirement to understand the challenges of this "new normal" and our commitment to secure our country. Solutions to many of our problems will be found when government answers the many "what" questions that are now in front of us. They should do so with private stakeholders at the table. Then they should facilitate leading industry voices to answer the "how" questions. That is the essence of *The Business of Counterterrorism: Public-Private Partnerships in Homeland Security*: what do we need to do, and how are we going to do it?

For those of us who were in the trenches in the beginning, I wish we would have had this common sense book to read. It would have helped to shape our thinking then, and it can absolutely do so now.

Admiral James Milton Loy (USCG, Ret.)
Acting Secretary, Department of Homeland Security, 2005
Deputy Secretary of Homeland Security, 2003–05
Administrator, TSA, 2002–03
Commandant, United States Coast Guard, 1998–2002

Acknowledgments

This book is an outgrowth of the Center for American Studies at Christopher Newport University's *Symposium on Homeland Security: Enhancing Public-Private Partnerships and Coordination*, which took place July 19–20, 2012.

This symposium featured a remarkable group of government and business leaders in homeland security, including Thad Allen, former Commandant of the U.S. Coast Guard and National Incident Commander for the BP Deepwater Horizon oil spill response; Bill Bratton, former commissioner of the New York Police Department; Bob Stephan, executive vice president at CRA, Inc. and former Assistant Secretary of Homeland Security for Infrastructure Protection; Thomas S. Winkowski, acting Deputy Administrator for U.S. Customs and Border Protection; and Terrie Suit, Secretary of Veterans Affairs and Homeland Security for the Commonwealth of Virginia.

We gratefully acknowledge these leaders' contributions to the symposium, as well as the symposium sponsors: the Hampton Roads Chapter of the National Defense Industrial Association (NDIA), Continuity First, Verizon Wireless, ABM, Lockheed Martin, ITA International, Bosch Global Services, Spectrum, and Mymic.

Outside of the symposium, we sought out many experts to provide us with background information on how government-business partnerships are transforming homeland security today. We especially thank Ami Abou-bakr, Mike Landefeld, Jim Loy, Sue Lynch, Elizabeth Mayo, Mark Milicich, Benjamin Muncy, Bob Newman, and Paul Byron Pattak for their time and expertise.

For their assistance with the cover design, we would like to thank Michael John and especially Amy Mayberry. For help with the references and bibliography, our thanks go to Ben Coffman and

Kelsey Nichols. We also thank Rebecca Francescatti for her services on indexing.

Finally, we thank our wives, Liz and Rachel, as well as our families and friends, whose love and encouragement made this book possible.

Abbreviations

ADS	Active Denial System
AMS	Automated Manifest System
BPS	Bulk Power System
CBP	Customs and Border Protection
CFAA	Computer Fraud and Abuse Act
CIA	Central Intelligence Agency
CIPAC	Critical Infrastructure Partnership Advisory Council
CRADA	Cooperative Research and Development Agreement
CSI	Container Security Initiative
C-TPAT	Customs Trade Partnership Against Terrorism
DHS	Department of Homeland Security
DNI	Director of National Intelligence
DOD	Department of Defense
ECPA	Electronic Communications and Privacy Act
EOC	Emergency Operations Center
EPA	Environmental Protection Agency
FAA	Federal Aviation Administration
FAST	Free and Secure Trade
FBI	Federal Bureau of Investigation
FEMA	Federal Emergency Management Agency
FERC	Federal Energy Regulatory Commission
FISMA	Federal Information Security Management Act

GAO	Government Accountability Office
HHS	Health and Human Services
HSDN	Homeland Security Data Network
HSIN	Homeland Security Information Network
HSPD	Homeland Security Presidential Directive
HUMINT	Human Intelligence
IC	U.S. Intelligence Community
ICS	Incident Command System
IED	Improvised Explosive Device
INTERPOL	International Criminal Police Organization
IP	Internet Protocol
IPS	Integrated Planning Strategy
ISAC	Information Sharing and Analysis Center
ISE	Information Sharing Environment
ISP	Internet Service Provider
IT	Information Technology
LEO	Law Enforcement Online
LRAD	Long Range Acoustic Device
MTA	New York City Metropolitan Transportation Authority
NASA	National Aeronautical and Space Administration
NCCIC	National Cybersecurity and Communications Integration Center
NCSA	National Cyber Security Alliance

NCSAM	National Cyber Security Awareness Month
NCTC	National Counterterrorism Center
NERC	North American Electric Reliability Corporation
NGA	National Geospatial-Intelligence Agency
NIDS	Network Intrusion Detection System
NIMS	National Incident Management System
NIPP	National Infrastructure Protection Plan
NMSAC	National Maritime Security Advisory Committee
NRF	National Response Framework
NRWA	National Rural Water Association
NSA	National Security Agency
NSC	National Security Council
NYPD	New York Police Department
NYSE	New York Stock Exchange
OIP	Office of Infrastructure Protection
PCCIP	President's Commission on Critical Infrastructure Protection
PII	Personally Identifiable Information
R&D	Research and Development
RFI	Request for Information
S&T	Science and Technology
SBINet	Secure Border Initiative
SCADA	Supervisory Control and Data Acquisition

SECURE	System Efficacy through Commercialization, Utilization, Relevance and Evaluation
SLA	Service Level Agreement
SNS	Strategic National Stockpile
SPP	Screening Partnership Program
SSCI	Senate Select Committee on Intelligence
TECS	Treasury Enforcement Communications System
TIDE	Terrorist Identities Datamart Environment
TSA	Transportation Security Administration
TSO	Transportation Security Officer
TWIC	Transportation Worker Identification Credential
UAV	Unmanned Aerial Vehicle
USCG	U.S. Coast Guard
USDA	U.S. Department of Agriculture
VACIS	Vehicle and Cargo Inspection System
VDEM	Virginia Department of Emergency Management
WMD	Weapon of Mass Destruction

Introduction

I want to just say this about the private sector. In my mind, the government is incapable of responding to its maximum ability without private sector support.
—Hon. Tom Ridge, Former Secretary, U.S. Department of Homeland
    Security, August 3, 2011

April 20, 2010 had been an otherwise typical day. At 9:49 pm, however, the first of several blasts shattered the night air over the Gulf of Mexico, ultimately killing 11 workers and crippling the Deepwater Horizon oil rig.[1] The explosion and subsequent oil spill eventually became the largest environmental catastrophe in U.S. history.[2] Over the following months, hundreds of government and private sector actors convened around the Gulf of Mexico, summoning an unprecedented amount of equipment and technical expertise to stop the oil flow from the Gulf's floor. BP, the National Oceanic and Atmospheric Administration, the U.S. Coast Guard and other Department of Homeland Security (DHS) entities, state governments, local governments, and hundreds of businesses and public sector agencies collaborated in response to the disaster.[3] BP and local officials launched initiatives enlisting local fishermen to assist in the waterborne clean-up effort.[4] The federal government used privately manufactured oil dispersants in recovery operations.[5] Throughout this process, the public and private sector worked closely together to restore a sense of normalcy in the Gulf.

The Deepwater Horizon incident provides a large-scale illustration of several important trends in homeland security. Although the DHS was initially created after the September 11th, 2001 terrorist attacks to coordinate federal counterterrorism efforts more effectively, the concept of "homeland security" has since evolved to address a host of man-made and natural disasters. "Homeland security" thus includes a wide range of subfields and functions, including critical infrastructure protection, cybersecurity, information sharing, port of entry security, and emergency management.[6]

In addition, as homeland security has evolved, public-private partnerships have increased in prominence. Although these partnerships are a major issue of discussion and study in businesses and government agencies involved in homeland security efforts, this issue has received a much less thorough treatment in scholarly literature on homeland security. This is surprising, as public-private partnerships are perhaps the most dynamic and important subjects for homeland security practitioners today.

Public-private partnerships have been defined as collaboration between a public sector (government) entity and a private sector (for-profit) entity to achieve a specific goal or set of objectives.[7] This collaboration results in government-business relationships that include service contracts, supply chains, ad hoc partnerships, channel partnerships, information dissemination partnerships, and civic switchboard partnerships.[8] These partnerships have been discussed in narrow ways in the scholarly literature in related disciplines (such as public administration broadly understood) and some of the various subfields of homeland security (such as emergency management or critical infrastructure protection). [9] For example, Sheffi suggests public-private partnerships are important for supply chain security under threat of international terrorism, a theme that Closs and McGarrell repeat.[10] Others underscore that private sector participation is integral in critical infrastructure protection and homeland security. [11] Discussion of the private sector's role within other subfields, such as intelligence, cybersecurity, transportation security, public health, and hazard mitigation shows increasing understanding of businesses' impact on homeland security.[12]

Overall, however, the scholarly literature has not yet caught up to the practitioner understanding of public-private partnerships' prominence in homeland security.[13] This book begins to fill a gap in homeland security scholarship by identifying the essential role that public-private partnerships are now taking in homeland security, and by examining the implications of this transformative shift in the field. As we will see, public-private partnerships hold great promise, but also face significant obstacles that will need to be overcome.

In this book we focus on five areas of homeland security— critical infrastructure protection, cybersecurity, information sharing, security at U.S. ports of entry, and disaster recovery—to illustrate how public-private partnerships are transforming homeland security as a whole. We chose these areas because they are among the most essential components of homeland security and, perhaps as a result of their importance, they also appear to be where public-private partnerships have developed the most in recent years. Although we acknowledge that these five areas do not cover every aspect of homeland security, it would be neither possible nor practical for us to cover every facet of public-private partnerships in homeland security in a single volume. Despite this limitation, we believe that the five areas of homeland security that we selected for this book serve as reliable indicators of how public-private partnerships influence homeland security today.

The book proceeds as follows. In Chapter 1, we trace the history of public-private partnerships in homeland security since America's founding, examine the impact of current partnerships between government and businesses in homeland security, and survey some of the challenges and opportunities facing public-private partnerships in homeland security as a whole.

In Chapter 2, we focus on critical infrastructure protection. Much scholarship has identified the advantages of public-private partnerships in critical infrastructure protection—including reduced duplication of effort, enhanced cross-sector communication, and increased efficiency. Such benefits suggest that public-private partnerships will be a significant and enduring part of critical infrastructure protection initiatives. However, we argue that a pattern is emerging that may lead to a fracture between the appearance and reality of public-private partnerships in critical infrastructure protection. Although some scholarship has focused on specific challenges in this subfield of homeland security, not enough attention has been paid to thinking through the issues facing critical infrastructure protection as a whole. We maintain that unless concrete steps are taken to bolster public-private partnerships in critical infrastructure protection, they will be much less effective than hoped for by homeland security analysts.

Chapter 3 argues that public-private partnerships are now essential to cybersecurity, and will remain so in the future, because of the converging interests of government and private sector actors in cybersecurity. Increasing attacks on U.S. government computer systems, as well as broader efforts to disrupt access to commercial websites, underscore the need for enhanced understanding of the principles of cybersecurity in the broader homeland security environment. Conceptually, however, there are key distinctions between types of "cyberattacks," which tend to become blurred in public discourse. Cyberterrorism, cyberespionage and cybercrime—while related—are notionally independent, though they often overlap, too. We seek to define these terms and discuss how information technology firms partner with government to bolster cybersecurity.

In Chapter 4, we argue that efforts to correct the information sharing failures of September 11th, 2001 have inadvertently created new problems: a trust deficit between the public and private sector, information overload for homeland security analysts, and a decline in information quality. The challenge for public-private partnerships now is to build cross-sector trust, control the flow of information, and manage information quality for decision-makers in government and business. The chapter examines the historic increase in post-September 11th information sharing within the federal government, as well as among local and state governments and businesses. It also addresses the emerging role of private sector partners in information sharing, and new opportunities for businesses and government to enhance information exchange for homeland security.

In Chapter 5 we turn to security at U.S. air, land, and sea ports, and discuss inspections of persons and cargo nationwide. Throughout this discussion, we underscore the role of businesses in helping to advance changes in homeland security operations. The chapter concludes with an overview of emerging challenges in port security, including inspection of cargo containers, urban and national rail security, transportation of hazardous materials, and the expanding role of the private sector to meet those challenges.

Chapter 6 assesses the effectiveness and limitations of the business community in post-disaster recovery efforts, including the 2011 Joplin, Missouri tornado and the 2010 Deepwater Horizon explosion and oil spill. What do FEMA and the business community perceive one another's role to be during large-scale incidents? What possible lessons for future public-private sector collaboration in disaster recovery can be learned from these cases? We end the chapter with a description of some of the essential elements of effective public-private sector collaboration in disaster recovery.

The final chapter of the book identifies key insights about public-private partnerships in homeland security, based upon the preceding chapters in the book. We underscore how critical the private sector is in homeland security operations, and argue that this arrangement forecasts a new operational framework for homeland security in the years ahead. Indeed, today's critical homeland security challenges demand that the private sector continue to partner closely with government for the foreseeable future.

Notes

1. BP, *Deepwater Horizon: Accident Investigation Report*, September 8, 2010, 29; National Commission on the BP Deepwater Horizon Oil Spill and Offshore Drilling, *Deep Water: The Gulf Oil Disaster and The Future of Offshore Drilling–Report to the President*, January 2011, http://www.oilspill commission.gov/sites/default/files/documents/DEEPWATER_Reporttothe President_FINAL.pdf.

2. National Commission on the BP Deepwater Horizon Oil Spill, *Deep Water*, 173.

3. Ibid., 1–398.

4. Ibid., 140.

5. Ibid., 145.

6. Throughout this book, the term "homeland security" refers to "[a]ctions taken at every level (federal, state, local, private, and individual citizen) to deter, defend against, or mitigate attacks within the United States, or to respond to other major domestic emergencies." See Dave McIntyre, "What Is Homeland Security? A Short Story," n.d., accessed April 12, 2012, http://www.homelandsecurity.org/bulletin/ActionPlan_WhatIsHLS.htm.

   The International Association of Emergency Managers (IAEM) defines emergency management as "[t]he managerial function charged with creating the framework within which communities reduce vulnerability to hazards and cope with disasters." Our use of the term "homeland security" also includes emergency management. See International Association of Emergency Managers, *Principles of Emergency Management Supplement*, September 11, 2007, http://www.iaem.com/publications/documents/Principles ofEmergencyManagement.pdf, 4.

7. Robert A. Beauregard, "Public-Private Partnerships as Historical Chameleons," in *Partnerships in Urban Governance: European and American Expe-*

rience, ed. Jon Pierre (London: MacMillan Press, 1997), 52–70; Pauline V. Rosenau, ed., *Public-Private Policy Partnerships* (Cambridge, MA: MIT Press, 2000); Peter V. Schaeffer & Scott Loveridge, "Toward an Understanding of Types of Public-Private Cooperation," *Public Performance & Management Review*, 26, no. 2 (December 2002): 169–189; Bonnie L. Regan, *Enhancing Emergency Preparedness and Response: Partnering with the Private Business Sector*, December 2009, Naval Postgraduate School Thesis, Homeland Security Digital Library, accessed March 4, 2012, 14–15.

8. Stephen Goldsmith and William D. Eggers, *Governing By Network: The New Shape of the Public Sector* (Washington, DC: Brookings Institution, 2004), 69–70.

9. Goldsmith and Eggers, *Governing By Network*; Beauregard, "Public-Private Partnerships as Historical Chameleons," 52–70; Regan, *Enhancing Emergency Preparedness and Response,* 14–15; Yossi Sheffi, "Supply Chain Management Under the Threat of International Terrorism," *International Journal of Logistics Management* 12, no. 2 (2001): 1–11; David J. Closs and Edmund F. McGarrell, "Enhancing Security Throughout the Supply Chain," Special Report Series, 2004, IBM Center for the Business of Government.

10. Sheffi, "Supply Chain Management Under the Threat of International Terrorism," 1–11; Closs and McGarrell, "Enhancing Security Throughout the Supply Chain," 1–56.

11. Stephen E. Flynn and Daniel B. Prieto, "Neglected Defense: Mobilizing the Private Sector to Support Homeland Security," Council Special Report No. 13, March 2006, Council on Foreign Relations; Phillip Auerswald, Lewis Branscomb, Todd La Porte, and Erwann Michel-Kerjan, eds., *Seeds of Disaster, Roots of Response: How Private Action Can Reduce Public Vulnerability* (New York, NY: Cambridge University Press, 2006); Myriam Cavelty and Manuel Suter, "Public-Private Partnerships Are No Silver Bullet: An expanded governance model for Critical Infrastructure Protection," *International Journal of Critical Infrastructure Protection* 2, no. 4 (December 2009): 179–187.

12. Ashton B. Carter, "The Architecture of Government in the Face of Terrorism," *International Security* 26, no. 3 (Winter 2001–2002): 5–23; Charles A. Stone and Anne Zissu, "Registered Traveler Program: The Financial Value of Registering the Good Guys," *Review of Policy Research* 24, no. 5 (September 2007): 443–462; Crystal Franco, Eric Toner, Richard Waldhorn, Thomas Inglesby, and Tara O'Toole, "The National Disaster Medical System: Past, Present, and Suggestions for the Future," *Biosecurity and Bio-*

terrorism: Biodefense Strategy, Practice, and Science 5, no. 4 (December 2007): 319–325; Mary C. Comerio, "Public policy for reducing earthquake risks: a US perspective," *Building Research and Information* 32, no. 5 (February 2005): 403–413.

13. Government documents, vis-à-vis the homeland security literature, place great emphasis upon the role of the private sector in homeland security operations. This reflects a greater understanding of public-private partnerships' importance for homeland security in the practitioner domain than in the scholarly domain, where knowledge is more limited. See The White House, *National Security Strategy* (Washington, DC, May 2010); U.S. Department of Homeland Security, *National Response Framework* (Washington, DC, 2008), 18–20; The White House, *National Incident Management System* (Washington, DC, 2008), 15-16; The White House, *National Infrastructure Protection Plan* (Washington, DC, 2009); The White House, *National Cyber Incident Response Plan* [Interim Version] (Washington, DC, September 2010); The White House, *National Disaster Recovery Framework* (Washington, DC, September 2011).

Chapter 1

Public-Private Partnerships in Homeland Security: Past and Present

Public-private partnerships have long been a part of homeland security in the United States. Today's public-private partnerships in homeland security are a natural outcome of this extensive history. And the ever-present threat of natural and man-made disasters continues to shape these partnerships in new and unexpected ways. In this chapter, we examine the current status of public-private partnerships in multiple homeland security subfields, including critical infrastructure protection, cybersecurity, information sharing, port security, and emergency management. We also identify many of the benefits of public-private partnerships for homeland security, as well as the challenges and opportunities that these partnerships present. The chapter concludes by offering suggestions to help make these partnerships more effective over the long term.[1]

Government and businesses' roles in homeland security can be traced back to America's founding. For example, in the *Federalist Papers*, James Madison was careful to underscore the importance of the federal government in "times of war and danger," while not diminishing the importance of the states in periods of "peace and security."[2] In 1803, following a devastating fire in Portsmouth, New Hampshire, Congress authorized the suspension of federal bond payments for merchants affected by the disaster.[3] For the first time, the U.S. government provided emergency relief for a community. Thus began an escalation of federal-level involvement that continues today, requiring close working relationships among the federal, state, and local levels of government, non-governmental organizations, and the private sector.

Public-private partnerships evolved in the 19th century, as various disasters prompted a re-calibration of government's role in emergencies. The Great Chicago Fire of 1871 burned a four square mile area in the southwestern part of the city, leaving one third of the city's population homeless.[4] While difficult to fathom today, the federal government's role was limited in recovery efforts. No appreciable amount of financial assistance flowed from Washington, D.C. to Chicago in the fire's aftermath.[5] Instead, the majority of recovery financing came from a combination of local and state governments, as well as charities and businesses.[6] The fire facilitated a shift in governmental involvement in emergency management. Subsequent 20th century disasters, including the 1906 San Francisco Earthquake and the 1927 Great Mississippi Flood, ratcheted up government support for response and recovery efforts.[7] Increasing amounts of funding changed hands between the public and private sectors to support post-disaster reconstruction.

From World War II through the end of the Cold War, public-private partnerships were an essential element in national defense. Citizens were trained by the federal government to watch for enemy aircraft, assist in preparation for nuclear attacks, and direct air raid drills in public spaces.[8] At the same time, U.S. manufacturing capacity adapted to emerging needs. Firms recycled and repurposed commercial products (e.g. rubber, steel, wood) to support the materiel needs of the armed forces. The private sector modified production to fill new demands. The Ford Motor Company, for example, built an entire complex to construct military aircraft.[9]

Public-private sector partnerships continued to develop in the late 20th and early 21st century. The Federal Emergency Management Agency (FEMA) was created during the Carter administration to consolidate disaster management functions previously scattered across the federal government.[10] Over time, businesses began taking a more expansive role in defense and security, from building out information technology (IT) infrastructure, to production of specialized equipment in law enforcement, to contracting out job functions in government offices.[11]

The September 11, 2001 terrorist attacks, Hurricane Katrina, and the Deepwater Horizon oil spill all highlight the prominence of public-private partnerships in what is today called homeland security. For example, following the 9/11 attacks, Verizon assumed a pivotal role in quickly rebuilding network infrastructure to re-open the New York Stock Exchange (NYSE).[12] In the aftermath of Hurricane Katrina, FEMA, in cooperation with the State of Louisiana, distributed $2.3 billion in public assistance funding to residents affected by the storm.[13] At the same time, Wal-Mart was instrumental in providing relief supplies—blankets, plastic tarpaulins, batteries, flashlights, water, and non-perishable food—to Gulf residents immediately following Katrina's impact.[14] Similarly, the Deepwater Horizon disaster required close coordination among government, non-profit, and private sector entities.[15] The American Red Cross sheltered and cared for displaced Gulf residents, while the private sector hired local fishermen to assist in cleanup efforts and worked with government agencies to stop the oil leak.[16] It is clear from these examples that businesses, alongside numerous government and non-governmental entities, now play an increasingly integrated role in homeland security.

I. The Emergence of Public-Private Partnerships in Homeland Security

Given the current expansive scope of public-private partnerships in homeland security as a whole, we limit our discussion below to select federal-level public-private partnerships, which have had enjoyed varying levels of success. However, it is important to note that homeland security includes efforts at the state and local levels, including fusion centers, non-profits, civic groups, professional associations, and individual citizens. As an "umbrella" concept, homeland security also touches on various subfields apart from those we discuss below, including immigration services, public health, and intelligence.[17] A comprehensive treatment of public-private partnerships in every aspect of homeland security is beyond the scope of this book. Nevertheless, the following discussion identifies some of the most significant trends in homeland security today.

Critical Infrastructure Protection

With approximately 85% of the nation's critical infrastructure under private sector control, alliances between government and businesses are essential for homeland security.[18] The U.S. Department of Homeland Security (DHS) creates coordination bodies to facilitate information exchange, planning, and situational awareness between the public and private sectors. The Office of Infrastructure Protection (OIP) within DHS works on threat and vulnerability analyses, national and local-level coordination with businesses and government agencies, and risk mitigation.[19] The OIP is responsible for coordinating information exchange and collaboration among six sectors: chemical, commercial facilities, critical manufacturing, dams, emergency services, and nuclear reactors, materials, and waste.[20] Given that private sector companies operate most of the facilities in these six sectors, public-private sector partnerships are indispensable to the OIP's mission.

The Critical Infrastructure Partnership Advisory Council (CIPAC), a strategic body, complements the OIP. The CIPAC is the basic organizational framework in which government and private sector representatives exchange information and coordinate critical infrastructure protection activities at the federal level. The CIPAC's membership roster reads as a veritable "who's who" of government agencies and industry leaders nationwide. Firms in the CIPAC include such companies as BASF Corporation, the Trump Organization, Verizon, the Boeing Company, Google, and the U.S. Oil and Gas Association. Government entities in the CIPAC include the U.S. Environmental Protection Agency, U.S. Department of Commerce, and U.S. Department of Justice.[21]

The CIPAC demonstrates substantial cooperation between public and private entities at the federal level related to critical infrastructure protection in homeland security. The existence of multiple coordination groups, as well as the presence of leading U.S. businesses within them, underscores that public-private partnerships are integral to achieving homeland security objectives in critical infrastructure protection.

Cybersecurity

Information technology (IT) firms are essential in achieving national cybersecurity objectives. Well-known companies routinely partner with government to share information and collaboratively address IT challenges with homeland security implications. For example, the National Cyber Security Alliance (NCSA) is an organization that raises awareness about cybersecurity issues, and empowers computer users to protect themselves against electronic threats.[22] Public-private partnerships are critical to the NCSA mission.[23] The NCSA board includes representatives from numerous national firms, including AT&T Services, Inc., Cisco Systems, Lockheed Martin, Microsoft, Google, Facebook, Bank of America, SAIC, and Visa.[24] Demonstrating linkages between the NCSA and federal government, the White House and DHS promoted the most visible NCSA initiative, known as National Cyber Security Awareness Month (NCSAM), in 2010.[25]

A recent hacking incident further highlights the interconnectedness of the public and private sectors in cybersecurity. In June 2011, Google publically disclosed that individuals in China illegally accessed the personal email accounts of several senior U.S. government officials.[26] This was allegedly done through use of "phishing," a method of fraudulently obtaining a user's information through fabricated emails asking for usernames, passwords, and related data. Google notified the FBI about the incident. The White House National Security Council (NSC), as well as DHS, followed up with Google to assess the incident's impact.[27] Understanding this attack's sources and methods provides greater knowledge of cybersecurity threats to public and private sector organizations. As this incident demonstrates, public-private sector partnerships, as well as information sharing, are critical to effective cybersecurity.

Information Sharing

The National Commission on Terrorist Attacks Upon the United States, more widely known as the 9/11 Commission, identified breakdowns in government information sharing as a key contributing factor that led to the 9/11 terrorist attacks.[28] Since then, government and businesses have made tremendous strides in bolstering information sharing efforts. For example, Infragard—a national organization created by the FBI in the late 1990s—brings public and private sector representatives together to share information about critical infrastructure.[29] The CIPAC, mentioned above, connects business leaders with DHS representatives. And new information sharing portals like the Homeland Security Information Network (HSIN) provide online platforms for government and business leaders to share threat information and best practices.[30]

This new emphasis on information sharing has yielded excellent results, leading to criminal prosecutions, new innovations, and a more complete understanding of the threats that the public and private sector face each day.

Port Security

America's ports are vital hubs of economic activity. In 2010 alone, nearly 263,000 metric tons of products passed through the port of Houston-Galveston, Texas.[31] During the same period, approximately 30 million passengers flew in and out of LaGuardia airport in New York City.[32] With such a high volume of goods and persons moving through U.S. ports of entry, port security is an urgent priority. Against this backdrop, the Customs Trade Partnership Against Terrorism (C-TPAT) is a government-business sector initiative that was created to enhance worldwide supply chain security.[33] Over 6,000 firms are certified through the C-TPAT program, meaning they enjoy close working relationships with U.S. Customs and Border Protection (CBP), are able to obtain government risk assessments of their supply chain, and can attend special government-sponsored supply chain security training sessions.[34] Programs like the C-TPAT are useful to homeland security in providing a broad administrative framework for regular public-private sector coordination.

On-the-ground security initiatives also impact this critical area of economic activity. The Transportation Worker Identification Credential (TWIC) program pre-screens workers with unescorted access to sensitive areas of America's ports to ensure that they do not pose a security threat.[35] This arrangement enhances supply chain security, and helps achieve port security objectives. As of 2009, over 500,000 workers were enrolled in the TWIC program.[36]

Technologies in use at America's ports underline the importance of public-private sector partnerships. Consider SAIC's Vehicle and Cargo Inspection System (VACIS). The VACIS is a device that emits low-level radiation, providing a rapid view of cargo containers' contents—not unlike an X-ray machine.[37] The VACIS permits government and private sector officials to quickly evaluate if a given container poses a threat. Similarly, new luggage and passenger screening machines produced by L-3 and GE Security bolster protection in U.S. airports.[38] While the latter continue to be the subject of vigorous public debate, it is worth noting that the so-called "full body scanners" are a private sector response to a governmental need—a clear example of public-private partnerships at work in homeland security.

Another public-private partnership in U.S. airports is the Screening Partnership Program (SPP). Under this initiative, screening companies that meet certain qualifications carry out TSA-like duties at U.S. airports. Additionally, individual airport executives may petition TSA for private sector employees to work as screeners in their facilities.[39] While the program's scope is limited—only 16 airports are participating—the SPP is proving a helpful alternative to TSA screening.[40] Mark VanLoh, Director of Aviation for Kansas City, Missouri, noted in Congressional testimony that the SPP enhances flexibility in personnel use, allows for greater employee cross-training, and is more effective in dealing with non-performing workers.[41] Like the use of new, privately manufactured screening technologies in airports, the SPP illustrates the increasing presence of public-private partnerships in port security.

Emergency Management

Emergency managers are increasingly engaged in all aspects of homeland security, including the previously discussed areas of critical infrastructure protection, cybersecurity, and port security.[42] But there is still a distinct area within emergency management that stands apart from these subfields: immediate, near-term response and recovery activities.[43] In such activities, FEMA has widely embraced the essential role of public-private partnerships.[44] Hurricane Katrina and the BP Deepwater Horizon oil spill illustrate why FEMA has embraced these partnerships.

Hurricane Katrina provides emergency management scholars and practitioners with a powerful lesson in what not to do. While popular blame for inadequate response initially fell upon FEMA, today researchers acknowledge systemic failures at all levels of government.[45] Despite these shortcomings, the private sector helped to address various government deficiencies in response and recovery efforts.[46] As the world's largest employer, Wal-Mart is proficient in logistics; that is, efficiently moving and distributing large quantities of goods over a wide geographic area. In anticipation of the storm's impact in 2005, Wal-Mart deployed trucks full of relief supplies to the Gulf region.[47] Clothing, diapers, toothbrushes, bottled water, ice, and non-perishable food items began rolling off Wal-Mart's fleet of trucks as the storm passed.[48] Government leaders took notice. A local official even suggested that FEMA use Wal-Mart's response as a model for its own efforts.[49] In the midst of a significant disaster, Wal-Mart filled governmental gaps in disaster recovery capabilities.

Like Katrina, the 2010 Deepwater Horizon oil rig explosion and spill affected a vast geographic area in the Gulf of Mexico. The initial response involved hundreds of local, state, and federal government actors, as well as representatives from the non-profit and private sectors. BP, which was a responsible party for the spill, worked with the federal government and veterans of the Exxon Valdez oil spill to assess its impact and facilitate clean-up efforts.[50] The public sector lacked the necessary combination of equipment and technical expertise to shut off the flow of oil from the Gulf floor.[51] Thus BP, which drilled the leaking undersea oil well in the first place, cooperated with the public sector in carrying out the work of halting the spill. Public-private sector partnerships were integral to the overall response and recovery effort.

FEMA has made public-private partnerships a high priority, and leads a major national initiative to forge closer ties with the business community. The agency's regional offices, which cover all 50 states and U.S. territories, house a private sector liaison officer charged with building alliances with firms.[52] FEMA Administrator Craig Fugate underscored the importance of the private sector for emergency management in recent public remarks:

> The private sector, from Fortune 500 companies to your local grocery store, is an essential member of the team....The faster we can help stores and businesses get back on their feet [after a] disaster, the more effective the rest of the team can be in focusing our resources on helping disaster survivors in areas that don't yet have access to those goods and services. Growing strong working relationships between emergency managers and the private sector is a good business decision for everyone—it helps us better serve survivors, rebuild our communities and boost local economies.[53]

These comments illustrate the degree of buy-in within FEMA oriented toward building relationships with businesses. Public-private partnerships are beneficial in enhancing firms' preparedness for disaster, as well as connecting them with government partners in advance of a large-scale emergency. From FEMA's leadership team to personnel in regional offices, public-private sector partnerships carry tremendous importance. This emphasis has real-world impacts in disaster response.

II. Benefits of Public-Private Partnerships for Homeland Security

Public-private partnerships can enhance hiring, resource utilization, specialization, cross-sector trust, and technological innovation. They are often able to cut across traditional bureaucratic divides within government. And they can enhance public protection in ways not possible for government or businesses acting independently. In this section, we will discuss each of these advantages, which suggest public-private partnerships will make ongoing contributions in homeland security.

Hiring

The private sector helps the public sector fill personnel needs more effectively than the government acting independently. Background checks for security clearances—a widespread requirement for prospective employees in the homeland security arena—are notoriously sluggish, sometimes taking years to complete.[54] This can create a significant time lag effect between an applicant being offered a position, and actually assuming that position. Compounding the issue, separate, human resources-oriented activities are also necessary to bring a new employee into the homeland security workforce. These background investigation and human resources processes frequently overlap. Businesses operating within the homeland security space are often able to bring in new employees faster, and more efficiently, than the public sector.[55] This, in turn, creates value for the public sector. This arrangement serves firms' business interests, as well as governmental personnel needs.

Today firms like SAIC, Booz Allen Hamilton, Northrop Grumman, and General Dynamics assign employees to work shoulder-to-shoulder with government counterparts in public sector homeland security offices.[56] As a result, the homeland security workforce benefits from the hiring speed of the private sector. These private sector employees perform traditionally government functions, from intelligence analysis, to emergency planning, to protecting critical infrastructure. Thus, businesses can augment the total homeland security workforce faster than government acting alone. This provides a swift, cost-effective solution to the need for more personnel in homeland security positions.

Resource Utilization

At any given time, firms have a fixed amount of human and physical capital with which to achieve business objectives. Resource utilization refers to these assets being directed toward a specific aim, and in so doing, forgoing other opportunities. By orienting resources toward homeland security applications, businesses, government, and the public can benefit. Firms' sales increase. Government gains from privately produced products and services, and public safety is enhanced.

A case from aviation security illustrates how focused resource utilization can benefit businesses, government, and the general public. In 2008, the Transportation Security Administration (TSA) announced that it would permit airline passengers to keep laptops in bags at security checkpoints, provided the bags adhere to a certain x-ray transparency standard.[57] TSA subsequently released a Request for Information (RFI) about bag requirements: they should have no metal components, such as zippers, buttons, or snaps that could interfere with the ability of an x-ray to "see" the laptop's components. To this end, Aerovation—a luggage producer—responded by designing a "checkpoint friendly" laptop bag.[58] In public-private partnerships such as this, a firm re-allocates research and development resources in order to meet government homeland security objectives, while at the same time serving its business interests. In theory, this would increase operational efficiency and reduce wait times for airline passengers in security queues. For this innovation to be effective, however, TSA personnel would also need to receive training to recognize these "checkpoint friendly" bags and allow passengers to keep their laptops in the bags. This training may not have sufficiently occurred yet. But through these and similar efforts to maximize resource utilization, public-private partnerships can work to achieve homeland security objectives.

Specialization

By participating in homeland security activities, private sector actors develop specializations in functional areas, enhancing public sector performance.[59] This process, in turn, can permit government agencies to focus more upon mission-essential activities. [60] For example, in 2009, TSA announced the award of an IT services contract to CSC, a firm based in Falls Church, Virginia.[61] The $493 million, five-year deal includes provisions for designing, maintaining, and upgrading TSA's IT infrastructure over time.[62] Serving one agency's IT needs in such a comprehensive way means that CSC develops increasing familiarity with TSA systems, software, hardware, and requirements. This knowledge creates efficiencies over time. On the one hand, CSC is able to anticipate TSA's needs in a more effective fashion. On the other hand, TSA is freed to devote personnel and resources to other critical activities. Increasing specialization by CSC increases aggregate effectiveness, serving both private sector and public sector interests in a mutually beneficial manner.

Building Trust, Increasing Effectiveness

Communication between the public and private sector can decrease officials' skepticism and mistrust of one another. Over time, repeated interaction and collaboration may actually build trust across the government-business divide. Whether developing plans for the future, or responding to an emergency, trust is invaluable in fostering effective, mutually beneficial outcomes.[63] So public-private partnerships have what might be called a "softer" benefit—the construction of relationships themselves. It is challenging to quantify the value of a public-private sector relationship in the same way that one might appraise a house or a car. But having excellent working relationships in place during routine operations, as well as crises, is invaluable.[64]

Technological Innovation

Public-private partnerships can also serve as catalysts for new technological innovations.[65] Two growing DHS initiatives stand out in their promotion of private sector innovation for homeland security-related challenges: the System Efficacy through Commercialization, Utilization, Relevance and Evaluation (SECURE) program, and its sister program, FutureTECH.[66] The SECURE program provides a pathway for private sector research and development (R&D) to occur without DHS financing the process itself. This departs from the traditional model of government-funded R&D, in that DHS provides clear requirements and design specifications to prospective vendors via public announcement. Firms, in turn, design technologies using their own resources, and attempt to sell them to the government at a competitive price.[67] This achieves public sector budgetary savings, permits firms to focus their R&D activities in a more effective way, and strives to deploy solutions in the short-term.

The FutureTECH program aims to enhance existing technologies to meet anticipated needs, taking a longer view of the innovation process. DHS identifies specific focus areas in which firms can continue to update and improve homeland security tools. These areas include detection of homemade explosives and waterborne improvised explosive devices. [68] By entering into a Cooperative Research and Development Agreement (CRADA) with DHS, firms can benefit from public sector subject matter experts who help to shape the design of a given product to meet precise requirements. In this sense, CRADAs require close coordination between a DHS Science and Technology (S&T) officer and business representatives.[69] Both SECURE and FutureTECH can advance innovation for homeland security by focusing private sector R&D activities to meet public sector needs. Despite the great promise of public-private partnerships in homeland security, they also have a number of shortcomings. We next address some of the ways in which public-private partnerships can fail, and outlines areas of governance in which public-private partnerships cannot function.

III. Potential Shortcomings of Public-Private Partnerships

Public-private partnerships can provide tremendous advantages for both government and businesses and can help the United States to meet its national security needs. There are, however, instances in which public-private partnerships are inappropriate due to the unique mandates of government. There have also been cases in which public-private partnerships fail to meet expectations or businesses do not comply with government recommendations. These issues demonstrate that while public-private partnerships are an important development in homeland security, they are imperfect, and there are certain roles that must be retained exclusively by the public sector.

The Limits of Public-Private Partnerships

There are certain functions that must remain squarely within the public sector domain. The decision to hire and fire government employees is clearly a public sector responsibility—and must remain an authority of the public sector. To be clear, private sector contractors can *assist* public sector entities in human resources-related processes, providing operational assistance, information, and expertise. But the actual *decision* to grow or shrink the workforce affects government in a deeply rooted way and requires a government employee's signature. To do otherwise would risk undermining the political process and would create severe conflicts of interest in the very contracts that are approved for the private sector. This would present an unacceptable and unethical quandary for government.

Procuring resources, managing crises, and securing contracts are clear public sector responsibilities that should not be placed in private sector hands. For accountability reasons, businesses cannot control public sector budgets. Firms can provide advice on budgeting decisions for government, but they cannot actually approve them. In order to avoid conflicts of interest, signatures on procurement orders must remain those of government employees. The public sector also relies on contracts for provision of goods and services, and government employees must sign those contracts. Outsourcing this function effectively places control of public dollars in private hands, undermining society's trust in government's stewardship of tax revenue. Similarly, crises often call for public safety-related decisions about the movement of people and resources. The democratic state's first duty is to protect its citizens, and it naturally follows that these types of choices—sending another police officer, opening and closing evacuation shelters— must ultimately be directed by governmental employees.

Unmet Expectations and Cost Overruns

Without proper management, contractual public-private partnerships can fail for many reasons, including unmet expectations and cost overruns. One component of DHS's Secure Border Initiative (SBINet), widely known as the "Virtual Fence," provides an excellent example of how this can happen. The "Virtual Fence" was to consist of a series of surveillance radars, cameras, and sensors to monitor the U.S.-Mexico border.[70] But the region's harsh terrain caused the equipment to malfunction, and the different technologies that made up the Virtual Fence were challenging to integrate.[71] These issues would be problematic enough on their own, but the project also ran into cost overruns. Although 2005 estimates showed that it would cost $7 billion for the fence to cover the *entire* 2,000 mile U.S. southern border, a pilot test of Virtual Fence technology cost $1 billion to cover *53 miles of the border*—just 2% of the total project.[72] In January 2011, DHS canceled the Virtual Fence project, noting that it "'did not meet current standards for viability and cost effectiveness.'"[73] The Virtual Fence project demonstrates how contractual partnerships between government and business can fall apart. Unmet expectations, poor execution and spiraling costs doomed the initiative. This underscores the importance of effective and transparent management of contracts in public-private partnerships.

Appearance Versus Reality of Cooperation

In 2008, teams of government scientists identified a cyber vulnerability in the U.S. Bulk Power System (BPS), drafted a list of remedies to address the vulnerability, distributed the list to electrical companies, and provided a timeline for implementation. Despite these proactive steps, and despite the apparent mutual interest in addressing these vulnerabilities, in reality there was minimal private sector compliance with these recommendations.[74] This example shows differences between public and private sector approaches to cybersecurity. It also suggests that, despite the appearance of public-private sector cooperation on cybersecurity initiatives, actual cooperation may be less common than one imagines.[75]

This example provides a cautionary tale for the public and private sectors. Public-private partnerships provide great value for both government and businesses. But there are fundamental limits to what public-private partnerships can do, and they sometimes fail to deliver as expected. In the following section, we discuss ongoing challenges for public-private sector partnerships for homeland security.

IV. Ongoing Challenges for Public-Private Partnerships

As the examples in the previous sections demonstrate, public-private sector partnerships are transforming the entire discipline of homeland security, but there are potential pitfalls from such partnerships as well. This trend toward public-private partnerships can therefore provide tremendous benefits, but it can also create organizational pathologies, long-term challenges, and many uncertainties. Several of the challenges discussed below are already emerging, while others may arise as public-private partnerships continue to evolve in homeland security. Scholars and practitioners will need to be mindful of these issues as the discipline of homeland security matures.

Evolving Governance and Responsibility

In public-private partnerships, traditional hierarchy yields to collaborative engagement. In addition to more traditional skills in overseeing and directing, managers will increasingly need to connect and coordinate the shared activities, resources, and capabilities of a host of new organizations and individuals. This arrangement suggests a shift in management and organizational accountability, raising salient legal and ethical questions.

Management and Accountability. Over time, public-private partnerships will undoubtedly affect the skill sets required for public sector managers. Supervisors will be more valued for their ability to foster collaboration among personnel and organizations than for hierarchical management skills. This transition toward a more coordinated public sector management is known as "networked governance."[76] Like most organizations broadly concerned with public safety, homeland security agencies have historically self-organized in a paramilitary-style, top-down structure. Networked governance suggests a flattening of this organizational structure over time.

In this sense, the need for collaborative management will ultimately drive changes in hiring and promotion practices. The spoils will go to those who can effectively communicate and coordinate the actions of many disparate actors—not to those that can simply command. The coordination-oriented manager's skills, values, and outlook then trickle down into the rest of the organization, eventually changing it from within. This adjustment from a hierarchical to a more horizontal organization would require excellent planning and execution by both public and private sector leaders to ensure continuing effectiveness. These potential organizational changes also connect with questions of accountability.

Who is calling the shots now? With more firms entering the homeland security space, delicate management questions become salient: is it ever appropriate for a private sector employee to direct a government civil servant to perform specific work functions? Under what circumstances might this hold true? Two members of Congress recently voiced reservations about this idea, underlining that it is government, not business, that must be ultimately be "in charge" of homeland security.[77] Is this always the case? What protections can government devise to ensure that it continues to direct homeland security operations, even with a substantial private sector presence? None of these questions are easy to answer. As the field of homeland security moves forward, these issues will continue to present difficult challenges for governmental and private sector specialists.

Legal and Ethical Challenges. Government can expand its presence and influence via public-private partnerships in homeland security. This carries legal implications worth considering. Jon Michaels refers to a phenomenon he calls "deputizing," in which the private sector, along with citizens and other organizations, serve as a force multiplier for homeland security purposes. He holds that this arrangement can place homeland security activities on ambiguous legal and regulatory ground.[78] For example, private security officers now outnumber police officers three to one in the United States.[79] Retaining private security firms can be financially advantageous for government. Guarding federal buildings or large-scale events increases long-term fixed costs for law enforcement agencies. Retaining firms to temporarily perform these duties saves time and money. It permits law enforcement agencies to reallocate resources to other priorities. Despite these benefits, this type of public-private partnership also raises serious constitutional questions.

There is a vigorous debate related to the legal powers of private security officers.[80] Private security firms may or may not act as government agents. Depending upon context, they may conduct limited searches of persons. It is not yet clear if these searches are uniformly constrained by the U.S. Constitution's fourth and fifth amendments.[81] Similarly, there are concerns about the chain of command within private security companies. To whom do private security officers ultimately report, and to whom are they ultimately accountable—a government authority or a business? And how does this distinction affect the way that they carry out their duties? These issues blur the legal boundaries between business and government. The implications here are significant. Use of private firms for law enforcement–like functions raises legal and organizational questions that must be balanced against financial advantages.[82]

Despite these challenges, proponents of public-private partnerships can point to a number of strategic advantages. Government can exert its influence through businesses in a beneficial way. For example, privately produced technologies scan citizens for explosives and contraband in airports. Moreover, scholars have also highlighted the many benefits of private sector participation in disaster response.[83]

Skeptics, however, can be apprehensive about the degree to which the state intrudes on private lives via public-private partnerships: surveillance cameras can capture one's every move in public; cell phone intercepts erase the notion of private information exchange; and invasive airport security screening is often interpreted as eroding individual liberties and initiating a slow shift toward more widespread draconian security measures. These are valid sources of concern and require clear responses from government and businesses.

The shifting of organizational and technological responsibilities to the private sector also prompts related questions about liability. If private sector technologies do not deliver, what does this mean from a legal perspective? For example, let us assume a sophisticated network of chemical sensors fails to detect a toxic agent in the Washington, DC-area Metro system. Who gets the blame? Absent indemnification agreements, can government sue the firm? Is it more appropriate for citizens' litigation to be directed toward government or the business itself? Joint action means sharing accountability for successes and failures in homeland security. Security, however, is the state's first duty. It is government, not business, that must ultimately make critical decisions and take decisive actions in homeland security. How to reconcile these positions? Does public-private sector collaboration mean mutual or individual culpability for mistakes? These lines of inquiry require further investigation. Additional liability questions arise when the public sector lacks the knowledge to make informed judgments and decisions.

The Deepwater Horizon oil rig explosion and spill show what can happen when government regulation breaks down. No public sector agency had a complete view of the problem, nor the expertise and equipment needed to solve it. Might the privatization of airport security functions create a similar dilemma? For instance, what happens if an explosive device slips through a security checkpoint, ultimately downing a commercial airliner? Will government be able to adequately explain to the public why the lapse occurred, and how to remedy it? Contractual consequences under this scenario prove worrisome, as well. If government homeland security capacity is "hollowed out" via outsourcing to private firms, then homeland security can be held hostage to the private sector.[84] Public sector agencies must guard against this possibility through diversifying contracts, incentivizing competition among private sector actors, and maintaining a minimum baseline of expertise in core competencies.

Increasing Need for Transparency. Public-private partnerships also raise concerns related to transparency, which refers to two distinct, yet related concepts. The first is governmental transparency, specifically agency reporting to Congress. The second is agency and business reporting to the general public. Both areas of transparency pose significant challenges. Legislative oversight is problematic for DHS.[85] As of January 2010, at least 108 committees or subcommittees address matters related to departmental operations.[86] Businesses in the homeland security space compound this challenge. For example, are private sector representatives held to the same standards of ethics and accountability as their public sector counterparts? If Congressional oversight of DHS is fractured, how effective is oversight of firms' activities? Robust monitoring of public and private sector homeland security actions is essential. Lawmakers will need to ensure that oversight evolves in parallel with the trend toward public-private partnerships in homeland security.

A second challenge relates to decreasing transparency in the privatization of national security functions.[87] Among the many volumes on the evolution of homeland and international security since 9/11, Dana Priest and William M. Arkin provide the most expansive treatment of this topic.[88] They raise several salient observations about the expansion of post-9/11 government contracts. Under the Bush administration, they argue that Congress was able to substantially grow government for national security reasons via private contracting.[89] At the same time, they note that

Congress tried to create the appearance government was not growing—presumably for political reasons.[90] There is also a span of control issue; top government officials admit the number of national security programs involving businesses has become unmanageable. [91] Cozy relationships between government and business representatives are uncomfortable for Priest and Arkin. These are best exemplified in the lavish conferences in which public and private sector officials mingle over expensive drinks, dinner, and entertainment. The purpose of these conferences is to build business relationships between the public and private sectors.[92] To Priest and Arkin, though, they appear to erode the sense of accountability and due diligence needed in government contracting. They argue that these trends are ultimately damaging to national security.

To a limited extent, we agree with Priest and Arkin's thesis. It is true that ineffective program management is fiscally irresponsible and is conducive to misdirection and error. It is also important for the public to know that program oversight is in place and that outcomes are being measured in a meaningful way. But the suggestion that there is something sinister here is unfounded. Priest and Arkin gloss over the efficiencies that public-private partnerships can create. As we have argued in this chapter, public-private partnerships can improve hiring, resource utilization, specialization of labor, and technological innovation. In public-private partnerships, firms seek profits, and government scales in a way that would be impossible if it were acting independently. In this sense, public-private partnerships enhance efficiencies in ways that government cannot produce on its own. This is not foul play; it is a case of rational action by both the public and private sectors.

In light of these challenges, the public and private sectors would be well served by showing why government-business partnerships are necessary, and how their existence benefits homeland security. A positive example of such efforts would be the work of Thomas Cellucci, former Chief Commercialization Officer at DHS, who publishes extensively on the benefits of public-private partnerships for government, businesses, and taxpayers.[93] For example, he makes the case for public-private partnerships, particularly in the context of DHS's SECURE program:

> The products that are developed through [the SECURE program] (even the ones that were not purchased by DHS) can be offered to other private sector entities, such as airport security, school and university security, and security for professional sports and concerts, many of whom support the defense of critical infrastructure and key resources nation-wide. There is then an increase in public safety and security, all while the private sector, public sector and taxpayer benefit from the partnership.[94]

In clear language, Cellucci demonstrates the benefits of public-private partnerships for businesses, government, and the public. Similar government reporting and explanation will help to allay concerns about the necessity of public-private partnerships.

Incentivizing Private Sector Participation

Public-private partnerships are easy when both government and businesses immediately benefit. In a service contract, for example, government is able to procure a needed good or service, and a company's bottom line increases. But what happens when government needs the private sector—such as in obtaining data on critical infrastructure vulnerabilities—but the private sector lacks incentives to cooperate with government? Working with public sector officials, while helpful for homeland security purposes, eats into firms' overhead expenses. Collecting data on a business' vulnerabilities requires time, labor, and material costs that are not profit-oriented. There is a financial disincentive for businesses to assist government in this case. This problem can be compounded if a company's competitor decides not to cooperate with government in the same way. The competitor can potentially provide services at a lower cost than the company that decides to "play ball."[95]

Public-private partnerships can also create proprietary and legal risks for companies. What assurances, for example, do firms have that government will protect proprietary or sensitive information? Recent events like the Edward Snowden case and the WikiLeaks scandal underline that classified national security information can quickly enter the public domain, damaging the national interest.[96] It is reasonable to suggest that firms' confidential information could be subject to similar disclosures while in government custody. Such leaks can rapidly erode a business' competitive edge. Other firms offering similar products or services gain valuable business intelligence from these data. Private sector actors may find their trust in government undercut by information leaks. *In extremis*, private sector cooperation with government on critical infrastructure protection could lead to a business' outright failure through breaches of confidentiality.[97]

Regulatory questions become salient during exchanges of sensitive information. Can businesses be targeted for punitive measures if they unwittingly turn over damaging information about their activities? There is a potential moral dilemma in businesses providing the government information on facilities and operations. By cooperating with government for homeland security purposes, firms may potentially risk shining a light on unsavory or illegal business practices. Government and businesses may need to develop clear guidelines on exchanging potentially damaging information for homeland security purposes.[98]

How to promote private sector engagement under these challenging circumstances? Peter Orszag argues that tax breaks make bad policy; they can provide benefits to firms that would have invested in security measures anyway, increasing the firms' budgetary costs but not actually providing extra security.[99] Moreover, he argues that tax credits do not distinguish between high-risk and low-risk sectors—for example, chemical plants versus shopping malls—when they logically should.[100] Similarly, James Lewis points out that voluntary cooperation from firms in the cybersecurity arena is inconsistent with other sectors of homeland security that require strict government regulation, including banking, commerce, and transportation.[101] Both of these examples show the difficulty of balancing regulatory tools and market forces to engage businesses in homeland security efforts. Scholars, public sector practitioners, and private sector representatives therefore aid homeland security by seeking new ways to encourage businesses' participation. Developing a menu of policy options to increase firms' involvement in homeland security will be an important priority for the years ahead.

Politics, Budgets, and Long-Term Planning

Politics, budgets, and long-term planning are interconnected in the homeland security context. The electoral process can impact homeland security in significant ways. Representatives' thinking about homeland security leads to adjustments in budgets and policies. While some hawkish elected officials may choose to funnel more resources toward homeland security, others might elect to trim budgets and focus more narrowly on specific strategic priorities. These shifts can alter, or even undermine, long-term planning in homeland security. The ongoing global financial crisis also impacts government and businesses' approaches to homeland security. In this dynamic environment, the public and private sectors must effectively plan for future threats and challenges in homeland security.

Politics affect public-private partnerships. For example, former Connecticut Senator Joseph Lieberman once expressed concern that private employees, rather than government officials, are making critical decisions at DHS.[102] After TSA halted an initiative in 2011 to expand businesses' roles in airport security, Florida Congressman John Mica vowed to investigate the decision, noting that "Nearly every positive security innovation since the beginning of TSA has come from the contractor screening program."[103] When politics challenges businesses in this way, firms can become increasingly reluctant to enter the homeland security space. Winning government contracts comes at significant overhead cost; research and development, labor, and negotiation expenses come out of firms' bottom lines. It makes little sense for firms to invest in homeland security if elected officials (vis-à-vis bureaucrats, with whom those firms routinely interact) can abruptly restrict or halt business. When companies hesitate to enter the homeland security arena, this reduces the size of the private sector homeland security market. With less competition in the game, firms that stay at the table can charge higher fees for government contracts. The public sector is left with a diminishing pool of choices for outsourcing, becoming increasingly beholden to a small number of businesses for products and services. Of course, with stifled competition, any cost increases are passed on to taxpayers.

Global financial markets influence agency budgets. Recently, the worldwide economic recession reduced the number of private contractors performing traditionally governmental functions. A 2009 DHS initiative began to examine the appropriate balance of government workers and contractors within the department.[104] By April 2011, DHS cut 3,200 contractor positions, converting them into 2,400 government jobs. The DHS 2012 fiscal budget included provisions to convert another 1,881 positions from the private sector to the public sector. [105] Current trends away from private contracting are not limited to DHS. In January 2011, then-Secretary of Defense Robert Gates announced an initiative to drastically thin the ranks of contractors within the Department of Defense, as well:

> [As] I have said before, this department has become far too reliant on contractors to perform functions that should either be done by full-time employees or, in some cases, to staff activities that could—and should—be discontinued....Overall, we will cut the size of the staff support contractor cadre by 10 percent per year for three years and realize nearly $6 billion in total savings.[106]

Reduced budgets affect public-private partnerships in homeland security, and will continue to change amidst efforts to revive the world's economies.

Businesses now face an uncertain future. Some firms find themselves in "survival mode," trimming staff because of operating costs. In 2011, icons of American industry with links to homeland security, including GM (official vehicles), Caterpillar (construction and debris removal equipment), Sprint Nextel (communications), and Home Depot (disaster recovery supplies) cut thousands of positions.[107] When firms trim budgets, they have fewer resources (human and physical capital) to produce products and deliver services. This means the range of possible business relationships for homeland security narrows. Complicating matters, when government budgets shrink, firms can find it difficult to plan for the future; revenue streams become dynamic, and this year's homeland security cash cow may not be there next year. These circumstances create a vicious circle effect for businesses. Government budget cuts eliminate business for the private sector, forcing firms to scale down. This trimming could restrict the ability of companies to operate in the homeland security space. For both the public and private sectors, then, there is an aggregate shrinking effect in homeland security capacity. This creates hardships for both sectors. Government may not be able to guarantee a consistent level of public protection, while businesses may find it difficult to sustain operations and grow effectively. Both sectors are burdened by the global financial crisis.

In light of these trends, government and businesses must effectively plan for the future of homeland security. Converting private sector jobs to public sector positions requires focused government effort. Competencies, skills, and knowledge must smoothly transfer from business to government hands. Yet there is little financial incentive for businesses to cooperate in this process. Doing so goes against firms' self-interest. After all, firms in the homeland security space make money from government contracts. For its part, government may find it has lost the capacity to perform in certain areas of homeland security. This may be due to over-reliance on the private sector—the "hollowing out" of government mentioned above. Further complicating this picture, there is a continual flow of homeland security officials between the public and private sectors. Firms' employees may join government to gain excellent benefits, promotion potential, and predictable work schedules. Public sector employees can gravitate toward the private sector for substantially higher salaries and fewer bureaucratic constraints. Downplaying or ignoring these trends hinders effective long-term planning in homeland security. Business and government officials should carefully consider these factors in their respective plans for the future.

V. Conclusions

This chapter shows that public-private partnerships are now integral to homeland security as a whole—not just its subfields. Government and business cooperation can provide distinct advantages in hiring, resource utilization, specialization, and techno-logical innovation. These partnerships also have significant impli-cations for management practices, legal and ethical challenges, transparency, building private sector participation, politics, budg-eting, and long-term planning.

From 9/11, to Hurricane Katrina, to the 2011 Joplin, Missouri tornado, to the 2013 Boston Marathon bombings, natural and man-made disasters continue to loom large in the national conscience. The private sector will continue to play a major role in addressing similar threats in the future. Public sector agencies benefit from working with businesses to strengthen U.S. resilience. And as we will see in subsequent chapters, these benefits can extend across a wide range of homeland security subfields.

Notes

1. Portions of this chapter are based on Nathan E. Busch and Austen D. Givens, Public-Private Partnerships in Homeland Security: Opportunities and Challenges," *Homeland Security Affairs* 8, Art. 18 (October 2012): 1–24.

2. James Madison, No. 45: The Alleged Danger from the Powers of the Union to State Governments considered for the Independent Fournal, in *The Fed-eralist Papers* (Yale Law School: The Avalon Project, 2008), http://avalon. law.yale.edu/18th_century/fed45.asp.

3. Suburban Emergency Management Project, "History of Federal Domestic Disaster Aid Before the Civil War," July 24, 2006, accessed April 4, 2012, http://www.semp.us/publications/biot_reader.php?BiotID=379.

4. Homeland Security Institute, *Financing Recovery from Catastrophic Events: Final Report*, March 30, 2007, accessed January 26, 2012, http://www.homelandsecurity.org/hsireports/Financing_Recovery_HSI_final _report.pdf, 22.

5. Ibid., 24.

6. Ibid., 21–26.

7. Ibid., 27–38.

8. Homeland Security National Preparedness Task Force, "Civil Defense and

Homeland Security: A Short History of National Preparedness Efforts," September 2006, accessed January 26, 2012, http://training.fema. gov/EMIWeb/edu/docs/DHS%20Civil%20Defense-HS%20-%20Short%20History.pdf.

9. Jenny Nolan, "Willow Run and the Arsenal of Democracy," *The Detroit News*, January 28, 1997, accessed January 26, 2012, http://apps.detnews. com/apps/history/index.php?id=73&category=locations.

10. Federal Emergency Management Agency, "FEMA History," August 11, 2010, accessed January 26, 2012, http://www.fema.gov/about/history.shtm.

11. For example, see Apptis, Inc., "About Us," 2012, accessed March 4, 2012, http://www.apptis.com/about/default.aspx; Taser, "About Taser," 2012, accessed March 12, 2012, http://www.taser.com/about-taser; Raytheon, "Raytheon Homeland Security," 2011, accessed March 12, 2012, http://www. raytheon.com/capabilities/homeland/.

12. Verizon, "World Trade Center—A Year Later," 2012, accessed January 27, 2012, http://newscenter.verizon.com/kit/wtc2/.

13. Federal Emergency Management Agency, "Louisiana Katrina/Rita Recovery," n.d., accessed June 8, 2012, http://www.fema.gov/pdf/hazard/ hurricane/ 2005katrina/la_progress_report_0810.pdf, 1.

14. Michael Barbaro and Justin Gillis, "Wal-Mart at Forefront of Hurricane Relief," *The Washington Post*, September 6, 2005, accessed March 27, 2012, http://www.washingtonpost.com/wp-dyn/content/article/2005/09/05/ AR2005090501598.html.

15. Austen Givens, "Deepwater Horizon Oil Spill Is An Ominous Sign for Critical Infrastructure's Future," *Emergency Management*, May 27, 2011, accessed March 27, 2012, http://www.emergencymgmt.com/disaster/ Deepwater-Horizon-Oil-Spill-Critical-Infrastructure-052711.html?page=1&.

16. American Red Cross, "Gulf Coast Beach Safety," June 21, 2010, accessed June 8, 2012, http://www.redcross.org/news/article/Gulf-Coast-Beach-Safety; Restorethegulf.gov, "Technical Assistance: Guide to Private/Nonprofit programs," 2012, accessed June 6, 2012, http://www.restorethegulf. gov/node/4621#redcross; Robbie Brown, "Fishermen Sign On to Clean Up Oil," *The New York Times*, April 30, 2010, accessed June 8, 2012, http://www.nytimes.com/2010/05/01/us/ 01marsh.html.

17. Dale Jones and Austen Givens, "Public Administration: The Central Discipline in Homeland Security," in *The Future of Public Administration, Public Management, and Public Service Around the World: The Minnowbrook Perspective*, eds. Rosemary O'Leary, David Van Slyke, and Soonhee

Kim (Washington, DC: Georgetown University Press, 2011), 67–78.

18. "Critical Infrastructure Sector Partnerships," U.S. Department of Homeland Security, 2011, accessed January 26, 2012, http://www.dhs.gov/files/partnerships/editorial_0206.shtm.

19. Ibid.

20. "More About the Office of Infrastructure Protection," U.S. Department of Homeland Security, 2010, accessed January 26, 2012, http://www.dhs.gov/xabout/structure/gc_1189775491423.shtm.

21. "Council Members, Critical Infrastructure Partnership Advisory Council," U.S. Department of Homeland Security, 2012, accessed January 26, 2012, http://www.dhs.gov/files/committees/editorial_0848.shtm.

22. "About the National Cyber Security Alliance," National Cyber Security Alliance, n.d., accessed January 26, 2012, http://www.staysafeonline.org/about-us/about-national-cyber-security-alliance.

23. Ibid.

24. National Cyber Security Alliance, "Board Members," n.d., accessed April 4, 2012, http://www.staysafeonline.org/about-us/board-members.

25. "National Cyber Security Awareness Month 2010 Results in Brief," National Cyber Security Alliance, January 14, 2011, accessed January 26, 2012, http://www.staysafeonline.org/sites/default/files/resource_documents/NCSAM%202010%20Short%20Report011411.docx.

26. Cecilia Kang and Ellen Nakashima, "Google says hackers based in China accessed U.S. officials' Gmail accounts," *The Washington Post*, June 1, 2011, accessed January 26, 2012, http://www.washingtonpost.com/business/technology/google-says-hackers-based-in-china-accessed-us-officials-gmail-accounts/2011/06/01/AGwgRmGH_story.html.

27. Ibid.

28. National Commission on Terrorist Attacks Upon the United States, "How To Do It? A Different Way Of Organizing The Government," *The 9/11 Commission Report*, 2004, accessed October 16, 2012, http://govinfo.library.unt.edu/911/report/911Report_Ch13.pdf

29. Federal Bureau of Investigation, "About Infragard," 2012, accessed October 16, 2012, http://www.infragard.net/about.php?mn=1&sm=1-0.

30. U.S. Department of Homeland Security, "Homeland Security Information Network," n.d., accessed October 16, 2012, http://www.dhs.gov/homeland-security-information-network.

31. "U.S. Waterborne Foreign Trade 2010: RANKING OF U.S. CUSTOMS DISTRICTS BY VOLUME OF CARGO," American Association of Port Au-

thorities, November 23, 2011, accessed January 26, 2012, http://aapa.files.cms-plus.com/Statistics/U.S.%20WATERBORNE% 20FOREIGN%20TRADE%202010%20RANKING%20OF%20U.S.%20CUST OMS%20DISTRICTS%20BY%20TRADE%20VOLUME.pdf.

32. "LaGuardia Airport Facts and Information," Port Authority of New York and New Jersey, 2012, accessed January 26, 2012, http://www.panynj.gov/airports/lga-facts-info.html.

33. "C-TPAT Overview," U.S. Customs and Border Protection, December 13, 2007, accessed January 26, 2012, http://www.cbp.gov/xp/cgov/trade/cargo_security/ctpat/what_ctpat/ctpat_overview.xml.

34. Adboulaye Diop and David Hartman, "Customs-Trade Partnership Against Terrorism Cost-Benefit Survey," U.S. Customs and Border Protection, August 2007, accessed January 26, 2012, http://www.cbp.gov/linkhandler/cgov/trade/cargo_security/ctpat/what_ctpat/ctpat_cost_survey.ctt/ctpat_cost _survey.pdf, 3; C-TPAT Overview.

35. "Federal Port Security Credential Now Available Nationwide," Transportation Security Administration, September 17, 2008, accessed January 26, 2012, http://www.tsa.gov/press/releases/2008/0917.shtm.

36. Testimony of Maurine Fanguy, Program Director, Transportation Security Administration, Before the U.S. House of Representatives Committee on Homeland Security, Subcommittee on Border, Maritime, and Global Counterterrorism, Transportation Security Administration, September 27, 2008, accessed January 26, 2012, http://www.tsa.gov/press/speeches/091708_fanguy_twic_depoyment_complete.shtm.

37. "Borders and Transportation Security," SAIC, 2012, accessed January 26, 2012, http://www.saic.com/natsec/homeland-security/border-security.html.

38. Joseph Straw, "New Views on Airport Screening," *Security Management*, 2012, accessed January 26, 2012, http://www.securitymanagement.com/article/new-views-airport-screening-004586?page=0%2C1.

39. House Committee on Homeland Security, Subcommittee on Transportation Security, *Screening Partnership: Why Is A Job Creating, Public-Private Partnership Meeting Resistance at TSA?*, 112th Cong., 1st sess., February 16, 2012.

40. Transportation Security Administration, "Screening Partnership Program," n.d., accessed June 8, 2012, http://www.tsa.gov/what_we_do/optout/index.shtm.

41. *Screening Partnership*, 12.

42. William L. Waugh and Gregory Streib, "Collaboration and Leadership for Effective Emergency Management," *Public Administration Review* 66, no. S1 (December 2006): 131–140. Comprehensive emergency management means all of a community's hazards are considered in mitigation, preparedness, response, and recovery activities.

43. Naim Kapucu, "Interorganizational Coordination in Dynamic Context: Networks in Emergency Response Management," *Connections* 26, no. 2 (2005): 33–48.

44. Elaine Pittman, "What Big-Box Retailers Can Teach Government About Disaster Recovery," *Government Technology*, November 28, 2011, accessed June 8, 2012, http://www.govtech.com/policy-management/Big-Box-Retailers-Teach-Disaster-Recovery.html.

45. Eric Bonabeau and W. David Stephenson, "Expecting the Unexpected: The Need for a Networked Terrorism and Disaster Response Strategy," *Homeland Security Affairs* 3, Article 3 (February 2007), accessed February 15, 2012, http://www.hsaj.org/?article=3.1.3.

46. Barbaro and Gillis, "Wal-Mart at Forefront of Hurricane Relief."

47. Ibid.

48. Ibid.

49. Ibid.

50. Harold F. Upton, *The Deepwater Horizon Oil Spill and the Gulf of Mexico Fishing Industry* (Washington, DC: Congressional Research Service), 2011, accessed June 8, 2012, http://www.fas.org/sgp/crs/misc/R41640.pdf, 8–9.

51. Givens, "Deepwater Horizon Oil Spill."

52. "About Industry Liaison Program," Federal Emergency Management Agency, 2010, accessed January 26, 2012, http://www.fema.gov/privatesector/ industry/about.shtm.

53. Federal Emergency Management Agency, "FEMA Administrator: Business Community is Critical Partner in Disaster Response and Recovery," November 4, 2011, accessed March 29, 2012, http://www.fema.gov/news/newsrelease.fema?id=59308. Fugate is FEMA's top official.

54. For example, see Edward T. Pound, "Security Clearance Challenges Defy Easy Fixes," *Government Executive*, August 14, 2007, accessed January 27, 2012, http://www.govexec.com/welcome/?zone=welcome&rf=http%3A%2F%2Fwww.govexec.com%2Fdailyfed%2F0807%2F081407nj1.htm; "Personnel Clearances: Key Factors for Reforming the Security Clearance Process," Statement of Brenda S. Farrell, U.S. Government Accountability Office, May 22, 2008, accessed January 27, 2012, http://www.gao.gov/assets/

130/120165.pdf; Letter to U.S. Senators Daniel Akaka and George Voinovich from Brenda Farrell, Director of Defense Capabilities and Management, U.S. Government Accountability Office, July 14, 2008, accessed January 26, 2012, http://www.gao.gov/new.items/d08965r.pdf; "Security Clear- ance Reform: Upgrading the Gateway to the National Security Community," Subcommittee on Intelligence Community Management, Permanent Select Committee on Intelligence, ASIS International, September 25, 2008, accessed January 27, 2012, http://www.asisonline.org/ councils/documents/ govt_secclearance.pdf; "Personnel Security Clearances: An Outcome-Focused Strategy Is Needed to Guide Implementation of the Reformed Clearance Process," U.S. Government Accountability Office, May 2009, accessed January 27, 2012, http://www.gao.gov/new.items/ d09488.pdf; Letter (with attachment) to Steven Aftergood, Federation of American Scientists from Dionne Hardy, FOIA Officer, U.S. Office of Management and Budget, May 20, 2011, accessed January 27, 2012, http://www.fas.org/irp/dni/irtpa-2011.pdf.

55. George Boyne, "Public and Private Management: What's the Difference?," *Journal of Management Studies* 39, no. 1 (January 2002): 97–122; Mary K. Feeney and Hal G. Rainey, "Personnel Flexibility and Red Tape in Public and Nonprofit Organizations: Distinctions Due to Institutional and Political Accountability," *Journal of Public Administration Research & Theory* 20, no. 4 (October 2010): 801–826.

56. See "Homeland Security," Booz Allen Hamilton, 2012, accessed October 3, 2011, http://www.boozallen.com/consultants/civilian-government/homeland -security-consulting; "Homeland Security," SAIC, 2012, accessed October 3, 2011, http://www.saic.com/natsec/homeland-security/; "Homeland Security," Northrop Grumman, 2012, accessed October 3, 2011, http://www.is. northropgrumman.com/by_solution/homeland_security/index.html; "Homeland Security," General Dynamics C4 Systems, 2012, accessed October 3, 2011, http://www.gdc4s.com/content/detail.cfm?item=a96ae1cb-eb74-47d6-bffc-bc7ada51469a.

57. "'Checkpoint Friendly' Laptop Bag Procedures," Transportation Security Administration, August 15, 2008, accessed January 26, 2012, http://www. tsa.gov/press/happenings/simplifying_laptop_bag_procedures.shtm.

58. "Aerovation Products," Aerovation, n.d., accessed January 26, 2012, http://aerovation.com/; "Laptop Bags: Industry Process and Guidelines," Transportation Security Administration, July 29, 2008, accessed January 26, 2012, http://www.tsa.gov/press/happenings/innovative_laptop_bag_

designs.shtm.

59. Goldsmith and Eggers, *Governing by Network*, 25–39.

60. Ibid.

61. "TSA Awards Contract for Information Technology Infrastructure," Transportation Security Administration, September 28, 2009, accessed January 27, 2012, http://www.federaltimes.com/article/20110131/ DEPARTMENTS 03/101310303/1050/PERSONNEL04.

62. Ibid.

63. Danny Peterson and Richard Besserman, "Analysis of Informal Networking in Emergency Management," *Journal of Homeland Security and Emergency Management* 7, no. 1 (January 2010): 1–14; Kathleen M. Kowalski-Trakofler, Charles Vaught, Michael R. Brinch Jr., Jacqueline H. Jansky, "A Study of First Moments In Underground Mine Emergency Response," *Journal of Homeland Security and Emergency Management* 7, no. 1 (January 2010): 1–28.

64. The authors thank an anonymous reviewer for this suggestion.

65. Goldsmith and Eggers, *Governing by Network*.

66. Thomas A. Cellucci, "Innovative Public-Private Partnerships: Pathway to Effectively Solving Problems," July 2010, U.S. Department of Homeland Security, 17–20.

67. Ibid.

68. "FutureTECH," U.S. Department of Homeland Security, accessed January 27, 2012, http://www.dhs.gov/files/programs/gc_1242058794349.shtm.

69. Thomas A. Cellucci, "FutureTECH: Concept of Operations," n.d., U.S. Department of Homeland Security, accessed January 27, 2012, http://www. dhs.gov/xlibrary/assets/st_commercialization_office_futuretech_conops.pdf.

70. Julia Preston, "Homeland Security Cancels 'Virtual' Fence After $1 billion Is Spent," *The New York Times*, January 14, 2011, accessed June 8, 2012, http://www.nytimes.com/2011/01/15/us/politics/15fence.html.

71. Daniel B. Wood, "Janet Napolitano halts funding for virtual border fence," *The Christian Science Monitor*, March 17, 2012, accessed June 8, 2012, http://www.csmonitor.com/USA/2010/0317/Janet-Napolitano-halts-funding-for-virtual-border-fence; Robert N. Charette, "Napolitano Cancels the US $1 billion SBINet Virtual Fence Project," *IEEE Spectrum*, March 2011, accessed June 8, 2012, http://spectrum.ieee.org/telecom/security/napolitano-cancels-the-us-1-billion-sbinet-virtual-fence-project.

72. Preston, "Homeland Security Cancels 'Virtual' Fence."

73. Ibid.

74. Hon. John D. Dingell, "Protecting the Electrical Grid from Cybersecurity Threats," testimony before the Subcommittee on Energy and Air Quality, of the Committee on Energy and Commerce, U.S. House of Representatives, 110th Cong., 2nd Sess., September 11, 2008, 128.

75. U.S. Chamber of Commerce, Business Software Alliance, TechAmerica, Internet Security Alliance (ISA), Center for Democracy and Technology, "Improving Our Nation's Cybersecurity through the Public-Private Partnership: A White Paper," March 2011, accessed April 2, 2012, https://www.cdt.org/files/pdfs/20110308_cbyersec_paper.pdf. This document supports the assertion that public-private partner-ships can be strengthened in multiple dimensions.

76. Goldsmith and Eggers, *Governing by Network*.

77. Gregg Carlstrom, "Senator: DHS Budget Begins 'Turnaround' Away from Contracting," *Federal Times*, February 24, 2010, accessed January 26, 2012, http://www.federaltimes.com/article/20100224/CONGRESS03/2240304/105 5/AGENCY; Stephen Losey, "TSA halts expansion of privatized airport screening," *Federal Times*, January 31, 2011, accessed January 26, 2012, http://www.federaltimes.com/article/20110131/DEPARTMENTS03/1013103 03/1050/PERSONNEL04.

78. Jon D. Michaels, "Deputizing Homeland Security," *Texas Law Review*, 88, no. 7 (2010): 1435–1473.

79. Kai Jaeger and Edward P. Stringham, "Private Policing Options for the Poor," National Center for Policy Analysis, December 15, 2011, accessed February 20, 2012, http://www.ncpa.org/pub/ba763.

80. For example, see Strickland, "Regulation Without Agency: A Practical Response to Private Policing in United States v. Day," *North Carolina Law Review* 89, no. 4 (May 2011): 1338–1363.

81. Ibid., 1340.

82. For one of the first of many studies on this subject, see P.W. Singer, *Corporate Warriors: The Rise of the Privatized Military Industry* (Ithaca, NY: Cornell University Press, 2003).

83. Ross Prizzia, "Coordinating Disaster Prevention and Management in Hawaii," *Disaster Prevention and Management* 15, no. 2 (June 2006): 275–285; Naim Kapucu, "Public-Nonprofit Partnerships For Collective Action in Dynamic Contexts of Emergencies," *Public Administration* 84, no. 1 (2006): 205–220; Camilla Stivers, "'So Poor and So Black': Hurricane Katrina, Public Administration, and the Issue of Race," *Public Administration Review* 67, no. 1 (Special Issue, December 2007): 48–56; Geoffrey T. Stewart, Ramesh

Kolluru, and Mark Smith, "Leveraging Public-Private Partnerships to Improve Resilience in Times of Disaster," *International Journal of Physical Distribution and Logistics Management* 39, no. 5 (2009): 343–364; Susan A. McManus and Kiki Caruson, "Emergency Management: Gauging the Extensiveness and Quality of Public and Private-Sector Collaboration at the Local Level," *Urban Affairs Review* 47, no. 2 (March 2011): 280–299.

84. For a classic treatment of this phenomenon, see R.A.W. Rhodes, "The Hollowing Out of the State: The Changing Nature of the Public Service in Britain," *The Political Quarterly* 65, no. 2 (August 1994): 138–151.

85. National Public Radio, "Who Oversees Homeland Security? Um, Who Doesn't?," July 20, 2010, accessed February 16, 2012, http://www.npr.org/templates/story/story.php?storyId=128642876.

86. Ibid.

87. To date, the most comprehensive and illuminating work on this topic is Dana Priest and William M. Arkin, *Top Secret America: The Rise of the New American Security State* (New York: Little, Brown and Company, 2011).

88. Ibid.

89. Ibid., 180.

90. Ibid.

91. Ibid., 187–188.

92. Ibid., 194–201.

93. For example, see Thomas A. Cellucci, *Partnership Program Benefits Taxpayers as well as Public and Private Sectors*, U.S. Department of Homeland Security, 2008.

94. Thomas A. Cellucci, and James W. Grove, *Leveraging Public-Private Partnership Models and the Free Market System to Increase Speed-of-Execution of High-Impact Solutions Throughout State and Local Governments*, U.S. Department of Homeland Security, August 2011, 10.

95. For a similar point, see Stephen Flynn, "The Brittle Superpower," in Auerswald et al., *Seeds of Disaster*, 30–31.

96. For an extended discussion of the Edward Snowden case, see Chapter 3. For more on the Bradley Manning case, see Scott Shane and Andrew Lehren, "Leaked Cables Offer Raw Look at U.S. Diplomacy," *The New York Times*, November 28, 2010, accessed February 24, 2012, http://www.nytimes.com/2010/11/29/world/29cables.html.

97. See Auerswald et al., *Seeds of Disaster*, for a thorough examination of public-private sector cooperation for critical infrastructure protection.

98. Ellen Nakashima, "Cybersecurity bill promotes exchange of data; critics say measure could harm privacy rights," *The Washington Post*, November 11, 2011, accessed March 27, 2012, http://www.washingtonpost.com/world/ national-security/cybersecurity-bill-promotes-exchange-of-data-white-house-civil-liberty-groups-fear-measure-could-harm-privacy-rights/2011/11/ 30/gIQAD3EPEO_story.html. Recent legislation seeks to limit firms' liability for sharing data with government. This is an example of an incentive for firms to exchange information with the public sector.

99. Peter R. Orszag, "Homeland Security: The Problems With Providing Tax Incentives to Private Firms," Testimony Before the House Committee on Small Business Subcommittee on Rural Enterprise, Agriculture, and Technology, 108th Cong., 2nd Sess., July 21, 2004.

100. Ibid.

101. Ibid. See also James A. Lewis, "Aux armes, citoyens: Cyber security and regulation in the United States," *Telecommunications Policy*, 29 (2005): 821–830.

102. Carlstrom, "Senator: DHS Budget Begins 'Turnaround'."

103. Losey, "TSA halts expansion of privatized airport screening."

104. "Mature and Strengthen the Homeland Security Enterprise," U.S. Department of Homeland Security, March 14, 2011, accessed January 26, 2012, http://www.dhs.gov/xabout/gc_1240838201772.shtm.

105. "Over Reliance on Contractors," Department of Homeland Security Appropriations Bill, 2012, Committee Reports (112th Congress), Senate Report 112-074, accessed January 26, 2012, http://thomas.loc.gov/cgi-bin/ cpquery/?&sid=cp112YCOmu&r_n=sr074.112&dbname=cp112&&sel=TOC_ 56275&. The 2012 Department of Homeland Security Appropriations Bill notes that DHS includes 110,000 private employees, vis-à-vis 221,000 federal employees. This effectively means that approximately one-third of DHS is privatized.

106. Robert Gates, "A Statement on Department Budget and Efficiencies," U.S. Department of Defense, January 6, 2011, accessed January 26, 2012, http://www.defense.gov/speeches/speech.aspx?speechid=1527.

107. "Big U.S. Companies Announce Massive Job Cuts," MSNBC, January 26, 2009, accessed January 26, 2012, http://www.msnbc.msn.com/id/28854051/ ns/business-stocks_and_economy/t/big-us-companies-announce-massive-job-cuts/.

Chapter 2

Public-Private Partnerships in Critical Infrastructure Protection

"Rush my Muslim brothers to targeting (sic) financial sites and the program sites of financial institutions, stock markets and money markets." That was the message posted online by Abu Suleiman Al-Nasser, a blogger working for Al-Qaeda, in January 2011—nearly ten years after the terrorist attacks of September 11th, 2001.[1]

In New York City, local and federal government counterterrorism officials quickly picked up on Al-Nasser's call for violence against financial institutions, and began to alert Wall Street bank representatives. Personnel from the Federal Bureau of Investigation (FBI) and New York Police Department (NYPD) briefed leaders from Citigroup, JP Morgan, Goldman Sachs, and Barclays about the threat, as well as measures that these firms could take to bolster security in light of the threat.[2] Since 9/11 large financial firms have shored up their protection against terrorist attacks. Information sharing between the public and private sector plays a significant role in this protection, since intelligence about terrorist threats can alter banks' preparedness plans directly. And since financial institutions are one of the sixteen critical infrastructure sectors that the U.S. Department of Homeland Security (DHS) identifies, this public-private sector information sharing also plays an important part in advancing critical infrastructure protection generally. But it is not just large banks that work with government agencies to advance critical infrastructure protection.

Today businesses nationwide partner with government agencies to help protect critical infrastructure. Private security guards patrol nuclear power plants.[3] Federal police officers monitor the Pentagon perimeter on standup motorized vehicles made by T3 Motion, Inc.[4] Consultants from Booz Allen Hamilton, a government contractor, work side-by-side with U.S. Coast Guard officials on port security projects.[5] The National Cybersecurity and Communications Integration Center (NCCIC), a DHS facility, includes representatives that communicate directly with large information technology companies during cyber incidents.[6]

These examples illustrate the private sector's prominent role in critical infrastructure protection. From banks, to nuclear power plants, to government facilities, to maritime ports, to computer networks, businesses are vital in promoting critical infrastructure protection. Since the terrorist attacks of September 11th, 2001, immense progress has been made in fostering public-private sector partnerships in critical infrastructure protection. Advisory groups made up of government and business representatives now meet regularly to exchange information about critical infrastructure protection priorities.[7] And there is clear, government-wide recognition of businesses' essential roles in this area.[8] But public-private partnerships in critical infrastructure protection are at an important crossroads.

To date, much governmental and scholarly attention has focused on the advantages of public-private partnerships in this area of homeland security.[9] Other research seeks to uncover and identify distinct challenges in cross-sector partnerships.[10] But this work overlooks an important point. Public-private partnerships in critical infrastructure protection are now in danger of stagnating.

In this chapter, we show that there is an emerging pattern of ineffective cross-sector partnerships. This fracture between appearance (i.e. effective partnerships) and reality (i.e. ineffective partnerships) can create a false perception of success, ultimately leading to organizational complacency. As a result, homeland security leaders should rigorously examine ongoing challenges in critical infrastructure protection and strive to bridge the divide between appearance and reality.

The chapter begins by briefly summarizing the history of critical infrastructure protection since 1997. It next analyzes four areas of critical infrastructure protection, makes the case that there is a gap between apparent and actual success in these areas, and explores the practical implications of these cleavages. The chapter then offers a few preliminary conclusions and discusses the need for further research in this area.[11]

I. The Evolution of Critical Infrastructure Protection

In 1997 the U.S. government and private sector leaders took the first steps in changing the U.S. approach to critical infrastructure protection.[12] Prior to that time there was recognition of critical infrastructure's importance, but only for its commercial implications, rather than in national security. The Clinton administration first saw the need to re-examine critical infrastructure in other contexts.[13] This led to the formation of the President's Commission on Critical Infrastructure Protection (PCCIP). By today's standards, the PCCIP's final report appears remarkably understated:

> [W]e have to think differently about infrastructure protection today and for the future....*We found that the nation is so dependent on our infrastructures that we must view them through a national security lens....*We also found the collective dependence on the information and communications infrastructure drives us to seek new understanding about the Information Age. Essentially, we recognize a very real and growing cyber dimension associated with infrastructure assurance.[14]

The PCCIP's membership also foreshadowed the proliferation of public-private partnerships in critical infrastructure protection; representatives from AT&T, IBM, the Association of American Railroads, and Pacific Gas and Electric Company all sat on the Commission alongside government representatives. Of course, in the years since the Commission's report, much has changed—in large part prompted by the September 11th, 2001 terrorist attacks.

The Aftermath of 9/11

The devastating attacks of September 11th reinforced the PCCIP's findings on U.S. critical infrastructure's importance in national security, profoundly underscoring the value of the PCCIP's being composed of both public and private sector officials. As Ami Aboubakr notes, 9/11 represented a catastrophic breach of national security that involved use of private resources in one critical infrastructure sector (i.e. commercial aircraft, part of the transportation sector) to attack multiple other public and privately controlled resources, including the World Trade Center, part of the commercial facilities and banking/finance sectors; the Pentagon, part of the government facilities and defense industrial base sectors; and associated critical infrastructure components in lower Manhattan, including electricity and steam distribution systems, telecommunications equipment, and components of the New York City subway system.[15] Thus 9/11 highlighted the importance of critical infrastructure protection to confront threats to both the public and private sectors, and it sparked a series of historic changes in government.

A new idea—U.S. homeland security—began rapidly altering the organization of government and the national approach to critical infrastructure protection. Less than a month after 9/11, the White House created an Office of Homeland Security, headed up by former Pennsylvania Governor Tom Ridge.[16] In 2002, DHS was established. [17] This new cabinet-level department brought 22 previously disparate agencies together under one administrative umbrella. It represented an extraordinary re-alignment of public sector resources to confront natural and man-made threats to the United States. Among its new responsibilities, DHS became the lead federal agency for coordinating critical infrastructure protection activities.[18] But as time passed, it became increasingly clear that the idea of "protection" itself needed to evolve. This gave rise to two important changes that continue to impact public-private partnerships in critical infrastructure protection today.

First, the idea of "protection" transformed into an ethos of "resilience." This broad concept suggests a more integrated role for the private sector in protecting critical infrastructure. Second, public-private sector collaboration became the "new normal" for this activity. There is recognition that joint action by government and businesses is needed to achieve resilience. For the public and private sectors, each of these shifts further developed and clarified understanding of how to protect critical infrastructure.

From Protection to Resilience: Engaging the Private Sector

The evolution from protection to resilience can be depicted as follows. In its original post-9/11 form, government protection of critical infrastructure narrowly focused on events and circumstances that came before an incident could occur. We hardened targets; we built walls around buildings; we posted armed guards; we installed surveillance equipment and intrusion alarms; we focused on stopping an incident before it started. In short, protection concerned the "before," rather than the "after." This was viewed as a largely government responsibility—what we will call the "government protects" model of critical infrastructure protection.

But the "government protects" model was soon shown to be insufficient. One of the most significant deficiencies was that it neglected the vital role of public-private partnerships in critical infrastructure protection. For example, dams, nuclear power plants, and commercial manufacturing facilities are remarkably complex systems. They make use of a host of private sector products and services. The notion that government alone could effectively protect this array of facilities ignores such complexities. Thus, a new, more inclusive approach—resilience—replaced the outmoded "government protects" model with an "everybody protects" model of critical infrastructure protection.[19]

Resilience places critical infrastructure protection within an immense network of public, private, non-profit, civic, and individual actors. This spreads the burden of protection among these stakeholders, and most significantly to businesses themselves, which own or operate some 85% of U.S. critical infrastructure.[20] The general public also participates in activities to enhance resilience. The New York City Metropolitan Transportation Authority (MTA), for example, launched a public awareness campaign in 2003 called "If You See Something, Say Something." This campaign places colorful posters on subway cars—which the U.S. Department of Homeland Security considers critical infrastructure—encouraging citizens to report suspicious behavior to police and MTA employees.[21] The "If You See Something, Say Something" campaign demonstrates the importance of public engagement in activities to promote critical infrastructure resilience. The Federal Emergency Management Agency (FEMA), too, actively encourages the public to prepare for disasters. Its advertisements stress the importance of having an emergency kit, preparing a family emergency plan, and remaining informed about ongoing emergencies.[22]

Individual preparedness can translate into societal preparedness, which can help to promote critical infrastructure resilience. By engaging multiple segments of society, including the private sector and the general public, resilience represents a conceptual improvement upon the idea of critical infrastructure protection.

Resilience also advances the idea of critical infrastructure protection in a temporal way. Whereas the "government protects" model of critical infrastructure protection focuses upon pre-incident prevention, resilience incorporates the idea of both pre-incident prevention and post-incident response. It concerns both the "before" and the "after."[23] In the abstract, resilience is generally helpful for both the public and private sectors—it means more comprehensive safety. But resilience also introduces difficult fiscal constraints. Someone has to pay for resilience to move from rhetoric to reality.

The current global financial crisis impacts U.S. critical infrastructure protection measures, including the adoption of resilience. Businesses are making painful choices about how to trim spending, including on security-related expenses. Fiscal constraints are further compounded by a lack of major disasters, because large-scale emergencies have a way of concentrating public policymakers' attention and freeing up money for protection initiatives.[24] But reduced budgets and infrequent major disasters mean policymakers' and business executives' attention is less attuned to critical infrastructure protection. Without this attention, critical infrastructure protection can become marginalized. Diminished importance means reduced budgets, which translate into eroding effectiveness.

Multiple forces, then, are now working against the move from protection to resilience, despite business and government recognition of this transformation's importance. It is in both the public and private sector's interests to embrace resilience, in spite of reduced spending. But under current circumstances, there is potential for a split between the appearance and reality of public-private partnerships, undermining the value of these partnerships in critical infrastructure protection.

Unless businesses and government actually deliver on their commitments to resilience, the actual value of public-private partnerships will remain in doubt. As things stand now, rewards could come from a hollow commitment to resilience, rather than genuine changes oriented toward truly achieving resilience.

II. Challenges That Threaten the Effectiveness of Public-Private Partnerships

Public-private sector coordination and information sharing are foundational in U.S. critical infrastructure protection. Since 9/11, there has been a remarkable surge in this activity across both the public and private sectors. For example, the CIPAC mentioned earlier provides a federal-level mechanism for public-private sector information sharing.[25] InfraGard is a Federal Bureau of Investigation (FBI)-led initiative that dates to 1996 and now brings together over 50,000 public and private sector representatives working in critical infrastructure protection nationwide.[26] The All Hazards Consortium, a not-for-profit organization, has hosted public-private sector workshops on critical infrastructure protection.[27] These are all positive signs that the public and private sectors recognize the importance of coordinating and sharing information, and that they are taking action to achieve mutually beneficial goals. However, there remain a number of challenges that government and businesses still need to overcome in this area of homeland security. Without greater attention from policymakers, these challenges will reduce the long-term value of public-private partnerships.

Obstacles to Cross-Sector Coordination

Effective public-private sector coordination in critical infrastructure protection continues to face challenges. These issues can result from imprecise contracts that can create a mismatch in expectations, a lack of centralized mechanisms for coordinating integrated actions, a tendency for each actor in a partnership to act purely out of self-interest, and the prospect of public or private sector actors leaving one another to bear the costs of the partnership. We see these obstacles in many areas of critical infrastructure protection, but to better illustrate these problems, we focus on specific concerns with contracts, the agricultural sector, and information technology.

While useful, contracts are imperfect instruments in defining public-private sector roles and facilitating coordination. Unanticipated issues can arise related to contractual scope, prompting government to demand more from a firm beyond the contract's original conditions.[28] In the short-term, this can lead to cost overruns, impacting companies' overhead expenses. These businesses' representatives may also push back against increasing demands from public sector clients. This is understandable—these firms must protect their own financial interests. But private sector pushback can sour relationships between businesses and government agencies. This can hamper coordination by temporarily slowing or reducing cross-sector communication. Repeatedly delivering goods and services beyond a contract's original terms can also lead to contract re-negotiation. This process requires time and labor. It risks delaying or stopping contractual provisions. Failures to clearly delineate roles and responsibilities for public and private sector actors have led to challenges in protecting two vital areas of critical infrastructure: the agricultural sector and the physical architecture of the Internet.

The U.S. food supply is recognized as critical to national security, yet the basic challenge of coordinating security efforts for it remains unsettled.[29] A 2011 Government Accountability Office (GAO) report shows that there is no centralized coordination mechanism for protecting the food and agriculture sector.[30] At the federal level, responsibility for food and agriculture security is primarily spread among DHS and the U.S. Departments of Agriculture (USDA), Health and Human Services (HHS), and the Environmental Protection Agency (EPA).[31] The USDA is charged under Homeland Security Presidential Directive (HSPD)-9 to develop a mass zoonotic disease vaccination program. The thinking behind this initiative is that terrorists could deliberately release diseases to kill substantial numbers of farm animals, endangering food supplies.[32] This would overwhelm the public sector, which is responsible for response, as well as the private sector, which produces the vaccines.[33]

Major coordination challenges in this area of critical infrastructure protection remain unresolved. Certain vaccines have not been produced for cost or logistical reasons. There are vaccine distribution problems at the state level. There is confusion about the distinct purposes of stockpiled vaccines for agricultural purposes, as opposed to the Strategic National Stockpile (SNS), which is a national cache of medical supplies for large-scale public health emergencies.[34] Numerous obstacles remain in coordinating action in this facet of critical infrastructure protection.

A very different area of critical infrastructure—the Internet's electronic backbone—shares strikingly similar coordination difficulties. Falling under the broad heading of the Information Technology (IT) sector, the Internet is the lifeblood of modern communication and commerce; coordination to protect the Internet's hardware is a truly global challenge. A vast network of undersea fiber optic cables link the Internet around the world from continent to continent.[35] In a study of this enormous web of equipment, Omer et al. examine the strength of the network's differing nodes with and without strategies for resilience. In this context, resilience means a network being able to absorb shocks or disruptions without cascading negative effects across the entire network itself. These disruptions could be caused by ship anchors, undersea earthquakes, or fish bites that damage or sever the underwater cables.[36] Ensuring the network's resilience is itself a "wicked problem."[37] It raises questions related to international relations, scientific and technical capacities, and economics.

For example: if a cable between the U.S. and Europe is cut by a ship's anchor, what nation is responsible for its repair? If a state is obligated to repair a cable, and lacks the resources to do so, what happens? Economically, what is the consequence of an undersea cable being cut? These questions underscore the importance of clear agreements—codified in contracts—among public and private sector stakeholders in critical infrastructure protection. Without a defined sense of responsibility for the Internet's physical components, there is increased potential for prolonged disruption. Role confusion among public and private sector actors is a real possibility under such a scenario. Resolving this role confusion would likely lead to delays in response time. Because of the Internet's profound influence on virtually every facet of modern life, every passing minute of downtime has the potential to negatively impact society in a substantial way. The effects of an Internet outage can easily spill into the economic realm (e.g. losing access to market data), medical arena (e.g. inability to pull up medical records through electronic databases), and public safety (e.g. inaccessibility of criminal history information). In this sense, poor coordination can have devastating consequences.

Persistent challenges in protecting the agricultural sector and the Internet point toward a disconnect between the appearance and reality of public-private partnerships. Agricultural security remains an important homeland security priority for government.[38] Billions of dollars hang in the balance for agricultural firms.[39] But coordinating public-private sector efforts related to animal vaccine production and distribution, as well as overall planning, is clearly uneven. This demonstrates a gap between appearance and reality. A false sense of security based upon appearances can lead to organizational apathy over time. Government and businesses have fewer incentives to enhance coordination. This perpetuates the status quo, meaning a continuation of unresolved coordination difficulties. The appearance of cross-sector coordination, then, carries at least two interrelated negative effects: first, it can lead to stagnation in true coordination levels; second, this stagnation has a way of "locking in" lower collective levels of security. Both of these pathologies harm critical infrastructure protection.

Gaps in Information Sharing

There is also an expectations gap in information sharing between the public and private sectors. Neither of the two sectors appears satisfied with the information they are receiving from the other. There is also a mutually acknowledged reluctance to exchange certain sensitive information. For example, a 2010 GAO report found that many private sector representatives feel the information they receive from government is generic, and therefore not actionable.[40] Additionally, the report noted that business officials expect to have access to sensitive government information related to critical infrastructure protection, but are not receiving it from government. How can we explain these findings?

Multiple variables can conspire to impede effective cross-sector information sharing.[41] There remains an unsettled organizational landscape in critical infrastructure protection. Personnel turnover and re-organizations can diminish or erode relationships among public and private sector actors. When one's colleagues and counterparts change, new working relationships need to form with new colleagues and new counterparts. This process takes time, and in the interim, can hamper communication. Moreover, fundamental questions of trust persist. It is extremely difficult to share sensitive information—whether proprietary or classified—absent trust. This is true whether that trust comes in the form of something tangible, such as a security clearance, or something less concrete, like a feeling of mutually shared confidence. There is also rarely an immediate payoff for businesses in information sharing. Prieto labels this the "quid pro quo" problem, in which private firms expect tangible benefits from information sharing, but do not receive them. [42] This can all be complicated by a sense among businesses that government is holding back information, and not providing them the "whole story." [43] Putting aside the *value* of information, these issues illustrate the more basic challenge of *actually sharing* information.

It is useless to talk about commitments to information sharing if that sharing cannot occur in a meaningful way. Over the long term, a false front of robust information sharing can hide dysfunction and poor results. After all, government can take satisfaction knowing that, in the eyes of its stakeholders (i.e. the public), it is "sharing information"—even when that information is generic, useless, and dated in the eyes of businesses. Similarly, businesses can relax, knowing they are good stewards of national security, simply by providing government minimal data on their security vulnerabilities. These approaches can entrench low levels of cross-sector engagement. Further information sharing beyond this low standard is unlikely if it requires increased overhead spending for firms and longer hours for government employees. This has the potential to stunt the growth of public-private partnerships and jeopardizes homeland security in the process.

Shortfalls in Private Sector Engagement in Critical Infrastructure Protection

Businesses need incentives to spend money on their own protection measures. To date, DHS has formed a number of helpful initiatives to boost firms' ability to enter the general homeland security arena—including the critical infrastructure space.[44] But it is important to distinguish these projects from how businesses spend money on protecting *their own operations*. Since these ideas are conceptually close to one another, it is easy to confuse a firm's work in developing critical infrastructure technologies with investing in self-protection.

Telling firms they must protect or perish may not be good enough anymore. Writing in 2005, Lewis and Darken state that firms will voluntarily opt-in to robust critical infrastructure protection measures.[45] They maintain that the notion of critical infrastructure protection being prohibitively expensive for the private sector is a kind of false choice.[46] Firms, the argument goes, have a vested interest in continuity of operations. Citing Hurricane Katrina's effects in the Gulf, they point out that severe business disruptions can force firms into bankruptcy. [47] In effect, they maintain that there is a built-in incentive for firms to invest in continuity of operations—not doing so risks a complete shutdown. While reasonable on its face, this argument does not hold up to scrutiny. In theory, businesses are indeed motivated toward self-preservation. But this ignores the sometimes illogical, non-linear decision-making patterns of human beings that operate and patronize those businesses.

- First, this idea brushes aside the notion of consumers gravitating toward most-affordable products and services, irrespective of reliability. A certain proportion of the population will always choose the cheaper option. Firms that invest less in security pass on fewer security-related expenses to consumers. This can provide a relative price reduction, making a less-reliable firm the more-affordable option toward which consumers gravitate. In this case, businesses have incentives to remain competitive, and not invest in additional protection.

- Second, in some areas of the United States, firms can have a natural monopoly on delivery of utilities like electricity, natural gas, or cable television.[48] In these cases, there is little profit-oriented incentive for firms to invest in protection. Whether a firm chooses to boost investment in security or not, it will continue to dominate the local market. Under these circumstances, and without effective regulation, firms can easily justify *not* investing in robust protection.

- Third, pointing to business failures in the wake of Hurricane Katrina is hardly sufficient to prompt firms to take protective actions. People tend to be optimistic and to forget negative evidence over time. This tendency impacts businesses and government entities' emergency preparedness efforts. There are enduring, well-documented disaster preparedness fallacies that plague both individuals and organizations. These include historical precedence (e.g. "It hasn't happened yet, so it likely won't happen"); fallacies of improbability (e.g. "That kind of thing doesn't happen here"); cost ("We just don't have the funding for it this year"); cognitive biases ("There have been no disasters recently, therefore, I am not actively thinking about emergency preparedness, so preparedness is unimportant");

cultural norms (i.e. particular populations are statistically less inclined to prepare for emergencies); and prioritization schema (e.g. "In the big picture, emergency preparedness is not that important right now"). Simply stating that it is in firms' best interests to invest in protection is not enough to overcome these fallacies.

- Fourth, the return-on-security-investment (ROSI) for a firm ultimately comes in the firm's ability to continue generating revenue in the midst of a crisis. This reality can make it difficult to initially justify the cost of emergency preparedness measures, for a firm can only fully understand why it is necessary to spend money on emergency preparedness measures when it is in the midst of an emergency. So while the value of investing in emergency preparedness measures is clear, connecting the initial expense of those measures to potential revenue can be a challenge.

- Fifth, this argument flies in the face of overwhelming evidence that individuals and organizations remain woefully unprepared for disasters, despite major disasters affecting businesses year after year.[49]

The argument that firms are naturally motivated to invest in protection, then, overlooks important subtleties. Businesses are supposed to keep their operations humming, even in the midst of disruptions. They should be self-motivated to do this and not require government intervention. In a competitive free-market environment, however, ensuring long-term continuity of operations may take a backseat to generating short-term revenue. This dynamic can also be exacerbated by other policy conditions, including a hands-off approach by government to critical infrastructure protection.

The George W. Bush administration took a market-driven stance on critical infrastructure protection, with little government intervention or regulation entering into the equation. Survey data reveals that this strategy failed to spur firms to action.[50] This is largely due to the need for businesses to keep costs low in order to be as competitive as possible. Commercial pressure is compounded by the general belief that enhanced security elevates costs, degrades efficiency, does not guarantee reliability, and limits consumer access to goods and services.[51] These assumptions about critical infrastructure protection provide little incentive for business leaders to invest in additional security measures. They also suggest that there may be a role for government in promoting businesses' engagement. However, it is not clear what actions or steps would be most helpful for government to take. There are also basic financial questions for the public and private sector that merit further consideration.

U.S. government appeals to morals, patriotism, or civic responsibility quickly lose their luster when they begin to eat into a firm's bottom line.[52] De Bruijne and Van Eeten point out that while government and business both agree on the importance of critical infrastructure protection, this consensus can be remarkably shallow.[53] Schneier notes that any business executive who suddenly announced he was increasing security spending by 25% for the good of the nation would almost certainly be fired.[54] Businesses may publicly promote their commitment to security, but behind closed doors, there is an upper limit to firms' security expenses. Beyond that limit, genuine (rather than rhetorical) investment in security is difficult to come by.

A 2008 Congressional hearing on private sector compliance with a government advisory body underlined the challenge of promoting firms' investment in critical infrastructure protection. Threats to the national power grid—technically known as the Bulk Power System (BPS)—are well-documented.[55] Less known is the delicate tension between government regulators and firms related to BPS security. A 2007 DHS laboratory test demonstrated the ease with which a hacker could compromise the BPS. In that test, technicians were able to remotely break into electrical grid components, and deliberately caused them to malfunction.[56] As a result of the test, the North American Electric Reliability Corporation (NERC) issued advisory guidance to national electricity producers.[57] This advisory guidance provided electrical power companies specific information on the vulnerability exploited by the test. It also included information on how to remedy the vulnerabilities. It was up to firms to comply with these recommendations.

The timeline for implementation of the guidance was 180 days. Over a year later, the Federal Energy Regulatory Commission (FERC) audited thirty electricity producers to check voluntary compliance with the advisory. Of the thirty, only two or three had fully complied with the guidance.[58] In Congressional testimony, much discussion focused on this gap in compliance.[59] Legislators and business officials recognize that a prohibitively high cost to implement the guidance may explain why corrections were not more widespread.[60] This instance of non-compliance with clear guidance for critical infrastructure protection shows why effective incentives are essential. Absent a clear business motivation for investing in security, it is unrealistic to think firms will arbitrarily spend on increased security measures—particularly if adjustments impact overhead expenses. There is also a second, related issue here, connected to the ongoing global economic crisis.

Short-term spending on security and protection reduces the availability of money for other expenses. Today, this is a difficult prospect for firms to consider. Lay-offs are increasing. Production is slowing. Revenues are shrinking.[61] Businesses are faced with the difficult choice between spending on short-term survival, or longer-term investments in protection. This choice means firms in dire straits must gamble. They can choose to maintain what remains of their operations, or cut into core business activities in the name of greater critical infrastructure protection. All but the most security-conscious businesses will choose survival over security. It does not make sense to worry about surveillance cameras when a company's financial core is melting down.

This trend does not bode well for public-private partnerships in critical infrastructure protection. It means that firms focusing on survival are not spending on security. Over time, and particularly as the economy begins to recover, this pattern of non-spending may become "sticky." A new norm of not expending firms' budgets to emphasize critical infrastructure protection may emerge. Of course, the public sector cannot shoulder the lion's share of critical infra-structure protection. Yet that is the logical outcome of long-term reductions in business' spending on security. For both the short and medium term, then, it is important to develop effective incentives to promote private sector engagement.

Consider Cavelty and Suter's suggestions of incentives to build public-private partnerships. It is up to government, they argue, to choose among regulation, financial incentives, definitions of liability, contracts, subsidies, loans, deficit guarantees, issuing licenses, state insurance, tax relief, and fines.[62] Of course, some of these tools could present a conflict for government itself. For example, government is a large consumer of electricity, but if through use of these policy tools, the government ends up getting charged more by electrical companies, then the government has helped to achieve one goal (i.e. better cooperation from the private sector) at its own expense. Nevertheless, this range of options provides tools for government to spur development of public-private partnerships. It also opens up a way of increasing private sector involvement in critical infrastructure protection that is more consistent with firms' business interests. Rather than appealing to good citizenship or other values, these choices simply make good financial sense. These options also come with caveats, however. It is far from certain if this list of policy tools is as comprehensive as it could be, or if its elements could potentially be implemented in an effective way. Despite these shortcomings, it underlines the pressing need to create workable incentives for private sector engagement in critical infrastructure protection.

A framework of incentives must support commitments to cross-sector collaboration. Without incentives, public-private sector partnerships' growth is stymied, because no business leader interested in maximizing profit will spend more on protection than what he perceives as the minimum amount necessary to sustain his firm's operations. Companies need more than appeals to emotion or goodwill to meaningfully engage with government in critical infrastructure protection. By developing effective incentives, government can help ensure the private sector's long-term commitment to this vital area of homeland security.

The Cyber Problem

Effective cybersecurity requires a cultural shift toward close and continuing public-private sector cooperation. And this has been occurring with increasing effectiveness since 9/11. As we first mentioned in Chapter 1, the National Cyber Security Alliance (NCSA) is an organization that increases public awareness of cybersecurity issues. [63] Public-private partnerships are at the center of the NCSA mission.[64] And in June 2011, Google alerted the FBI that a number of senior U.S. government officials' personal email accounts had been illegally accessed by hackers in China.

The clear national security implications of this incident underline why strong working relationships between the public and private sectors are so essential in critical infrastructure protection. These relationships can help to foster closer cooperation and information sharing between the public and private sectors, and they can permit both the public and private sector to work together more efficiently.

But in spite of these positive steps, there still remain challenges to effectively addressing cybersecurity considerations. Government cybersecurity recommendations to private industry, as well as other government agencies, can be inconsistently implemented. These unresolved challenges risk eroding public-private sector partnerships' potential value in cybersecurity initiatives.

There are also challenges in the implementation of best practices for cybersecurity. In a survey of control system operators—that is, personnel managing software that regulates industrial processes—Permann et al. learned that common security procedures were not being consistently followed.[65] Permann et al.'s work highlights an important gap between appearances and reality in cybersecurity. While agencies and businesses may appear to collaborate using relatively uniform cybersecurity standards, this is not necessarily the case. This pattern is also seen in the context of the nation's electrical grid.

The 2008 House of Representatives hearing on the BPS addressed in the previous section underlines the difficulty of integrating IT security into other protection initiatives.[66] In that discussion, teams of government scientists identified a clear electronic vulnerability in the BPS. These officials drafted a list of remedies to stop the vulnerability, distributed the list to electrical companies, and provided a timeline for implementation. Despite these proactive steps, firms' actual compliance with recommendations remained low.[67] This gap shows differences between public and private sector approaches to cybersecurity. It suggests that, despite the appearance of public-private sector cooperation on cybersecurity initiatives, actual cooperation may be less common than one imagines.[68]

A recent government report adds weight to the idea that effective cybersecurity practices are not as common as they might seem. In 2009, the GAO found that while significant efforts are underway to integrate cybersecurity planning throughout DHS, sector-specific plans not being updated to the degree that they should.[69] Indeed, most of these plans date to 2007.[70] Tellingly, these plans also continue to focus primarily on physical threats, rather than cyber threats.[71] This is despite increasing evidence of the persistent threat posed by electronic crimes and attacks on public and private sector information systems.[72] Like the deficiencies in closing BPS vulnerabilities, this GAO report demonstrates a widening gap between public and private sector approaches to cybersecurity. Government and businesses inadvertently undermine public-private partnerships by publicizing their mutual commitment to cybersecurity initiatives, yet cooperating or adopting these measures in a minimal way.

Government emergency management documents show a similarly uneven approach to cybersecurity. Emergency managers will be increasingly needed to handle "cyber disasters," but important U.S. emergency management documents do not reflect this new reality. Despite an increasing number of cyber incidents four years ago, the 2008 National Response Framework (NRF) and National Incident Management System (NIMS) core documents—foundational doctrinal publications for emergency managers—hardly addressed cybersecurity.[73] The NRF describes a cyber attack scenario as part of a broader discussion related to emergency planning.[74] NIMS does not mention cyber issues at all. The 2009 National Infrastructure Protection Plan (NIPP), by contrast, comprehensively integrates discussion of cybersecurity.[75] Focused tactical documents, such as DHS' Configuring and Managing Remote Access for Industrial Control Systems, also show an analogous level of concern for cybersecurity issues.[76] The disconnect between these emergency management and infrastructure protection documents is striking, and worth further exploration.

It is reasonable to suppose that the gap between the NRF/NIMS and NIPP reflects differences in disciplinary focus. Emergency managers, and those with an otherwise strong connection to incident response, may not yet view cybersecurity as a high priority issue—although this is slowly changing. By contrast, the NIPP's authors—clearly concerned with critical infrastructure protection—recognize that IT security is an essential facet of modern life.

This gap is arguably the crux of the cyber problem in critical infrastructure protection. Effective cybersecurity requires a shift in culture. It is not enough to consider cybersecurity in an emergency context; it must instead be viewed as a unifying thread that transcends organizations' entire operations. Scholars and practitioners working in critical infrastructure protection (vis-à-vis emergency management) already recognize the importance of this cultural change.[77] The reason for this is simple: IT is itself a critical infrastructure sector. But it is actually emergency managers and other practitioners who do *not* normally focus exclusively on critical infrastructure protection that *most* need to make cybersecurity part of their organizational cultures. Fortunately, future releases of the NRF and NIMS will likely integrate additional discussion of cybersecurity. These updates will help place government and corporate emergency managers in a better position to understand the relevance of cybersecurity to their respective operations. Public-private sector approaches to cybersecurity may become more integrated as a result. This can lead to greater cross-sector uniformity in planning and incident response, ultimately benefitting all critical infrastructure protection activities.

Solving the cyber problem, then, involves several overlapping areas of concern. It is a given that basic cybersecurity principles need to be followed by businesses and government agencies. But emergency managers, and other specialists that do not typically focus on critical infrastructure, are in the best position to benefit from these changes. After all, IT experts do not need to be convinced of cybersecurity's importance. Rather, non-IT experts will benefit the most from greater knowledge of cybersecurity threats. Without alignment among IT and non-IT experts in both government and business, the public and private sectors' approaches to cybersecurity will be out of sync and will lose effectiveness.

This lack of synchronicity threatens to lower the potential value of public-private partnerships. Either the public or the private sector will be in a perpetual game of catch-up with the other. The process of catching-up, and re-aligning approaches to cybersecurity, causes delays. These delays mean that vulnerabilities to electronic threats remain open for longer periods of time, increasing the possibility of their being exploited for nefarious purposes. This harms public-private partnerships and negatively impacts society's electronic defenses as a whole.

III. Enhancing the Effectiveness of Public-Private Partnerships in Critical Infrastructure Protection

As we have argued, public-private partnerships in critical infrastructure protection are at an important crossroads. Despite the potential benefits of public-private partnerships in this area of homeland security, there are numerous organizational pathologies creating the conditions for public-private partnerships to fall short of analysts' expectations.

Structural challenges beneath these surface-level characteristics show that public-private partnerships are actually on shaky ground. The definition of critical infrastructure is constantly evolving, which challenges cross-sector coordination efforts and information sharing. There is a frustrating lack of robust financial incentives to promote businesses' engagement in critical infrastructure protection. Uneven public and private sector approaches to cybersecurity show that protection efforts are out of alignment.

Left unchecked, these pathologies promote organizational complacency. Government can reap rewards from a veneer of partnership with the private sector, including positive media attention, political praise, and increased budget allocations. Businesses can also benefit from the appearance of cooperating with government, through expanded contracts and increased sales. These gains reinforce a superficial commitment to public-private partnerships. They imply that beyond a certain threshold of commitment to cross-sector cooperation, further action by either sector no longer carries discernible benefits. Rational actors will not extend themselves beyond that threshold. Of course, public-private partnerships hold great potential for deep systemic change in critical infrastructure protection. But achieving this full potential requires coordinated action by each sector.

We would suggest five initial steps that can help in beginning to remove these pathologies:

- **Choose collaborative leadership, not regulation.** It is clear that the private sector must fully participate in critical infrastructure protection in order for both government and businesses to achieve the broader homeland security mission. The BPS vulnerability discussed above underlines the importance of private sector participation in critical infrastructure protection, even when the payoffs for that participation are not immediately obvious. Firms are faced with a basic choice of resisting this participation, which may eventually lead to government regulation, or engaging in collaborative leadership with government, which involves jointly re-assessing mutually shared goals, strategies, and tactics. We support the latter, and excellent research has already been conducted to inform these efforts. Flynn argues for collaborative leadership across the public-private sector divide. Government, his case goes, must directly engage with the private sector to promote critical infrastructure protection, rather than rely on purely market forces to dictate solutions.[78] Another scholar extends this thinking further and proposes a spectrum of government engagement levels with the private sector.[79] Values on this spectrum range from total state control of infrastructure, to a hybrid model of delegation and negotiation with businesses, to purely market forces dictating protection levels.[80] Using this research, government and businesses can develop a baseline understanding of what goal-oriented cooperation should look like, and how their respective roles can evolve in partnerships over time. This is helpful in bolstering public-private sector collaboration. It provides a foundation of shared understanding for what needs to be done to achieve objectives.

- **Measure what is really happening—not what appears to be happening.** Business executives and government administrators should rigorously examine what is really occurring in public-private partnerships, rather than what appears to be occurring. The current gaps in information sharing for critical infrastructure protection demonstrate that there is potential for public-private partnerships to appear to be more beneficial than they actually are. To help correct this, there must be consensus on what both the public and the private sectors need from public-private partnerships to bolster critical infrastructure protection efforts. With this mutual understanding in mind, metrics can develop to measure genuine levels of cooperation and information sharing, as well as outcomes from cross-sector coordination. This basic re-examination of objectives will work to confirm that public-private partnerships are oriented toward common goals. New measurements can then track if public-private partnerships are producing what they are intended to for both government and businesses.

- **Focus on quality, not quantity, of information.** The gaps in information sharing above show that both government and businesses are dissatisfied with the information they are receiving from one another. The public sector generally seems to perceive that firms are "holding back" data on their own critical systems and facilities. Companies appear to find the government's information on critical infrastructure protection threats to be dated, watered-down, and of little use. This suggests that both businesses and government are following a process-oriented approach, meaning they are sharing for the sake of sharing, without paying much attention to *what* they are sharing. A goal-oriented approach, by contrast, emphasizes the quality of information. A "meeting of the minds" on the type, timeliness, and specific level of detail desired by government and businesses in information would go a long way toward reducing these mutual frustrations.

- **Increase awareness of cybersecurity issues in the emergency management community.** The post-9/11 world is all about breaking down silos among disparate security functions. But it is clear that aspects of U.S. cybersecurity (one silo) have not fully made their way into important federal-level emergency management publications (another silo). This suggests that there may be an underdeveloped awareness in the U.S. emergency management community of the increasingly important role cybersecurity plays in emergencies. Further integrating information on cybersecurity into emergency management training materials would help to raise conscientiousness of this issue. This, in turn, should help increase the penetration of cybersecurity-related information into emergency management documents.

- **Figure out resilience.** It remains to be seen if resilience will prove to be more than just a new buzzword in homeland security circles. While its use remains in vogue, important questions need to be grappled with by the public and private sectors, individually and jointly: What precisely does resilience mean to us? What are the challenges we face in embracing resilience? How will adopting resilience actually change the way we operate on a daily basis? And perhaps most importantly, can this change be measured? Our analysis suggests that significant costs will be associated with the evolution from critical infrastructure protection to resilience. At this early stage, it would be helpful for businesses and government to determine exactly what those costs are, and who will bear them.

While these preliminary steps will not solve all problems for public-private partnerships in critical infrastructure protection, they will be positive steps forward for this area of homeland security. Given the very necessary role these partnerships will play in critical infrastructure protection, policymakers should now help them to achieve all that they should.

IV. Conclusions and Suggestions for Further Research

Strong steps are being taken in all critical infrastructure sectors to bolster coordination and information sharing across the government-business divide. But despite these gains, a great deal needs to be thought through about public-private partnerships in critical infrastructure protection. Scholars and policymakers need to directly engage these challenges for public-private partnerships to realize their full potential. What follows are a few of the unresolved questions in critical infrastructure protection that merit further examination:

- **What measurable benefits do government and industry leaders reap from public-private partnerships in critical infrastructure protection?** The "tragedy of the commons" discussed above, in which individual actors in a public-private partnership tend to behave in self-interested ways, highlights the need for success stories in public-private partnerships for critical infrastructure protection. These success stories— accounts of measurable benefits for participants in public-private partnerships—can help to promote partnership-oriented behavior by individual actors in public-private partnerships. If a participant in a public-private partnership can see clearly how acting for the good of the partnership can also benefit him and his organization directly, then this can prompt him to act more for the good of the partnership than for his own organization. To generate these success stories, focus groups with business representatives and public sector officials can help explore the difference between the rhetorical and genuine benefits of public-private partnerships. These groups can also be an excellent setting in which to examine the advantages and frustrations of cross-sector partnerships. These data are useful for scholars and practitioners alike.

- **How do middle managers and front-line practitioners perceive public-private partnerships in critical infrastructure protection?** Analyses of public-private partnerships in this chapter derive mostly from high-level views of organizational activities. But workers at the middle and front lines of organizations tend to have a more detailed view of operational realities than more senior leaders. Quantitative analyses of these data can be particularly helpful in identifying emerging trends and challenges that may not be readily apparent to leaders in either sector.

- **What metrics measure success for public-private partnerships in critical infrastructure protection?** The information sharing gaps highlighted in this chapter underscore the need for metrics to measure the progress of public-private partnerships in critical infrastructure protection. Important scholarship needs to be done to identify metrics for success in public-private partnerships. This challenge is distinct from the identification of success stories and benefits mentioned above. It is essential to *define* the particular advantages conferred on critical infrastructure protection activities by public-private partnerships. But to be truly meaningful, it is vital to actually *measure* the strength and effectiveness of those same advantages.

Critical infrastructure protection remains an enduring challenge in homeland security, and government-business partnerships are indispensable to these protection efforts. While numerous gains have been achieved in public-private partnerships in critical infrastructure protection since 9/11, these relationships can also hide inconvenient truths about genuine effectiveness. It is now important for public and private sector leaders to examine if their partnerships are actually achieving all that they should.

Notes

1. Jonathan Dienst, "Exclusive: Wall Street Execs on New Terror Threat Info," nbcnewyork.com, February 7, 2011, accessed June 26, 2013, http://www.nbcnewyork.com/news/local/Exclusive-Wall-Street-Execs-On-New-Terror-Threat-Info-114985979.html.

2. Deb Feyerick, "Wall Street banks alerted of potential terrorist threat," cnn.com, February 1, 2011, accessed June 26, 2013, http://www.cnn.com/2011/CRIME/02/01/new.york.banks.threat/index.html.

3. Peter Stockton, *Nuclear Power Plant Security: Voices From Inside the Fences*, Project on Government Oversight, September 12, 2002, accessed June 26, 2013, http://www.pogo.org/our-work/reports/2002/nss-npp-20020912.html.

4. Eric Loveday, "Pentagon deploys T3 Series electric three-wheeler for perimeter security," autoblog.com, January 12, 2011, accessed June 26, 2013, http://green.autoblog.com/2011/01/12/pentagon-t3-series-electric-three-wheeler-security/.

5. Marc Gerencser, Jim Weinberg, and Don Vincent, *Port Security War Game: Implications for U.S. Supply Chains*, Booz Allen Hamilton, 2002, accessed June 26, 2013, http://www.boozallen.com/media/file/Port_Security_War_Game.pdf.

6. U.S. Department of Homeland Security, "DHS Highlights Two Cybersecurity Initiatives to Enhance Coordination with State and Local Governments and Private Sector Partners," dhs.gov, November 18, 2010, accessed June 26, 2013, http://www.dhs.gov/news/2010/11/18/dhs-highlights-two-cybersecurity-initiatives-enhance-coordination-state-and-local.

7. U.S. Department of Homeland Security, "Critical Infrastructure Partnership Advisory Council," n.d., accessed June 26, 2013, http://www.dhs.gov/files/committees/editorial_0843.shtm.

8. The White House, *National Security Strategy*, 2010, accessed June 26, 2013, http://www.whitehouse.gov/sites/default/files/rss_viewer/national_security_strategy.pdf.

9. For example, in government documents, see The White House, *National Security Strategy*; U.S. Department of Homeland Security, *National Infrastructure Protection Plan*, 2009; U.S. Department of Homeland Security, *National Cyber Incident Response Plan*, September 2010; U.S. Department of Homeland Security, *Quadrennial Homeland Security Review Report: A Strategic Framework for a Secure Homeland*, February 2010. See also, see Phillip Auerswald, Lewis Branscomb, Todd La Porte, and Erwann Michel-Kerjan, eds., *Seeds of Disaster, Roots of Response: How Private Action Can Reduce Public Vulnerability* (New York, NY: Cambridge University Press, 2006); Sue E. Eckert, "Protecting Critical Infrastructure: The Role of the Private Sector," in *Guns and Butter: The Political Economy of International Security*, ed. Peter Dombrowski (Boulder, CO: Lynne Rienner, 2005).

10. Mark de Bruijne and Michel Van Eeten, "Systems That Should Have Failed: Critical Infrastructure Protection in an Institutionally Fragmented Environment," *Journal of Contingencies and Crisis Management* 15, no. 1 (March 2007): 18–29; Myriam Cavelty and Manuel Suter, "Public-private partnerships are no silver bullet: An expanded governance model for Critical Infrastructure Protection," *International Journal of Critical Infrastructure Protection* 2, no. 4 (December 2009): 179–187; Mayada Omer, Rosanak Milchiani, and Ali Mostashari, "Measuring the Resilience of the Global Internet Infrastructure System," in *2009 IEEE International Systems Conference Proceedings*, Vancouver, British Columbia, Canada, March 23–26, 2009, accessed June 26, 2013, http://www.stevens.edu/csr/fileadmin/csr/Publications/Omer_Measuring_the_Resilience_of_the_Global_Internet__Infrastructure.pdf, 156–162; Ted Lewis and Rudy Darken, "Potholes and Detours in the Road to Critical Infrastructure Protection Policy," *Homeland Security Affairs* 1, no. 2 (August 2005): 1–11; Stephen E. Flynn, "The Brittle Superpower," in *Seeds of Disaster, Roots of Response: How Private Action Can Reduce Public Vulnerability*, eds. Phillip Auerswald, Lewis Branscomb, Todd La Porte, and Erwann Michel-Kerjan (New York: Cambridge University Press, 2006), 26–36.

11. Portions of this chapter appeared in Austen D. Givens and Nathan E. Busch, "Realizing the Promise of Public-Private Partnerships in U.S. Critical Infrastructure Protection," *International Journal of Critical Infrastructure Protection* 6, no. 1 (March 2013): 39–50.

12. Throughout the article, we use "critical infrastructure" in the singular to represent the 16 sectors identified as critical by the U.S. Department of Homeland Security.

13. President's Commission on Critical Infrastructure Protection, *Critical Foundations: Protecting America's Infrastructures, Report of the President's Commission on Critical Infrastructure Protection*, October 1997, accessed June 25, 2013, http://www.fas.org/sgp/library/pccip.pdf.

14. Ibid., viii, emphasis ours.

15. Ami Abou-bakr, *Managing Disaster: Public-Private Partnerships as a Tool For Mitigation, Preparedness, Response & Resiliency in the United States*, Ph.D. Dissertation, Department of Political Economy, King's College London, London, United Kingdom, 2011, 10. For an excellent overview of public-private partnerships in disaster management, see also Ami J. Abou-bakr, *Managing Disasters Through Public-Private Partnerships* (Washington, D.C.: Georgetown University Press, 2013).

16. The White House, "Executive Order Establishing the Office of Homeland Security," October 8, 2001, accessed June 26, 2013, http://georgewbush-whitehouse.archives.gov/news/releases/2001/10/20011008-2.html.

17. U.S. Department of Homeland Security, *Homeland Security Act of 2002*, November 25, 2002, accessed June 26, 2013, http://www.dhs.gov/xabout/laws/law_regulation_rule_0011.shtm.

18. U.S. Department of Homeland Security, *Homeland Security Presidential Directive 7: Critical Infrastructure Identification, Prioritization, and Protection*, December 17, 2003, accessed June 25, 2013, http://www.dhs.gov/xabout/laws/gc_1214597989952.shtm.

19. U.S. Department of Homeland Security, National Infrastructure Advisory Council, "Critical Infrastructure Resilience: Final Report and Recommendations," September 8, 2009, accessed June 26, 2013, http://www.dhs.gov/xlibrary/assets/niac/niac_critical_infrastructure_resilience.pdf, 19–23.

20. U.S. Department of Homeland Security, "Critical Infrastructure Sector Partnerships," n.d., accessed June 26, 2013, http://www.dhs.gov/files/partnerships/editorial_0206.shtm.

21. New York City Metropolitan Transportation Authority, "If You See Something, Say Something," n.d., accessed June 26, 2013, http://web.mta.info/ mta/security.html.

22. U.S. Federal Emergency Management Agency, "Make A Plan," June 11, 2013, accessed June 26, 2013, http://www.ready.gov/make-a-plan.

23. Aaron Wildavsky, "Riskless Society," *The Concise Encyclopedia of Economics*, 2002, accessed June 26, 2013, http://www.econlib.org/library/Enc1/RisklessSociety.html.

24. Brian Lopez, "Critical Infrastructure Protection in the United States Since

1993," in *Seeds of Disaster, Roots of Response: How Private Action Can Reduce Public Vulnerability*, eds. Phillip Auerswald, Lewis Branscomb, Todd La Porte, and Erwann Michel-Kerjan (New York, NY: Cambridge University Press, 2006), 48.

25. U.S. Department of Homeland Security, "Council Members, Critical Infrastructure Partnership Advisory Council," n.d., accessed June 26, 2013, http://www.dhs.gov/files/committees/editorial_0848.shtm.

26. Federal Bureau of Investigation, "Infragard: A Partnership That Works," March 8, 2010, accessed June 26, 2013, http://www.fbi.gov/news/stories/2010/march/infragard_030810.

27. All Hazards Consortium, "Critical Infrastructure Protection," 2013, accessed June 26, 2013, http://www.ahcusa.org/critical_infrastructure.htm.

28. Donald Kettl, "Managing Indirect Government," in *The Tools of Government: A Guide to the New Governance*, ed. Lester M. Salamon (New York: Oxford University Press, 2002), 495.

29. U.S. Department of Homeland Security, "Critical Infrastructure," n.d., accessed June 26, 2013, http://www.dhs.gov/files/programs/gc_1189168948944.shtm.

30. U.S. Government Accountability Office, *Homeland Security: Actions Needed to Improve Response to Potential Terrorist Attacks and Natural Disasters Affecting Food and Agriculture*, Report to the Chairman, Subcommittee on Oversight of Government Management, the Federal Workforce, and the District of Columbia, Committee on Homeland Security and Governmental Affairs, U.S. Senate, August 2011, accessed June 26, 2013, http://www.gao.gov/assets/330/322674.pdf.

31. Ibid., 8.

32. Ibid., 10.

33. Ibid.

34. Ibid., 10–13.

35. Omer, Milchiani, and Mostashari, "Measuring the Resilience," 156–162.

36. Ibid.

37. See Horst Rittel and Melvin Webber, "Dilemmas in a General Theory of Planning," *Policy Sciences* 4, no. 2 (March 1973), accessed June 26, 2013, http://www.uctc.net/mwebber/Rittel+Webber+Dilemmas+General_Theory_of_Planning.pdf, 155–169. By definition, wicked problems are multidimensional challenges that are difficult to grasp and lack tidy solutions. This is highly relevant to discussions of public-private partnerships, where hosts of at times contradictory variables can conspire against policymakers.

38. U.S. Department of Agriculture, "Homeland Security-Overview," n.d., accessed April 2, 2012, http://www.usda.gov/wps/portal/usda/usdahome? navid=HOMELANDSECU&navtype=CO; U.S. Department of Homeland Security, "Food, Agriculture, and Veterinary Defense Division," n.d., accessed April 2, 2012, http://www.dhs.gov/xabout/structure/gc_ 1234195670177.shtm.

39. Albert J. Allen, Albert E. Myles, Porfirio Fuentes, Safdar Muhammad, "Agricultural Terrorism: Potential Economic Effects on the Poultry Industry in Mississippi," paper presented at the Southern Agricultural Economics Association Annual Meeting, Tulsa, Oklahoma, February 14–18, 2004; Jim Monke, "Agroterrorism: Threats and Preparedness," Congressional Research Service, March 12, 2007, accessed April 2, 2012, https://www.fas.org/ sgp/crs/terror/RL32521.pdf, 3–11.

40. U.S. Government Accountability Office, *Critical Infrastructure Protection: Key Private and Public Cyber Expectations Need to Be Consistently Addressed*, July 2010, accessed June 25, 2013, http://www.gao.gov/assets/ 310/307222.pdf, 13.

41. Daniel Prieto, "Information Sharing With the Private Sector," in *Seeds of Disaster, Roots of Response: How Private Action Can Reduce Public Vulnerability*, eds. Phillip Auerswald, Lewis Branscomb, Todd La Porte, and Erwann Michel-Kerjan (New York, NY: Cambridge University Press, 2006), 410.

42. Ibid., 410.

43. Ibid., 414–415.

44. U.S. Department of Homeland Security, "SECURE (System Efficacy Through Commercialization, Utilization, Relevance and Evaluation) Program," n.d., accessed June 26, 2013, http://www.dhs.gov/secure-system-efficacy-through-commercialization-utilization-relevance-and-evaluation-program; U.S. Department of Homeland Security, "FutureTECH," n.d., accessed June 26, 2013, http://www.dhs.gov/futuretech.

45. Lewis and Darken, "Potholes and Detours," 1–11.

46. Ibid., 8.

47. Ibid.

48. For example, see Robert Panasci, "New York State's Competitive Market for Electricity Generation: An Overview," *Albany Law Environmental Outlook Journal* 6, no. 1 (Fall 2001): 25–32.

49. "Most Americans Unprepared for Disasters," *Security Magazine*, March 1, 2012, accessed June 26, 2013, http://www.securitymagazine.com/articles/

82813-most-americans-unprepared-for-disasters-; Angus Loten, "Most Business Owners Unprepared for Natural Disasters," *Inc. Magazine*, April 24, 2006, accessed June 26, 2013, http://www.inc.com/news/articles/200604/disaster.html; Courtney Rubin, "Why You Should Stop Reading This and Go Get a Data Backup Plan," *Inc. Magazine*, September 15, 2011, accessed June 26, 2013, http://www.inc.com/news/articles/201109/small-businesses-unprepared-for-data-disaster.html.

50. Flynn, "The Brittle Superpower," 30.

51. Ibid.

52. de Bruijne and van Eeten, "Systems That Should Have Failed," 18.

53. Ibid.

54. Bruce Schneier, *Beyond Fear: Thinking Sensibly About Security In an Uncertain World* (New York, NY: Copernicus Books, 2003), 41; de Bruijne and van Eeten, "Systems That Should Have Failed," 18–29.

55. "Securing the Modern Electrical Grid From Physical and Cyber Attacks," Hearing before the Subcommittee on Emerging Threats, Cybersecurity, and Science and Technology, of the Committee on Homeland Security, U.S. House of Representatives, 111th Congress: First Session, July 21, 2009, accessed June 25, 2013, http://www.empactamerica.org/13%20Transcript%20of%20Homeland%20Security%20SubCom%20Hearing.pdf; North American Electric Reliability Corporation and U.S. Department of Energy, *High-Impact, Low Frequency Event Risk to the North American Bulk Power System: A Jointly-Commissioned Summary Report of the North American Electric Reliability Corporation and the U.S. Department of Energy's November 2009 Workshop*, June 2010, accessed June 26, 2013, http://www.nerc.com/files/HILF.pdf.

56. SecurityFocus, "DHS Video Shows Potential Impact of Cyberattack," September 27, 2007, accessed June 26, 2013, http://www.securityfocus.com/brief/597.

57. "Protecting the Electrical Grid from Cybersecurity Threats," Hearing before the Subcommittee on Energy and Air Quality, of the Committee on Energy and Commerce, U.S. House of Representatives, 110th Congress: Second Session, September 11, 2008, accessed June 25, 2013, https://house.resource.org/110/org.c-span.281056-1.pdf, 2.

58. Ibid., 128.

59. Ibid., 58.

60. Ibid.

61. Patti Domm, "Corporate Layoffs Increase as Economy Sputters," cnbc.com,

August 1, 2011, accessed June 26, 2013, http://www.cnbc.com/id/43977352/ Corporate_Layoffs_Increase_as_Economy_Sputters.

62. Cavelty and Suter, "Public-private partnerships are no silver bullet," 183.

63. National Cyber Security Alliance, "About Us," 2013, accessed June 25, 2013, http://www.staysafeonline.org/about-us/.

64. Ibid.

65. Max Permann, John Hammer, Kathy Lee, and Ken Rohde, "Mitigations for Security Vulnerabilities Found in Control System Networks," Presented at the 16th Annual Joint Instrumentation, Systems, and Automation Society POWID/EPRI Controls and Instrumentation Conference, 2006, accessed June 25, 2013, http://www.inl.gov/scada/publications/d/mitigations_for_vulnerabilities_in_cs_networks.pdf.

66. "Protecting the Electrical Grid from Cybersecurity Threats."

67. Ibid., 128.

68. U.S. Chamber of Commerce, Business Software Alliance, TechAmerica, Internet Security Alliance (ISA), Center for Democracy and Technology, "Improving Our Nation's Cybersecurity through the Public-Private Partnership: A White Paper," March 2011, accessed June 25, 2013, https://www.cdt.org/files/pdfs/20110308_cbyersec_paper.pdf. This co-authored white paper supports the assertion that public-private partnerships can be strengthened in multiple dimensions.

69. U.S. Government Accountability Office, *Critical Infrastructure Protection: Current Cyber Sector-Specific Planning Approach Needs Re-Assessment*, September 2009, accessed June 25, 2013, http://www.gao.gov/new.items/d09969.pdf.

70. Ibid., 3.

71. Ibid.

72. Mike Lennon, "Threat from Cyber Attacks Nearing Statistical Certainty," *SecurityWeek*, June 22, 2011, accessed June 25, 2013, http://www.securityweek.com/threat-cyber-attacks-nearing-statistical-certainty/.

73. U.S. Department of Homeland Security, *National Response Framework*, 2008; U.S. Department of Homeland Security, *National Incident Management System*, 2008.

74. U.S. Department of Homeland Security, *National Response Framework*, 2008, 75.

75. U.S. Department of Homeland Security, *National Infrastructure Protection Plan*, 2009.

76. U.S. Department of Homeland Security, *Configuring and Managing Remote*

Access for Industrial Control Systems, November 2010, accessed June 25, 2013, http://www.hsdl.org/?view&did=7974.

77. Lizzie Coles-Kemp and Marianthi Haridou, "Insider Threat and Information Security Management," in *Insider Threats in Cyber Security*, eds. Christian Probst, Jeffrey Hunker, Dieter Gollman, Matt Bishop (New York: Springer, 2010), 59; Dan Lohrmann, "5 Reasons Cybersecurity Should Be a Top Priority," *Governing*, December 2010, accessed June 26, 2013, http://www.governing.com/topics/technology/five-reasons-why-cybersecurity-should-be-priority-public-officials.html.

78. Flynn, "The Brittle Superpower," 34–35.

79. Dan Assaf, "Conceptualising the Use of Public-Private Partnerships as a Regulatory Arrangement in Critical Information Infrastructure Protection," in *Non-State Actors as Standard Setters*, eds. Anne Peters, Lucy Koechlin, Till Förster, Gretta Fenner Zinkernagel (New York: Cambridge University Press, 2009), 65.

80. Ibid.

Chapter 3

Public-Private Partnerships in Cyberterrorism, Cybercrime, and Cyberespionage

In late May 2013 *The Washington Post* reported that Chinese hackers had stolen several advanced U.S. weapons systems designs from private defense firms and U.S. government agencies.[1] These stolen designs included plans for the U.S. missile defense system in Asia, which was built to shoot down nuclear missiles aimed at the United States and its allies, as well the U.S. Navy's widely-used F/A-18 fighter jet.[2] Senior U.S. government officials claimed that these thefts were part of a huge ongoing Chinese government cyberespionage campaign.[3] A groundbreaking 2013 report by Mandiant, a cybersecurity consultancy, stated that "Our research and observations indicate that the Communist Party of China...is tasking the Chinese People's Liberation Army...to commit systematic cyber espionage and data theft against organizations around the world."[4] The report noted that the Chinese government targets both public and private sector computer networks for what Mandiant labels "harmful 'computer network operations'"—principally the theft of information.[5]

Though the Mandiant report included significant new details on the extent of Chinese cyberespionage, the thefts were not exactly surprising. In 2012 former Director of National Intelligence (DNI) Mike McConnell, former Secretary of Homeland Security Michael Chertoff, and former Deputy Secretary of Defense William Lynn characterized the Chinese cyber threat bluntly in a *Wall*

Street Journal opinion column, noting that "[t]he Chinese are the world's most active and persistent practitioners of cyber espionage today."[6] Further underscoring the scope of Chinese cyberespionage, a 2013 Department of Defense (DOD) report to Congress indicated that in 2012, numerous U.S. government and private sector computer networks were targeted for intrusions for the purpose of data exfiltration, "some of which appear to be attributable directly to the Chinese government and military."[7]

Today's cyber threats do not stop with China, however. In May 2013 the *Wall Street Journal* reported that Iranian hackers had electronically broken into several U.S. energy companies' computer networks.[8] The hackers appeared to be surveilling these firms' computer networks for electronic vulnerabilities. With knowledge of these vulnerabilities, hackers could launch a future cyberattack to exploit these vulnerabilities.[9] These were not isolated attempts by Iranian entities. The reports of Iranian hacking into U.S. energy firms followed a separate October 2012 report that Iranian hackers had broken into the computer networks of Saudi Aramco, an oil company, and caused millions of dollars in damage to equipment and systems.[10]

The Chinese and Iranian examples above illustrate many of the challenges posed by emerging cyber threats. The Chinese attempts show how easy it can be to steal significant amounts of information from businesses using electronic tools, and the Iranian case demonstrates how an adversary could infiltrate and potentially damage U.S. critical infrastructure. And both cases prompt questions about government jurisdiction for investigation and prosecution purposes: where do we try cybercriminals? What evidence is needed in which jurisdiction to secure convictions? What steps should the United States take to retaliate against other governments' cyberattacks? It is not just theft and electronic sabotage that raise these issues, either. The world is increasingly threatened by cyberterrorism, cyberespionage, and cybercrime.

This chapter will argue that public-private partnerships are now essential to cybersecurity, and will remain so in the future, because of the converging interests of government and private sector actors. The argument proceeds in three steps. We first introduce cyberterrorism, cyberespionage, and cybercrime as distinct-yet-related topics. The chapter then describes how public-private partnerships successfully mitigate cyberterrorism, cyberespionage, and cybercrime, and we explore some of the challenges facing public-private partnerships in these areas. The chapter concludes by offering a few predictions about the future of public-private partnerships in cybersecurity.

I. Distinguishing Among Cyberterrorism, Cyberespionage, and Cybercrime

It is possible to distinguish among the different types of cybersecurity threats by examining the separate risks arising from cyberterrorism, cyberespionage, and cybercrime. In the case of cyberterrorism, there is increasing potential for a nefarious actors to use electronic networks to launch attacks against nations. When this occurs, electronic networks can be used to induce political change within a society or government.

Foreign intelligence services now steal secrets over the Internet and other electronic networks. Espionage is nothing new, but the way in which it is done in the cyber domain *is* new and unique. In theory, an actor thousands of miles away from a target can use malware, hacking, or social engineering to steal secrets stored in electronic form. And this threat is very real. DOD Deputy Undersecretary for Policy William J. Lynn III recently noted that DOD networks are attacked thousands of times per day.[11]

Cybercrime refers to the use of computers to commit what would otherwise be conceived of as conventional criminal acts. Foremost among these is theft. Cybercrime is big business; Symantec—a well-known computer security firm—estimates that $114 billion is stolen through cybercrime each year.[12] Moreover, cybercrime's costs now exceed those of the combined global black market in marijuana, cocaine, and heroin.[13] In their own ways, cyberterrorism, cyberespionage, and cybercrime are indicative of a more general trend in society. That is, in the future, computers and electronic networks will be increasingly used as instruments for acts of terrorism, espionage, and crime, and these acts may ultimately outnumber conventional incidents of terrorism, espionage, and crime.

And it is hard to see how this *couldn't* happen given current trends: 85% of all information technology infrastructure in the United States is controlled by the private sector. Moreover, the public sector—be it DOD, the Federal Bureau of Investigation (FBI), or other agencies—now has a deep interest in countering cyberterrorism, cyberespionage, and cybercrime. Since the majority of U.S. information technology infrastructure is owned and managed by the private sector, and government's first duty is to protect its citizens, this confluence of variables suggests that public-private partnerships will play a central and significant role in federal cybersecurity initiatives for the foreseeable future.

Cyberterrorism

Cyberterrorism refers to the exploitative use of computer systems to bring about political change. As with real world terrorism, cyberterrorism can impact government and military computer systems, as well as computer systems of civilian organizations and individuals. Scholars have defined this emerging threat in different ways. Cavelty says cyberterrorism is an unsettled idea. Absent understanding of the term and evidence of its existence, she argues, it is difficult to say if cyberterrorism will ever actually materialize.[14] In a 2004 study, Prichard and MacDonald found that most computer science texts paid short shrift to the topic, despite its significance for national security and private sector employment opportunities.[15] Relatedly, Thomas Rid believes the term "cyber war" is a misnomer, because there is no violence in a cyberattack like in conventional war; for Rid, the idea of cyber war has more in common "with the war on obesity than with World War II."[16]

Other scholars accept cyberterrorism as reality. Hardy compares U.S. cyberterrorism laws with similar laws from Commonwealth states (Canada, New Zealand, Australia, and the United Kingdom) and he argues that U.S. definitions for cyberterrorism are more finely calibrated than those of the Commonwealth states.[17] There seems to be emerging consensus around what cyberterrorism is, for these states' definitions include important similarities. A curious event in 2008 further sharpened our understanding of cyberterrorism, as well as the prominent role of public-private partnerships in combatting it.

Logic bombs are a form of malware. They undermine computer systems by triggering a "new logic" that disrupts normal functions. In 2008, government and private sector officials discovered logic bombs planted by foreign governments on the U.S. Bulk Power System (BPS). (They did not disclose precisely which governments were responsible for it.) This discovery was widely reported in popular media. *The Wall Street Journal* carried a front-page headline about the logic bombs.[18] Former White House cybersecurity czar Richard Clarke warned about the bombs' potential impact in his own book, *Cyber War*.[19] By potentially disrupting the BPS, these logic bombs would also disrupt daily life. Practically every aspect of modern society relies on electricity in some form, from life support systems in hospitals, to databases in commercial banks, to mass transportation systems. Public-private partnerships played a significant role in identifying these logic bombs on the BPS, as well as in developing measures to reduce or eliminate the threat they pose.

Firms generate most of the electricity produced in the United States. So it is no surprise that electrical companies in particular stand to lose quite a bit if these types of logic bombs function as intended. And the consequences could be devastating, not only from a commercial standpoint—businesses without power would have to close for some period of time—but also for private citizens who rely on electricity for activities of daily living. But what of cyberterrorism in other contexts? What might cyberterrorism's impact be on government and commercial operations? And what are the implications of those types of attacks for public-private partnerships?

Cyberterrorism threatens numerous systems apart from the BPS. The list of potential targets is long and can include Supervisory Control and Data Acquisition (SCADA) systems, bank databases, and organizational data storage facilities. For each of these systems there is potential for harm in the event of a cyberterrorist attack. And this harm takes multiple forms. There is first an immediate harm, which is the disruption of whatever service is being provided by that system. For example, if a cyberterrorist disrupts a SCADA system at a wastewater treatment plant, the wastewater treatment plant may shut down. Second there is political harm. Cyberterrorism coerces political change. The precise nature of these changes can vary. A cyberterrorist may want to bring about the withdrawal of armed troops from a geographic area under perceived occupation.[20] A cyberterrorist may want to alter economic policy, promote re-distribution of wealth, or lower taxes. Thus cyberterrorism causes at least two distinct harms: one immediate and tangible, one longer-term and political. And both of these harms are strikingly similar to the effects of conventional terrorism. A related, but no less serious, cyber threat concerns one of the oldest practices of statecraft: stealing secrets.

Cyberespionage

The Chinese and Iranian hackings discussed at the beginning of this chapter underscore the extent to which sensitive computer networks remain vulnerable. Foreign governments, as well as non-state actors like Anonymous, can conduct electronic surveillance to gather information about how best to penetrate those networks.[21] Exploiting holes in network security, they can then steal information that can be used to gain strategic advantages. And the U.S. government knows this all too well.

DOD's computer networks are attacked daily.[22] These attacks are designed to spot and exploit weaknesses in DOD computer networks. Doing this can help a foreign intelligence service to steal sensitive information and damage U.S. national security in the process. But public-private partnerships help to mitigate the impact of these intrusions.

DOD relies on contracts with private companies to operate its IT infrastructure and to prevent the theft of secrets. These companies are well-known; they include Dell, Microsoft, Cisco Systems, McAfee, and Symantec.[23] These firms sell tens of millions of dollars worth of equipment and other IT resources to DOD, and can play a critical role in defending against cyberespionage. For example, Microsoft builds firewalls that can prevent computer users from accessing a computer network without permission.[24] Over 30 companies have collaborated with DOD to build effective network intrusion detection systems (NIDS), which function like burglar alarms for computer networks.[25] In this way, private companies partner with DOD to restrict external and internal access to DOD networks.

Theft of proprietary industrial secrets is also a problem today. Security experts have advised businesses that the Russian and Chinese governments are stealing trade secrets, research, and other corporate data in order to gain a competitive economic advantage over the United States. [26] Businesses partner with government to counter this trend. For example, the FBI will train business officials on how to spot and avoid espionage, whether that espionage comes from external electronic breaches or business insiders working for a foreign government. The FBI also develops relationships with industry officials to collect reports on suspected business espionage.[27] In this way, private sector representatives can serve as a "force multiplier" for counterintelligence efforts. Thus public-private partnerships help to decrease the theft of trade secrets and research from U.S. firms. This furthers the national interest, because government is better able to prevent espionage, and businesses retain their own competitive advantage by preventing theft of data and research. This "win-win" scenario exemplifies the value of public-private partnerships in countering cyber espionage. And a related area of cybersecurity—cybercrime—is now a multibillion dollar problem.

Cybercrime

Albert Gonzalez was a brilliant hacker. And he was scared. After police arrested Gonzalez for using stolen bank card numbers in 2003, he agreed to help the U.S. Secret Service in chasing down other cybercriminals in order to avoid prosecution. The information he passed on to the U.S. Secret Service was valuable; it helped indict a dozen members of a hacking ring that Gonzalez had been affiliated with. Remarkably, while working as a paid informant for the U.S. Secret Service from 2003–2008, Gonzalez also stole millions of debit and credit card numbers from well-known U.S. firms, including JC Penney, TJ Maxx, 7-Eleven, and Target. Using this information, Gonzalez pilfered millions of dollars.[28] But his duplicity caught up with him. In 2010, a judge handed Gonzalez a 20-year prison term—the longest sentence for computer crimes in U.S. history.[29]

The Gonzalez case is not unique. For example, in 2011, police arrested members of an international organization that duped nearly a million computer users into purchasing security software that did not work.[30] Or consider another case, in which a hacker named Jonathan James pilfered $1.7 million worth of specialized software from NASA.[31] These actions demonstrate the wide range of possibilities available to cybercriminals. Today financial investigators from private firms play an essential role alongside their government counterparts in reducing theft via computer networks. These employees routinely partner with government law enforcement officials, including those from the local, state, and federal level, to investigate and prosecute financial crimes.[32] Through such partnerships, government and business officials share information, collect evidence for prosecution purposes, and help secure convictions of cybercriminals.

Cyberterrorism, cyberespionage, and cybercrime undermine U.S. national security. Public-private partnerships not only play a role in responding to these threats, but more importantly, help to prevent them from occurring in the first place. The next section discusses the importance of public-private partnerships in mitigating cyberterrorism, cyberespionage, and cybercrime.

II. Opportunities for Public-Private Partnerships in Cybersecurity

Public-private partnerships are essential in mitigating the effects of cyberterrorism, cybercrime, and cyberespionage. Cyberterrorism can instill fear in the population and coerce political change. Cyberespionage harms U.S. national security and erodes economic vitality. Cybercrime permits rapid theft of substantial sums of money and provides a new avenue for criminals to destroy data. Given the private sector's huge share of all IT infrastructure, it is literally impossible for government acting independently to reduce these threats. So it is helpful to examine precisely what benefits public-private partnerships bring in mitigating cyberterrorism, cybercrime, and cyberespionage.

Opportunities for Public-Private Partnerships to Mitigate Cyberterrorism

Like conventional terrorism, cyberterrorist attacks require detailed preparation. There are seven recognized "signs" of conventional terrorism, and these provide a useful guide for what cyberterrorist attack preparation might look like. The seven "signs" are surveillance, elicitation, tests of security, acquiring supplies, suspicious persons, trial runs, and deploying assets.[33] Using these preparation phases as a framework for analysis, one gains a clearer sense of how public-private partnerships work to interdict cyberterrorism.

Surveillance in Cyberterrorism. In conventional terrorism, surveillance could involve a would-be terrorist covertly photographing a potential target, or loitering around a guardhouse at night to get a sense of what his target's physical security is like. But in cyberterrorism, surveillance might mean a nefarious actor scanning ports—the electronic equivalent of a thief checking for unlocked cars in a parking garage—to assess vulnerabilities in computer networks. These same vulnerabilities, the thinking goes, can be exploited later for an attack. The private sector builds network intrusion detection products that can identify when a port is being scanned. The alerts from these network intrusion detection products notify government computer network administrators. The government computer network administrators can then intervene to halt the scan. In this way, private sector products help to reduce or eliminate surveillance in cyberterrorism.

Elicitation in Cyberterrorism. Elicitation means attempting to gain information about a target or facility. A conventional terrorist might casually ask about a facility's physical security or employees' work schedules, for example. But a cyberterrorist can do this by posing as a legitimate organization's employee over the phone and using a technique called social engineering. The would-be cyberterrorist telephones multiple offices in an organization. He claims to be an employee of the organization, often using corporate jargon to establish credibility. A typical telephone conversation might go as follows:

> Cyberterrorist: Yeah, hi, this is John down in IT. We got a report about a computer virus circulating in your division. You know anything about this?

> Employee: No, John, I don't know anything about that. Who reported it?

> Cyberterrorist: Uh, I think it was Jane...or maybe Dan....sorry, it's written on a Post-It here, I can't quite make out the writing. (Sigh.) Hey, do me a favor would you? Could you go into your system preferences and tell me what version of Windows you're using?

> Employee: Uh...sure, no problem....can you walk me through how to do it?

The cyberterrorist repeats this type of telephone call many times. He contacts different employees and different departments within the organization. Through multiple conversations, he is able to stealthily gain a sense of an organization's internal vocabulary and structure. He may learn employee names and responsibilities, leading him to make additional calls in a kind of snowball effect that is familiar to academic researchers. Depending upon how the cyberterrorist frames his own phony responsibilities during these calls, he can gather other information about network vulnerabilities that can be used to carry out an attack. The private sector, however, produces tools that can prevent this from happening.

Perhaps the simplest of these tools is caller ID, which can show precisely who is attempting to call someone within an organization. Displaying inbound phone numbers provides a helpful security check against social engineering. Another tool made available through public-private partnerships is administrative rights on software. Here is how administrative rights work. Most organizations' IT departments impose restrictions on installing software. For example, it is likely that your employer's IT department limits your ability to install software on your office desktop computer. This is for good reason—it prevents less-than-reputable software from being installed on your computer, which if flawed, infected by a virus, or corrupted could compromise the security of your employer's entire computer network. Social engineering attacks' effects are limited by administrative rights. A would-be cyberterrorist cannot ask his interlocutor to install software on his computer, because—again, by design—the interloctuor's IT department prevents him from installing software. Thus two simple tools—caller ID and administrative rights—reduce the risk of elicitation. And this helps to prevent cyberterrorism.

Tests of Security in Cyberterrorism. To test security in conventional terrorism, a would-be terrorist might deliberately act in an unruly way on an airplane—cursing, shouting, or walking up the aisle when he is not allowed to do so. By doing this, the would-be terrorist learns how passengers and flight attendants respond, and can use this information to attack at a later time. But to test security in cyberspace, the would-be cyberterrorist may attempt to penetrate one node in a computer network but not take any action after that penetration. This is like a burglar walking alongside a chain link fence outside a business, looking for bends or openings in the metal that could be crawled through. In testing security, the would-be cyberterrorist is performing two discrete tasks: he confirms that a vulnerability exists and verifies that he can exploit that vulnerability to attack. However, he does not actually attack.

Public-private partnerships foil tests of security in several ways. Privately manufactured firewalls installed on government computer networks restrict access to those networks. Network intrusion detection software, as mentioned earlier, can notify network administrators that their systems are being tested by a nefarious actor. This information can help prompt protective actions by computer network administrators. Moreover, privately produced encryption programs can encode data that needs to remain secret on government computer networks. This means that even if a cyberterrorist penetrates a firewall and somehow eludes network intrusion detection software, he will still have a hard time accessing data he means to destroy. In these ways, private sector innovation prevents cyberterrorists from successfully testing government computer network security.

Acquiring Supplies for Cyberterrorism. Acquiring supplies for a conventional terrorist attack is different than acquiring supplies for a cyberterrorist attack. In the former case one thinks of chemicals, bomb parts, or weapons. But in cyberterrorism acquiring supplies could include purchase of specialized software or recruitment of individuals with particular programming skills. This activity is easily hidden. Therefore it is difficult to make a strong analogy between acquiring supplies for a conventional terrorist attack and a cyberterrorist attack. This demonstrates that while there are important parallels between cyberterrorism and conventional terrorism, they are not perfect analogs.

Suspicious Persons in Cyberterrorism. The "suspicious persons" sign of terrorism refers to individuals engaging in suspicious activity near a potential terrorist target. For example: a group of unknown men show up at a guard station outside a nuclear power plant, or a worker with suspicious credentials attempts to inspect a server room in a data center. But unlike conventional terrorism, this activity is more difficult to detect in the cyber domain. Since a cyberterrorist attack will likely be launched remotely, cyberterrorists do not have to be physically present at the attack site in order to carry out the attack. Thus the analogy between conventional terrorism and cyberterrorism does not hold here. There are clear differences between suspicious persons in conventional terrorism and suspicious persons in cyberterrorism.

Trial Runs in Cyberterrorism. In conventional terrorism a trial run (alternately called dry run) means a live walk-through of a terrorist attack's execution. This could involve driving a vehicle up to a building, for example, or having a team of men enter a shopping mall in a pre-defined pattern. The trial run is supposed to provide the most accurate possible rehearsal of a terrorist attack without actually carrying out the attack itself. But in cyberterrorism, this might involve port scanning instead of driving a vehicle up to a building or having a team of men enter a shopping mall. It could also involve temporarily disabling a website by overloading it with data—a technique called a "denial of service" attack. These steps mimic the execution of a cyberterrorist attack because they re-create the steps that a cyberterrorist attack could require. Yet they do not completely follow through with the attack; they stop short of causing lasting damage. Public-private partnerships can help identify and halt trial runs of this nature.

Network intrusion detection systems reside on network servers and identify attempts to scan ports. Hosted intrusion detection systems are similar to network intrusion detection systems, but instead of residing on network servers, they are installed on individual computers and protect those computers alone. Suspicious activity reporting procedures between the public and private sectors also work to ensure that activity consistent with a trial run is identified and reported to the appropriate government agencies—particularly DHS's National Cybersecurity and Communications Integration Center (NCCIC). Via public-private partnerships, government and businesses detect cyberterrorism trial runs with greater ease and are able to halt them faster.

Deploying Assets in Cyberterrorism. The final sign of terrorism is most grave—deploying assets. This refers to the detection of a terrorist attack-in-progress. For example, in 2010, a T-shirt vendor in Times Square discovered Faisal Shazad's car emitting smoke. In this case, Shazad set off an incendiary bomb in his car, but it did not detonate properly.[34] This terrorist attack-in-progress exemplifies the "deploying assets" sign of terrorism. In cyberterrorism, the signs of an attack-in-progress may be more subtle than a car belching smoke. Websites may go down for no apparent reason. Computer networks could become inaccessible. Network and hosted intrusion detection systems might ring at full alarm. Important data may vanish mysteriously. And presumably this would occur on a significant scale, affecting entire organizations, states, or clusters of states. Public-private partnerships play a significant role in identifying cyberterrorist attacks-in-progress.

Software packages, like anti-virus and anti-spyware applications, network intrusion detection systems, and firewalls are important in identifying a cyberterrorist attack-in-progress. Moreover, public-private information sharing and coordination are indispensable for an effective response. In this context, reporting between affected organizations and the NCCIC—which is in charge of coordinating national responses to cyberattacks—is profoundly important. Otherwise, due to gaps in knowledge and awareness, the response to a cyberattack becomes disjointed and misaligned. Sharing access to databases or making physical computer equipment available for investigation purposes would be essential in these circumstances. Personnel may also cross between the public and private sectors, such that firms' employees are detailed to a government office and public sector employees are assigned to a private firm's office. This exchange of personnel facilitates information sharing. And public-private partnerships are also valuable in stopping cyberespionage.

Opportunities for Public-Private Partnerships to Mitigate Cyberespionage

Much of the work involved in halting cyberespionage is quite similar to that involved in stopping cyberterrorism. To better understand how public-private partnerships can stop cyberespionage, it is helpful to use conventional spying, also known as human intelligence (HUMINT), as a framework for analysis. The HUMINT cycle traditionally consists of six phases: spotting, assessing, developing, recruiting, asset handling, and termination. Using this six phase process as a framework for analyzing cyberespionage, it becomes clear that public-private partnerships are an essential bulwark against cyberespionage.

Spotting and Assessing an Intelligence Asset in Cyberspace. In traditional spycraft, a person who provides intelligence is called an "intelligence asset." Spotting refers to an intelligence officer identifying a person as a *potential* intelligence asset. Assessing means evaluating whether that person has access to information the intelligence officer requires and determining whether that person might be vulnerable to coercion. Applying these principles to cyberespionage, a number of interesting parallels emerge. For example, a foreign intelligence service may decide that it wants to know all about the latest U.S. Unmanned Aerial Vehicle (UAV) designs. The foreign intelligence service then develops a list of firms and government agencies involved in these projects in the United States. These firms currently include Boeing, Lockheed Martin, Northrop Grumman, BAE Systems, General Atomics, and AeroVironment.[35] The same foreign intelligence service then might also list the U.S. Air Force and Central Intelligence Agency (CIA) as prime targets for cyberespionage, as they are the government agencies most involved in UAV operations. To assess whether these firms have access to data on UAV designs, the foreign intelligence service might comb these organizations' websites for information on their UAV-related work.

Public-private partnerships can help to identify spotting and assessing early on. For example, using analytical software, network administrators at Lockheed Martin might discover an unusual number of website views from China, Russia, or Iran—all of whom are known to target the United States for espionage. The network administrator can flag this activity for further investigation. He can also set up an automated alert that emails him when Lockheed Martin's website is viewed by computer users in China,

Russia, or Iran an unusually high number of times. This provides an early-warning mechanism for additional suspicious activity. The network administrator may later report the incident to his superiors. Having a fuller picture of Lockheed Martin's operations, the firm's leaders might connect the network administrator's report with similar information from other divisions of the firm, such as Lockheed Martin employees being persistently approached by Chinese, Russian, or Iranian nationals while abroad. Putting these pieces of information together, this suggests a concerted intelligence gathering effort against the firm. This is certainly troubling, and may prompt Lockheed's leadership to notify the Federal Bureau of Investigation (FBI), which investigates espionage, as well as Lockheed Martin's partners in the U.S. Air Force and CIA. In this way, public-private partnerships form part of a wide network that detects and shares information on potential cyberespionage.

Developing and "Recruiting" an Intelligence Asset in Cyberspace. Development and recruitment refer to an intelligence officer forging a relationship with a potential intelligence asset. Traditionally this might involve social gatherings like formal business meetings (intelligence officers almost always work undercover), cocktail parties or dinners, along with simple information exchanges, such as the asset passing non-sensitive reports to the intelligence officer. Gradually the intelligence officer asks the potential asset for more and increasingly sensitive information, and pushes their meetings into dark corners—out-of-the-way bars, restaurants, hotel rooms, and alleys. By taking these actions, the intelligence officer and his asset begin to behave in a way that closely mirrors a true spy-asset relationship. Once this pattern is well-established, the officer then makes a recruitment pitch to the would-be asset: would you like to work for us? Applying these ideas to cyberespionage, the development phase might involve assessing businesses and government agencies' computer networks for vulnerabilities. For example: What does a port scan of BAE Systems reveal about network vulnerabilities? Are the U.S. Air Force's computer networks in Nevada, where much UAV piloting takes place, behind well-designed firewalls? Is it possible to determine if any of their data is unprotected? The "recruitment" phase of cyberespionage acts on this information. Once it becomes clear that a network can be penetrated, and that the network contains the information the foreign intelligence service needs, then the foreign intelligence service commits to penetrating the network and collecting the information. This can happen using existing electronic tools, or the foreign intelligence service can develop new technologies and methods to collect data.

Public-private partnerships are invaluable in thwarting cyberespionage development and recruitment activity. Like the discussion of cyberterrorism above, network and hosted detection intrusion systems can notify network administrators of suspicious activity, including port scanning and pinging, which might indicate networks are being probed for intelligence-gathering purposes. Firewalls can head off efforts to identify network vulnerabilities. Anti-malware software can stop foreign intelligence services from covertly siphoning data from government computer networks. Moreover, companies and government agencies can share information about these suspicious network activities, increasing mutual awareness and understanding of these activities. Public-private partnerships help stop cyberespionage in this way.

Asset Handling in Cyberspace. The next phase of the HUMINT cycle—asset handling—is the crux of espionage itself. It refers to the act of collecting information from an intelligence asset over a period of time. In traditional spycraft, this can happen any number of ways: through "dead drops," where an asset leaves packets of information for the officer to pick up; through transfer of electronic files on USB drives; or through verbal conversations in out-of-the-way hotel rooms. In cyberespionage, asset handling refers to the foreign intelligence service actively stealing information from a computer network. Using the earlier example, this could mean that the foreign intelligence service penetrates computer networks at Boeing and begins electronically transferring data files to the foreign intelligence service's headquarters. Similar intelligence gathering methods might be used on government computer networks at the U.S. Air Force and CIA. In collecting information, the foreign intelligence service achieves its objective by gathering information about the topic that prompted the intelligence cycle to begin in the first place.

Working together, government and businesses can shut down cyberespionage activities-in-progress. For example, Boeing's network administrator may discover a pattern of unusual activity on a computer network, such as large amounts of data streaming out of the firm. He may investigate this further and discover that a foreign intelligence service is stealing the data. The network administrator can then stop this by electronically adjusting firm's firewalls and notifying other government partners. Upon invitation from Boeing, public sector officials could also assist Boeing in investigating the source of the espionage activity and assessing what data was stolen.

Termination. Termination is the final phase of the human intelligence cycle. The relationship between an intelligence officer and his asset can be severed for a host of reasons. The officer may be transferred or retire—normal workplace events, in other words. The asset may prove unreliable, unstable, or too great a risk to be associated with. In extreme cases, the asset is caught by his own government and imprisoned or executed for treason; frequently the officer who handled the agent is simultaneously expelled from the country (most intelligence officers work under diplomatic cover, affording them diplomatic immunity from prosecution abroad). In cyberespionage, similar circumstances may also occur. The well of information may run dry—it could be that all available information on a computer network that could be stolen has been stolen. It is possible that the owner of the penetrated computer network discovers the security breach and promptly halts it, effectively shutting out a foreign intelligence service. An organization may also decide to move information to another non-secure network or an encrypted file directory while still unaware that its data is being stolen. When this happens, the foreign intelligence service's access to the information is cut off.

Public-private partnerships can still contribute to countering cyberespionage, even after a foreign intelligence service steals secrets. There are after-effects—traces of cyberespionage—that can spark public and private sector officials to investigate suspicious occurrences. Assume that a great deal of unusual activity begins taking place with UAVs in Afghanistan. Their navigation systems begin to fail at an alarming rate; many crash into the ground without warning. This circumstance might reasonably prompt U.S. Air Force or CIA officials to wonder if the UAV navigation systems have been somehow compromised. By investigating further, the U.S. Air Force or CIA might discover evidence of cyberespionage on their computer networks. Public and private sector officials can work together to examine this digital forensic evidence, identify those responsible for the data theft, and secure networks that may still be vulnerable. In this way, public-private partnerships can limit the damage from cyberespionage and prevent further cyberespionage. And in a similar way, thwarting cybercrime requires close coordination between government and business actors.

Opportunities for Public-Private Partnerships to Mitigate Cybercrime

Since most IT infrastructure is privately manufactured or controlled, effectively prosecuting cybercrime—a largely government function—requires private sector assistance. All crimes can be divided into three distinct stages: the prelude, the incident, and the aftermath.[36] Using these phases as a general framework for analyzing cybercrime, public-private partnerships' importance for thwarting cybercrime becomes clear.

The Prelude to a Cybercrime. All cybercrimes require some preparation. This may involve purchase and installation of software, studying computer hardware, gathering intelligence about a potential target, or designing new computer programs or scripts. Public-private partnerships have a role to play in each of these situations. For example, cybercriminals can buy things online or in person. Buying items online generates an electronic paper trail, because even criminals require a credit card number or PayPal account to buy things online. This electronic paper trail can be subpoenaed by police. Purchasing software in person also generates data. But privately manufactured cameras and cash registers can record cybercriminals' actions. This leaves a trail for investigators to follow.

A cybercriminal may go online to study computer hardware, or actually purchase the hardware himself. Whether examining data on a screen or physical hardware, the cybercriminal must act to obtain this information. But police can subpoena subscriber web-browsing data held by Internet Service Providers (ISPs)—data that can later substantiate that a cybercriminal was studying physical hardware online. Web browsers on individual computers can hold Internet browsing histories that investigators can later retrieve.

Thus Internet research leaves a trail that investigators can use to reconstruct a cybercrime. Like the software purchases mentioned above, buying physical computer hardware generates transactional data. These data could be in the form of credit card records or in-store receipts. Police and businesses can work together to retrieve these data for investigation and prosecution purposes.

A cybercriminal can gather intelligence in numerous ways about an individual or organization that he wishes to defraud. For instance, the cybercriminal might ping or port scan the target, techniques which help the cybercriminal learn of electronic vulnerabilities. But these actions can leave traces on privately manufactured firewalls and network intrusion detection systems. Network administrators can examine these traces of data, which can alert them to a pattern of suspicious behavior. The network administrator can then take action, like blocking ports on a network or prohibiting scans from certain Internet Protocol (IP) addresses. He can also provide information about the suspicious scans to his organization's leaders, as well as to intelligence and law enforcement agencies.

Cybercrime can also require a would-be hacker to write specific programs to execute prescribed actions. A recent hacking incident exemplifies this: in summer 2012, hackers stole millions of passwords from the social media website LinkedIn and posted the passwords on a third-party website. [37] To accomplish this, the hackers designed a script—a task-specific computer program—to vacuum up millions of LinkedIn passwords. Writing programs or scripts like this takes time, resources, and talent. Hackers often must solicit others' assistance to achieve their programming goals. This requires communication—communication that travels over largely private computer networks. This communication leaves behind digital evidence for business and government officials. When businesses and government share this information, intelligence agencies can pinpoint hackers and crime investigators can develop evidence for criminal prosecution purposes. If public and private sector officials discover this activity early enough, they can interdict a cybercrime before it occurs. But what if a cybercrime does occur? Public-private partnerships can again play a starring role in reducing their potential impact.

The Incident: A Cybercrime-in-Progress. Public-private partnerships can thwart cybercrimes as they happen. Examining phishing—a common cybercrime—emphasizes this point. Phishing involves a computer user receiving an official-looking email that asks the recipient to act. Often the message content contains urgent-sounding language to reinforce the point. The email message also contains a link. By clicking on the link, the user believes he is acting according to the email's instructions. He expects to be directed to an "official" website. But this actually opens the door to a number of crimes. Clicking on the link may covertly download software to the user's computer. This software secretly exports data to criminals about the computer user's activities. For example, the software can capture passwords or birthdates that criminals can exploit to defraud and steal. A more common possibility is that by clicking on the link, the user is led to an official-looking website, and asked to input information about himself—often a social security number, a birthdate, or a password. The trick is that this phony website is built for crime. It is used to dupe users into disclosing sensitive information. The computer user then unwittingly enters his information onto the phony website. Once he reveals his birthdate, password, or social security number, criminals can potentially use the information to steal his money and his identity.[38]

Public-private partnerships can decrease phishing. Firms whose corporate identities are used in phishing attacks alert the public.[39] Gmail, Google's popular email service, sets up filters to block phishing messages.[40] The FBI, working with businesses, publishes warning information about phishing and investigates phishing incidents.[41] And public-private sector organizations like the Anti-Phishing Working Group alert their members to phishing scams.[42] These incident-specific actions by the public and private sector lessen phishing's impact. And even if cybercrimes are successful, public-private partnerships are essential in investigations and prosecutions.

The Aftermath of a Cybercrime. Public-private partnerships help cybercrime investigators and prosecutors. For example, the Zotob computer virus first appeared in 2005. It attacked Windows server software, and in the United States, the virus affected CNN, ABC, and *The New York Times'* computer systems.[43] Microsoft and police from Morocco, Turkey, and the United States worked together to track down the writers and distributors of the Zotob virus.[44] In a different case, prosecutors used evidence provided by Microsoft to convict Robert Soloway of illegally spamming millions of people.[45] Governments and firms work together internationally to investigate cybercrime, too. The FBI sends digital forensic examiners abroad to train local police agencies in other countries; and it partners with firms to investigate cybercrimes. In training other law enforcement agencies, then, the FBI serves as a de-facto ambassador for the value of public-private partnerships in mitigating cybercrime.

It is clear that public-private partnerships have a powerful effect on cybercrime. They can thwart a nascent cybercrime, stop cybercrimes-in-progress, and help convict cybercriminals. But while helpful, public-private partnerships are not a cure-all for cybercrime, cyberterrorism or cyberespionage. We next explore some of the persistent challenges facing public-private partnerships in each of these areas.

III. Challenges for Public-Private Partnerships in Cybersecurity

While public-private partnerships hold great promise in reducing cyberterrorism, cyberespionage, and cybercrime, there are a number of important questions that remain unresolved. These questions are not unique to any of these three threats—they relate to *all* of them. A still-growing framework of local, state, and federal cybersecurity laws leaves open gaps for prosecuting crimes and advancing civil suits. Government and business interests do not align perfectly, leading to potential conflicts. Sharing resources and information can be difficult. And the public and private sectors must deepen their cooperation with one another to avoid complacency. To be sure, none of these issues spells impending doom for public-private partnerships in cybersecurity. For public-private partnerships to be successful, though, government and businesses will have to navigate these challenges.

Developing a Legal Framework for Cybersecurity

There is an underdeveloped system of cybersecurity laws in the United States. Legislation at all levels of government has not kept pace with changes in technology. This leaves important legal questions about cyberterrorism, cyberespionage, and cybercrime unanswered.

We do not know of a single local government law that specifically addresses cybersecurity threats. A smattering of state-level laws exist. [46] In California, for example, the Notice of Security Breach Act requires government agencies, firms, and non-profits that collect personal data to notify everyone in their database if that data is accessed without authorization.[47] This applies regardless of an organization's physical location; even organizations in other states must notify Californians if their personal data may have been stolen.[48]

In Massachusetts, a similar law requires any organization that owns or licenses personal information about a state resident to implement a comprehensive information security program.[49] This is no small undertaking. Under this law, even small businesses must designate an information security officer, maintain an information security training plan for employees, and monitor information systems for unauthorized intrusions.[50] But these state-level laws are exceptions; most states do not have similar laws.

At the national level, the U.S. Senate recently defeated the Cybersecurity Act of 2012, which would have imposed baseline cybersecurity standards for critical infrastructure operators and bolstered public-private sector information sharing.[51] But other federal laws lay groundwork for future cybersecurity legislation. For example, the Federal Information Security Management Act (FISMA) governs information security requirements for federal agencies.[52] Another law—the Computer Fraud and Abuse Act (CFAA)—addresses unauthorized access to computer systems, use of computers to commit fraud, and transmission of malware that can damage information systems.[53] A third law, the Electronic Communications Privacy Act (ECPA), covers crimes that have "no close 'traditional crime' analog."[54] In this vein, the ECPA addresses hacking, boosts computer users' privacy rights, and lets police use electronic surveillance to investigate possible computer crimes.[55]

It is likely that updates to existing laws and new laws will emerge to address cybersecurity threats. But it is also obvious that the distribution of cybersecurity laws skews to the federal level of government. Given the complexity of cyberterrorism, cyberespionage, and cybercrime, this still-developing system of laws leaves important questions unresolved.

Jurisdictional Challenges in Cybersecurity

Substantial jurisdictional questions hover over the future of public-private partnerships in cybersecurity. Overlapping jurisdictions make investigating and prosecuting cyberterrorism, cyberespionage, and cybercrime difficult. For example, a cyberterrorist attack that appears to come from an IP address in California may actually have been launched from Russia.[56] This is done using a technique called "IP spoofing." Who investigates this crime? The government of California? The FBI? The Russian government? All of them? And if a cyberterrorist uses a private ISP's resources in an attack, and the ISP captures important data about the attack, how does the ISP know with whom to cooperate in the investigation? How might the investigation change if the ISP is located in a place other than where the attack occurred?

International relations also come into play, particularly where the United States has a vested interest in prosecuting cyberterrorism, cyberespionage, and cybercrime. There are no clear legal norms for extraditions in cases of cybercrime, nor is there a well-defined role for international groups like the International Criminal Police Organization (INTERPOL) in dealing with cybercrime, nor is it obvious that specific international laws can be applied to cybercrime, nor if those same laws can be used for prosecution purposes in international tribunals. And could a court try a cyber-criminal in absentia? Or if an act of cyberterrorism were somehow to kill people, could an international human rights tribunal become involved? These ambiguities demonstrate how difficult it is to manage international jurisdictions in cybersecurity.

Post-trial questions also emerge. If a cyberterrorist is convicted of a crime, given that the cyberterrorist does not need to be where he attacks, where is he jailed? In his victim's jurisdiction, or the jurisdiction where he was located when he carried out the crime? Can a private sector victim of cyberterrorism—a Microsoft, Dell, or Apple—sue a cyberterrorist? These types of practical questions show how difficult it may be for judicial systems to deal with cyberterrorism. Unlike conventional terrorists, who plan, acquire supplies, cause destruction, and ultimately leave behind tangible evidence for investigators, cyberterrorists can manipulate their every step, so that a cyber attack appears to come from a place other than its true origin. This makes investigating and prosecuting cyberterrorism more difficult than conventional terrorism.

Cyberespionage presents similar jurisdictional challenges. If software companies' products fail to prevent intrusions on private or public sector networks, how liable are they for this failure? If a Chinese intelligence officer steals information from a protected DOD network, is there any hope of prosecuting him, especially if he is located in China? Does a foreign intelligence officer conducting cyberespionage enjoy diplomatic immunity from prosecution? And what international conventions might govern this diplomatic immunity?

Cybercrime can be lucrative for cybercriminals. And like cyberterrorism and cyberespionage, it is not always obvious what jurisdiction should lead in cybercrime investigations and prosecutions. If a cybercriminal steals one thousand Mastercard numbers, where will he stand trial? Can victims sue the cybercriminal, and if so, where? Assume for a moment that those credit card numbers are used to purchase televisions and DVD players from Target and Best Buy. Does the cybercriminal stand trial for fraud for *those* crimes, too? Where might *that* trial take place? Since Target and

Best Buy must then eat the cost of the televisions and DVD players, can they then sue Mastercard for poor security?

It is obvious that numerous legal questions surround public-private partnerships in cybersecurity. This is partly a function of legal system complexity; the world's political and economic connections grow every minute. But it is also the product of local, state, and federal laws not keeping up with emerging technology.

Unmet Expectations and Cost Overruns in Cybersecurity

Government and business expectations do not always align. This means that their approaches to cyberterrorism, cyberespionage, and cybercrime will also differ. And this can be problematic for public-private partnerships. For example, there may be misaligned expectations about the timing of service delivery between businesses and government. This can sour public-private sector relationships and lead to re-evaluation or outright cancellation of contracts. Moreover, controlling costs remains an important priority for government, particularly given the current national economic crisis. But public-private sector contracts frequently experience "scope creep;" that is, a slow and informal expansion of contractual terms. Scope creep generally increases costs and, by adding to a firm's responsibilities without providing support, scope creep can hamper firms' ability to fulfill their contractual obligations. The public and private sectors will have to carefully navigate these concerns for cybersecurity initiatives to be successful.

Sharing Sensitive Information for Cybersecurity

Government and businesses share cybersecurity information, but for each sector, the quality and timing of that information remains unsatisfying. Many business representatives maintain that the information they receive from government is watered down.[57] Government officials, too, are not exactly thrilled with the information they receive from businesses.[58] This is understandable for several reasons. From the private sector's perspective, there is a gap between information sharing and business results. Gathering, analyzing, vetting, and distributing information eats into overhead costs. Industry leaders also worry about proprietary information leaking to competitors or the public. What"s to keep a member of Congress, just briefed about a company's trade secrets, from accidentally disclosing this information in a press conference?

From the public sector's perspective, there are ethical, political, and legal concerns about sharing information with firms. Is it ethical for government to give sensitive information to a firm which provides that firm a competitive advantage in the marketplace? If business A receives sensitive government information, but business B does not—even for legitimate reasons—business B's leaders might wonder why they are left out. This can erode trust and damage public-private sector relationships. And government officials must be careful about sharing sensitive or classified information with businesses. Recipients must have an active security clearance that is at or above the classification level of the information, and recipients must be in a position to safeguard the information. These issues demonstrate that it will take substantial trust, built up over many mutually beneficial exchanges of information, to advance public-private sector information sharing in cybersecurity.

Integrating Public-Private Sector Cybersecurity Operations

There are legal, financial, and technical challenges to integrating public-private cybersecurity operations. As discussed above, there are tight restrictions on government sharing classified information with businesses. But businesses may need this information to act effectively, particularly in responding to cyber incidents. So what are government and businesses to do in this situation? Moreover, during criminal investigations, it may be illegal for firms to have access to investigation materials like physical evidence, personal data, or internal police reports. Yet to prosecute cybercriminals, police may need to give firms access to physical evidence, personal data, or internal police reports.

It costs money to integrate public and private sector cybersecurity operations. Robinson and Gaddis posit a spectrum of collaboration based upon opportunity costs for collaborating entities. At the low end of their spectrum, simple information sharing imposes few opportunity costs on collaborators. This could be termed low-level collaboration. At the high end of their spectrum, personnel sharing places high opportunity costs on collaborators. This could be called high-level collaboration. Thus cybersecurity activities ranging from information sharing to personnel sharing can all be called collaboration. But the truly hard work of collaboration—conducting in-person meetings among public and private sector representatives, for instance—is less common because of its high opportunity costs.[59] But it is precisely this sort of challenging, high opportunity cost activity that actually builds trust among collaborators.[60]

Technical integration of public and private sector cybersecurity operations is also difficult. Access rules, developed for security reasons, can shut out private sector employees from searching government databases or accessing government networks. Similar rules can block government employees from gaining access to important private sector databases and networks. For both the public and private sector, then, there is a delicate balance between information security and access to information on computer networks and databases. And there is a question of hardware, too. If a firm's employee is detailed to U.S. Cyber Command, who pays for his desktop computer? Where does the employee go for technical support? There are not immediate answers to these questions. But they illustrate the degree to which public and private sector integration for cybersecurity needs to be fine-tuned. Integration of public-private sector operations, however, raises concerns about loss of information or intentional leaks by private sector employees.

Loss of Information and Intentional Leaks

In June 2013 Edward Snowden, an employee of the government contracting company Booz Allen Hamilton, deliberately leaked classified information about two huge National Security Agency (NSA) surveillance programs to two major newspapers. [61] The disclosure of these programs caused a public outcry. Some analysts commented that, in light of these disclosures, public-private sector collaboration in homeland security should be re-thought. [62]

However, the call for scrapping government contracting to private companies may be misguided. It is important to remember that leaks occur from direct federal employees at least as much as from the private sector. For example, at the time of this writing, U.S. Army Private Bradley Manning is on trial for leaking thousands of classified documents to WikiLeaks, a news website. [63] Former CIA officer Aldrich Ames, FBI agent Robert Hannsen, NSA analyst Ronald Pelton, and U.S. Navy civilian Jonathan Pollard are also currently sitting in jail, each convicted of selling classified information to foreign governments over the last thirty years. [64]

The problem, then, is not the trustworthiness of private sector employees doing government intelligence work. It is the loss of information, or intentional leaks of information, by people with security clearances. Only the federal government can issue a security clearance. Private sector employees like Edward Snowden obtain their clearances from the federal government, not their private sector employers. Being granted one of these clearances requires that a person submit to a lengthy background investigation, a polygraph examination, and a drug test. Snowden had to submit to the same background investigation, polygraph examination, and drug test that other federal employees working for the NSA must submit to.[65] Moreover, Snowden worked in an NSA office in Hawaii—not a Booz Allen Hamilton office. His top secret security clearance, issued by the federal government, gave him access to incredibly sensitive federal government documents. So despite being employed by Booz Allen Hamilton, Snowden was, in effect, a de facto NSA employee.

Leaks and information loss will plague intelligence work for the foreseeable future, regardless of whether or not the private sector is involved. Firms involved in intelligence work must ensure that their corporate security standards meet the same security standards of the federal government and federal employees. Yet firms can only do so much. Private sector personnel and government employees are bound by the same regulations and laws requiring them to safeguard classified information. The federal government, not the private sector, decides who is sufficiently trustworthy to access classified information. But ultimately individuals decide whether or not to divulge classified information.

Developing Incentives for the Private Sector

With the exception of public-private sector contracts for goods or services, there are few incentives for businesses to cooperate with government in cybersecurity. There are no immediate payoffs, and collaboration is not necessarily profit-oriented. By contrast, there is no profit motive in government. The public sector protects citizens. This creates a lopsided arrangement in which the private sector needs financial incentives to partner with government, but government does not need financial incentives to partner with the private sector. For example, it costs money for the private sector to share information: a firm's employees must gather data, vet it, convert it to a form that is useful for government, and transmit the data to public sector partners. Each of these discrete steps imposes an opportunity cost; it is time spent away from other tasks that could increase revenue. Similarly, meetings between public and private sector representatives pull a firm's employees away from the office, monopolizing their time and preventing them from making money for the firm. But the story is different for public sector employees—sharing information with the private sector is necessary to be effective. And meetings with private sector representatives are completely aligned with governmental responsibilities in cybersecurity.

In light of this disparity between the public and private sector's motives in cybersecurity, the public sector needs to develop new creative incentives for the private sector to partner with it. These incentives need to apply specifically to circumstances that have nothing to do with a contract for a good or a service, because contracts already make money for firms—there is no need for additional incentives in contracts. By contrast, these *new* incentives need to focus on high opportunity cost activities without a clear financial return for businesses, such as personnel exchanges, meetings, information exchange, and sharing technical resources. It is not reasonable to expect the private sector to voluntarily cooperate with government, except when that cooperation advances the firm's business interests. Developing sound incentives, then, remains an important priority for the future of public-private partnerships in cybersecurity.

Appearance Versus Reality

There is a public value in cross-sector cooperation: the public sector benefits in political capital; the private sector benefits from the perception of its being a "team player," which can result in increased revenue. But there is a clear difference between the seeing and the being. For example, in Chapter 2 we discussed a vulnerability in the U.S. Bulk Power System (BPS) that homeland security officials discovered in 2008. These officials notified electricity companies about the vulnerability, and they identified remedies for the vulnerability. Despite this proactive notification, electricity companies failed to address the vulnerability sufficiently.[66] This shows that *genuine* public-private sector cooperation may not be as common as *apparent* public-private sector cooperation.[67] If the public and private sectors benefit substantially from *apparent* cooperation, this reduces the need for them to deepen their cooperation in more substantive ways. This can reinforce a superficial commitment to cooperation that fails to deliver the full potential value of public-private partnerships. Avoiding complacency in public-private partnerships means that government and businesses must commit to mining their relationships for their full worth.

IV. Future Implications of Public-Private Partnerships in Cybersecurity

Given the relative newness of cyberterrorism, cyberespionage, and cybercrime, it is difficult to forecast the future of public-private partnerships in this area of homeland security. But in light of recent events and current challenges, there are a number of trends that we will increasingly see in cybersecurity, which we discuss below.

General Expansion of Public-Private Partnerships in Cybersecurity

Expect public-private partnerships in cybersecurity to grow in number and scope. The data on cyberattacks, cyberespionage, and cybercrime all point upward. These threats will increasingly dominate policymakers' attention, and it follows that greater cooperation between government and businesses will be needed to prevent, respond to, and recover from them. At a minimum, then, we can expect public-private partnerships in cybersecurity to expand over time.

Growth of Public-Private Partnerships in Hardware and Software Design

Security has long been viewed as an afterthought in building computer software and hardware. Yet there is growing recognition that building security into the design of software and hardware— from the ground up—is a less costly and more effective method for achieving cybersecurity goals. Given this recognition, public-private partnerships will increasingly figure into hardware and software product design. Teams of government and business representatives may meet to review current cybersecurity threats, and how to mitigate those threats, at the early design stages of a product. These conversations will be valuable for at least two reasons. First, they will increase awareness of current threats to cybersecurity. Second, they will ensure that even if a comprehensive consideration of cybersecurity threats is not built into a product's design, at least a partial consideration of cybersecurity threats *will* make it into the design, which is certainly better than the status quo. There is already a formal arrangement for this kind of approach to product design: DHS's SECURE program, which pairs DHS representatives and industry leaders for research and development projects.[68] We can expect this and similar programs to pop up and expand in the coming years.

Public-Private Partnerships for Cybersecurity in Financial Institutions

Financial institutions' reliance on computer networks makes them particularly vulnerable to cybercrime. Effectively investigating and prosecuting cybercrimes involving financial institutions requires close cooperation between the public and private sectors. A financial institution can first detect and report something amiss to government investigators. Conversely, public sector officials can sometimes identify financial irregularities during the course of an investigation, leading them to alert banks to possible fraud or theft. As these types of crimes increase, greater integration of public and private sector operations will rise to meet growing need. And this stands to transform not only financial institutions' approaches to cybercrime, but also the relationship between financial institutions and government regulatory agencies generally. On the heels of the global financial crisis, it is fair to say that the relationship between banks and regulators has been strained. Each side views the other with greater suspicion; banks may see government as a heavy-handed financial policeman, and government may see banks as reckless, irresponsible risk takers. But with the rise in cybercrime involving financial institutions, partnerships will become the "new norm" for the industry—neither government nor financial institutions have much of a choice. Lines of communication between financial institutions and government will become more open. And it may well be that tensions between financial institutions and public sector regulators ease over time, too. This is beneficial not only for cybersecurity objectives, but also for economic activity in the United States.

More Private Sector Leaks of Government Information

As more government functions are outsourced to the private sector, there is increased potential for private sector leaks of sensitive or classified government information. This can happen in at least three ways: external electronic data breaches, internal electronic data breaches, and conventional human disclosures. In an external data breach, a third-party actor—neither government nor the private sector—forces its way into an electronic network to steal information. A classic example of this is a foreign intelligence service breaking into a computer network. It may be that a private sector firm, lacking adequate network protection, has sensitive or classified information stolen from it by a foreign intelligence service; this is the electronic equivalent of a burglar picking an easy-to-defeat lock. When external data breaches like this occur, there are important legal and civil ramifications for government and the private sector. There are legal consequences in the sense that an investigation could reveal that the firm broke the law by not safeguarding government information. There are civil consequences in the sense that government could (but likely won't) take civil action against the firm for damage caused by the leak.

An internal electronic data breach is equally possible. A standard example of this is a private sector employee accessing data that he should not access. To underscore the point, in 2009 a group of U.S. State Department employees and contractors were indicted for improperly viewing the passport files of celebrities and other high-profile public figures.[69] This incident demonstrates that leaks of confidential information—which years ago would have only occurred on the government's watch—can today be linked to public sector employees, private sector employees, or employees of both sectors.

There is a third, more conventional possibility for leaking government information—what we call conventional human disclosures. Two examples of this include the cases of Bradley Manning and Edward Snowden, which we discussed earlier in this chapter. Given the increasing potential for private sector leaks of sensitive or classified information, it is reasonable to expect government to impose more regulations on contractors. Moreover, as the private sector presence grows in cybersecurity, expect a corresponding rise in government scrutiny of its contractors' operations. These changes are both for good reason. First, it is in government's interest to ensure that the private sector safeguards sensitive information. Second, as more private sector employees perform traditionally government functions, there is a need for greater government oversight of private sector operations. Whether this means an expansion of legal authorities for DHS or increased reporting requirements for businesses, government will need to know more about how its own budget is being expended for cybersecurity purposes.

Cross-Sector Personnel Exchanges

Intergovernmental personnel exchanges for cybersecurity are already taking place. For example, DHS details some of its employees to U.S. Cyber Command, and U.S. Cyber Command details some of its own employees to DHS.[70] Although employee swaps between businesses and the public sector are not yet commonplace, it is reasonable to expect more of this over time as cybersecurity needs evolve. For example, representatives from Microsoft, Dell, Google, and Apple might find themselves working alongside DHS and DOD employees in Washington, DC for 6-9 months at a time. Similarly, cybersecurity experts from the FBI might spend time in Silicon Valley. There are numerous benefits to these personnel exchanges. They build relationships across the public-private sector divide; they promote information sharing; they serve as a valuable buffer during inter-organizational conflicts; they increase cross-organizational knowledge; they bolster trust; and they increase the effectiveness of both sectors' cybersecurity operations. Cross-sector personnel exchanges clearly hold great potential for the future of cyber-security.

Predicting specific changes for the future of public-private partnerships in cybersecurity is challenging. But current trends show that the number and complexity of public-private partnerships will certainly grow.

V. Conclusions and Suggestions for Further Research

Public-private partnerships hold great promise in countering cyberterrorism, cyberespionage, and cybercrime. They can increase the possibility of thwarting these activities during their preparatory stages. Public-private partnerships can make it easier to halt these activities while they are in progress. And after the fact, public-private partnerships can enhance the effectiveness of a criminal investigation and prosecution. Despite these benefits, public-private partnerships in cybersecurity face numerous challenges; and more importantly, public-private partnerships will shape the future of cybersecurity, too.

Since cybersecurity remains an emerging area of study, there are abundant opportunities for future research in this area. It would be helpful for scholars to examine how workplace culture affects public and private sector representatives' interactions and ability to cooperate with one another. For instance, it may be that the slower, more bureaucratic machinations of government are ill-suited to cyber incident management, and therefore the private sector can provide a model for a faster, more adaptable way for government to approach cybersecurity. There is also a pressing need for government and the private sector to share cybersecurity information. But a number of obstacles impede progress in this area. One line of research inquiry here could explore the current effectiveness of information sharing, and another could begin to tease out concrete ways to enhance that effectiveness. This research would be valuable for both scholars and practitioners. Finally, as discussed above, the private sector needs new incentives to cooperate with government. Researchers from numerous disciplines, including business, finance, and public policy, can develop measurable incentives for businesses to partner with government in cybersecurity.

Public-private partnerships provide one solution for addressing cyberterrorism, cyberespionage, and cybercrime. And there is no doubt that these partnerships carry benefits for both government and businesses. But their future success now depends upon a mutual commitment to overcoming shared challenges. This stands to usher in a new phase of cybersecurity operations—one in which public-private partnerships simultaneously address tangible cybersecurity threats, as well as less-tangible threats to the partnerships themselves. Given the increasing trust, information sharing, and operational synergies that today's public-private partnerships generate, government and businesses appear well-prepared for the road ahead.

Notes

1. Portions of this chapter appear in Austen D. Givens and Nathan E. Busch, "Integrating Federal Approaches to Post-Cyber Incident Mitigation," *Journal of Homeland Security and Emergency Management* 10, no. 1 (August 2013): 1–28; Ellen Nakashima, "Confidential reports lists weapons system

designs compromised by Chinese cyberspies," *The Washington Post*, May 27, 2013, accessed June 26, 2013, http://www.washingtonpost.com/world/national-security/confidential-report-lists-us-weapons-system-designs-compromised-by-chinese-cyberspies/2013/05/27/a42c3e1c-c2dd-11e2-8c3b-0b5e9247e8ca_story.html.

2. Ibid.

3. Ibid.; Department of Defense, *Annual Report to Congress: Military and Security Developments Involving the People's Republic of China, 2013*, accessed June 26, 2013, http://www.defense.gov/pubs/2013_china_report_final.pdf, 51–53; Ellen Nakashima, "U.S. said to be target of massive cyber-espionage campaign," *The Washington Post*, February 10, 2013, accessed June 26, 2013, http://www.washingtonpost.com/world/ national-security/us-said-to-be-target-; David E. Sanger, "U.S. Blames China's Military Directly for Cyberattacks," *The New York Times*, May 6, 2013, accessed June 26, 2013, http://www.nytimes.com/2013/05/07/world/ asia/us-accuses-chinas-military-in-cyberattacks.html.

4. Mandiant, *APT1: Exposing One of China's Cyber Espionage Units*, 2013, accessed June 26, 2013, http://intelreport.mandiant.com/Mandiant_APT1_Report.pdf, 7.

5. Ibid., 3.

6. Michael McConnell, Michael Chertoff, and William Lynn, "China's Cyber Thievery Is National Policy—And Must Be Challenged," *The Wall Street Journal*, January 27, 2012, accessed June 26, 2013 via ABI/Inform Complete.

7. Department of Defense, *Annual Report to Congress*, 36.

8. Siobhan Gorman and Danny Yadron, "Iran Hacks Energy Firms, U.S. Says; Oil-and-Gas, Power Companies' Control Systems Believed to Be Infiltrated; Fear of Sabotage Potential," *The Wall Street Journal*, May 23, 2013, accessed June 26, 2013 from ProQuest.

9. Ibid.

10. Nicole Perlroth, "In Cyberattack on Saudi Firm, U.S. Sees Iran Firing Back," *The New York Times*, October 23, 2012, accessed June 26, 2013, http://www.nytimes.com/2012/10/24/business/global/cyberattack-on-saudi-oil-firm-disquiets-us.html.

11. William J. Lynn III, "Defending a New Domain," *Foreign Affairs* 89, no. 5 (September/October 2010): 97–108.

12. Reuters, "Global cybercrimes cost $114 billion annually: Symantec," September 7, 2011, accessed September 4, 2012, http://www.reuters.com/

article/2011/09/07/us-symantec-idUSTRE7861DP20110907.

13. Ibid.

14. Myriam Dunn Cavelty, "Cyber-Terror—Looming Threat or Phantom Menance? The Framing of the US Cyber-Threat Debate," *Journal of Information Technology & Politics* 4, no. 1 (2007): 9–36.

15. Janet J. Prichard and Laurie E. MacDonald, "Cyber Terrorism: A Study of the Extent of Coverage in Computer Security Textbooks," *Journal of Information Technology Education* 3 (2004): 279–289.

16. Thomas Rid, "Cyber War Will Not Take Place," *Journal of Strategic Studies* 35, no. 1 (February 2012): 5–32.

17. Keiran Hardy, "WWWMDs: Cyber-attacks against infrastructure in domestic anti-terror laws," *Computer Law & Security Review* 27, no. 2 (April 2011): 152–161.

18. Siobhan Gorman, "Electricity Grid in U.S. Penetrated By Spies," *The Wall Street Journal*, April 8, 2009, accessed September 4, 2012, http://online. wsj.com/article/SB123914805204099085.html.

19. Richard A. Clarke and Robert A. Knake, *Cyber War: The Next Threat to National Security and What To Do About It* (New York, NY: HarperCollins Publishers, 2010).

20. Robert A. Pape, *Dying to Win: The Strategic Logic of Suicide Terrorism* (New York, NY: Random House, 2005), 80–101.

21. Anonymous is a leaderless, stateless, amorphous group of political activist hackers, or "hacktivists." See Radio Free Europe, "What Is 'Anonymous' And How Does It Operate?" February 29, 2012, accessed June 26, 2013, http://www.rferl.org/content/explainer_what_is_anonymous_and_how_does _it_operate/24500381.html.

22. Sean Lawson, "Just How Big Is The Cyber Threat To The Department of Defense?" forbes.com, June 4, 2010, accessed September 4, 2012, http://www.forbes.com/sites/firewall/2010/06/04/just-how-big-is-the-cyber-threat-to-dod/. The precise number of attacks varies depending upon how one defines an attack.

23. "Transforming the federal government for the future," dell.com, 2012, accessed September 4, 2012, http://content.dell.com/us/en/fedgov/fed.aspx?c =us&l=en&s=fed&cs=RC974327&~ck=bt&redirect=1; "Microsoft in Government," microsoft.com, 2012, http://www.microsoft.com/government/en-us/dod/pages/default.aspx; "US Department of Defense (DoD) Unified Capabilities (UC) Approved Products List (APL)," cisco.com, n.d., accessed September 4, 2012, http://www.cisco.com/web/strategy/government/security

_certification/net_business_benefit_secvpn_dod.html; "DoD Antivirus PEO-MA/IA Tools," Defense Information Systems Agency, n.d., accessed September 4, 2012, http://www.disa.mil/Services/Information-Assurance/HBS/Antivirus/Downloads-and-Resources.

24. "The United States Government Configuration Baseline (USGCB) – Windows 7 Firewall Content," National Institute of Standards and Technology, June 21, 2012, accessed September 4, 2012, http://usgcb.nist.gov/usgcb/microsoft/download_win7firewall.html.

25. "DoD works with industry on automated network intrusion detection system," infosecurity-magazine.com, March 21, 2011, accessed September 4, 2012, http://www.infosecurity-magazine.com/view/16745/dod-works-with-industry-on-automated-network-intrusion-defense-system-/.

26. Nicole Perlroth, "Traveling Light In a Time of Digital Thievery," *The New York Times*, February 10, 2012, accessed September 4, 2012, http://www.nytimes.com/2012/02/11/technology/electronic-security-a-worry-in-an-age-of-digital-espionage.html?pagewanted=all.

27. "Safety and Security for the Business Professional Traveling Abroad," fbi.gov, n.d., accessed September 4, 2012, http://www.fbi.gov/about-us/investigate/counterintelligence/business-brochure; "The FBI's Business Alliance Initiative," fbi.gov, n.d., accessed September 4, 2012, http://www.fbi.gov/about-us/investigate/counterintelligence/us-business-1.

28. James Verini, "The Great Cyberheist," *The New York Times*, November 10, 2010, accessed September 4, 2012, http://www.nytimes.com/2010/11/14/magazine/14Hacker-t.html; The Associated Press, "20-Year Sentence in Theft of Card Numbers," *The New York Times*, March 25, 2010, http://www.nytimes.com/2010/03/26/technology/26hacker.html.

29. The Associated Press, "20-Year Sentence."

30. Kim Zetter, "$74 Million Scareware Ring Raided," wired.com, June 23, 2011, accessed September 4, 2012, http://www.wired.com/threatlevel/2011/06/scareware-raid/.

31. Kevin Poulsen, "Former Teen Hacker's Suicide Linked to TJX Probe," wired.com, July 9, 2009, accessed September 4, 2012, http://www.wired.com/threatlevel/2009/07/hacker/.

32. U.S. Senate Committee on the Judiciary, *Cybercrime: Updating the Computer Fraud and Abuse Act to Protect Cyberspace and Combat Emerging Threats*, Statement of Pablo A. Martinez, U.S. Secret Service, 112th. Cong., 1st Sess. (September 7, 2011), accessed August 30, 2012, http://www.

dhs.gov/news/2011/09/06/statement-record-usss-senate-committee-judiciary-hearing-titled-cybercrime-updating.

33. Virginia Fusion Center, "7 Signs of Terrorism," 2007, accessed September 4, 2012, http://www.vsp.state.va.us/FusionCenter/7-Signs.shtm.

34. William K. Rashbaum and Al Baker, "Smoking Car to an Arrest in 53 Hours," *The New York Times*, May 4, 2010, accessed August 12, 2013, http://www.nytimes.com/2010/05/05/nyregion/05tictoc.html.

35. Oxford Analytica, "Drone Aircraft Market Surges in U.S.," forbes.com, July 30, 2009, accessed September 4, 2012, http://www.forbes.com/2009/07/29/aircraft-drone-market-business-oxford-analytica.html.

36. Marcus Felson and Rachel A. Boba, *Crime and Everyday Life: Fourth Edition* (Thousand Oaks, CA: Sage Publications, Inc., 2010), 132–133.

37. Colleen Curry, "6.4 Million Passwords Reportedly Stolen From LinkedIn Website," abcnews.com, June 6, 2012, accessed September 4, 2012, http://abcnews.go.com/US/linkedin-hacked-64-million-user-passwords-reportedly-leaked/story?id=16508728.

38. "Fraudulent E-mail examples," chase.com, 2012, accessed September 4, 2012, https://www.chase.com/index.jsp?pg_name=ccpmapp/privacy_security/fraud/page/fraud_examples.

39. For example, see "Defending Against Fraud," fedex.com, 2012, accessed September 4, 2012, http://www.fedex.com/us/security/prevent-fraud/index.html; "How to Avoid Phishing Scams Through Fraudulent E-mails," dell.com, October 20, 2010, accessed September 4, 2012, http://support.dell.com/support/topics/global.aspx/support/kcs/document?c=us&l=en&s=gen&docid=DSN_202A15BC34B7EFC2E0401E0A55174C77&isLegacy=true; "Active Facebook Phishing Warning! – Friends posting links to your wall which urge you to watch a video," facebook.com, February 26, 2011, accessed September 4, 2012, http://www.facebook.com/note.php?note_id=191956910837067.

40. Thomas Claburn, "Google's Gmail Blocks Phishers Sending Forged eBay, PayPal E-Mail," *Information Week Security*, July 8, 2008, accessed September 4, 2012, http://www.informationweek.com/news/security/client/208803181.

41. "New E-Scams and Warnings," fbi.gov, n.d., accessed September 4, 2012, http://www.fbi.gov/scams-safety/e-scams/.

42. "Anti Phishing Working Group (APWG) Public Education Initiative," n.d., accessed September 4, 2012, http://education.apwg.org/index.html.

43. "Worm strikes down Windows 2000 systems," cnn.com, August 17, 2005,

accessed September 4, 2012, http://articles.cnn.com/2005-08-16/tech/computer.worm_1_latest-worm-new-worm-zotob?_s=PM:TECH.

44. Jean-Christophe Le Toquin, "Public-private partnerships against cybercrime," Organisation for Economic Co-Operation and Development, n.d., accessed September 4, 2012, http://www.oecd.org/internet/consumerpolicy/42534994.pdf, Slide 2.

45. Ibid.; Jim Popkin, "Robert Soloway Exits Prison, Disavows 'Spam King' Ways," wired.com, March 3, 2011, accessed September 4, 2012, http://www.wired.com/business/2011/03/spam-king-robert-soloway/.

46. Tom Kemp, "Buckle Up With Cybersecurity...It's the Law," forbes.com, February 1, 2012, accessed September 4, 2012, http://www.forbes.com/sites/tomkemp/2012/02/01/buckle-up-with-cybersecurity-its-the-law/; Michael J. Glennon, "State-level cybersecurity," *Policy Review* 171 (February and March 2012): 85–102.

47. James F. Brelsford, "California Raises the Bar on Data Security and Privacy," findlaw.com, March 26, 2008, accessed September 4, 2012, http://corporate.findlaw.com/law-library/california-raises-the-bar-on-data-security-and-privacy.html.

48. Ibid.

49. Standards for the Protection of Personal Information of Residents of the Commonwealth, 201 CMR 17.00, *Laws of Massachusetts*, 2010, http://www.mass.gov/ocabr/docs/idtheft/201cmr1700reg.pdf.

50. Ibid.

51. Brendan Sasso, "After defeat of Senate cybersecurity bill, Obama weighs executive-order option," thehill.com, August 4, 2012, accessed September 4, 2012, http://thehill.com/blogs/hillicon-valley/technology/242227-with-defeat-of-cybersecurity-bill-obama-weighs-executive-order-option.

52. *Federal Information Security Act (FISMA) of 2002*, Public Law 107-347, http://www.gpo.gov/fdsys/pkg/PLAW-107publ347/pdf/PLAW-107publ347.pdf.

53. *Fraud and related activity in connection with computers*, 18 U.S.C. § 1830, http://www.law.cornell.edu/uscode/text/18/1030.

54. Dominic Carucci, David Overhuls, and Nicolas Soares, "Computer Crimes," *American Criminal Law Review* 48, no. 2 (Spring 2011): 402–403.

55. Ibid.

56. Matthew Tanase, "IP Spoofing: An Introduction," symantec.com, November 2, 2010, accessed September 4, 2012, http://www.symantec.com/connect/articles/ip-spoofing-introduction.

57. "Critical Infrastructure Protection: Key Private and Public Cyber Expectations Need to Be Consistently Addressed," U.S. Government Accountability Office, July 2010, 13.

58. Daniel Prieto, "Information Sharing With the Private Sector," in *Seeds of Disaster, Roots of Response: How Private Action Can Reduce Public Vulnerability*, eds. Phillip Auerswald, Lewis Branscomb, Todd La Porte, and Erwann Michel-Kerjan (New York, NY: Cambridge University Press, 2006), 410.

59. Scott E. Robinson and Benjamin S. Gaddis, "Seeing Past Parallel Play: Measures of Collaboration in Disaster Situations," *The Policy Studies Journal* 40, no. 2 (May 2012): 256–273.

60. Ibid., 266.

61. Glenn Greenwald, "NSA collecting phone records of millions of Verizon customers daily," *The Guardian*, June 5, 2013, accessed June 26, 2013, http://www.guardian.co.uk/world/2013/jun/06/nsa-phone-records-verizon-court-order; "NSA slides explain the PRISM data collection program," *The Washington Post*, June 6, 2013, accessed June 26, 2013, http://www.washingtonpost.com/wp-srv/special/politics/prism-collection-documents/.

62. Sue Mi Terry, "How to Prevent the Next Edward Snowden," foreignaffairs.com, June 17, 2013, accessed June 26, 2013, http://www.foreignaffairs.com/articles/139516/sue-mi-terry/how-to-prevent-the-next-edward-snowden.

63. Charlie Savage, "Former Hacker Testifies at Private's Court Martial," *The New York Times*, June 4, 2013, accessed June 26, 2013, http://www.nytimes.com/2013/06/05/us/bradley-manning-court-martial.html.

64. Federal Bureau of Investigation, "Aldrich Hazen Ames," n.d., accessed June 26, 2013, http://www.fbi.gov/about-us/history/famous-cases/aldrich-hazen-ames; Federal Bureau of Investigation, "Robert Phillip Hannsen Espionage Case," February 20, 2001, accessed June 26, 2013, http://www.fbi.gov/about-us/history/famous-cases/robert-hanssen; U.S. Department of Energy, "Ronald William Pelton," n.d., accessed June 26, 2013, http://www.hanford.gov/c.cfm/oci/ci_spy.cfm?dossier=118; Shushannah Walshe, "Who Is Jonathan Pollard? Obama Heckled Over Spy For Israel," abcnews.com, March 21, 2013, accessed June 26, 2013, http://abcnews.go.com/blogs/politics/2013/03/who-is-jonathan-pollard-obama-heckled-over-spy-for-israel/.

65. At the time of this writing the Snowden case is still unfolding. Questions are being raised about the rigor of Snowden's background investigation prior to working for the NSA. See Richard Lardner and Kimberly Dozier,

"Watchdog Faults Background Check of NSA Leaker," *The Associated Press*, June 21, 2013, accessed July 2, 2013, http://bigstory.ap.org/article/report-nsa-can-keep-us-records-indefinitely.

66. Nathan E. Busch and Austen D. Givens, "Public-Private Partnerships in Homeland Security: Opportunities and Challenges," *Homeland Security Affairs* 8, Art. 18 (October 2012): 1–24; "Protecting the Electrical Grid from Cybersecurity Threats," U.S. House Subcommittee on Energy and Air Quality of the Committee on Energy and Commerce, statement of Hon. John D. Dingell, 110th Cong., 2nd Sess. (September 11, 2008).

67. U.S. Chamber of Commerce, Business Software Alliance, TechAmerica, Internet Security Alliance (ISA), Center for Democracy and Technology, "Improving Our Nation's Cybersecurity through the Public-Private Partnership: A White Paper," March 2011, accessed April 2, 2012, https://www.cdt.org/files/pdfs/20110308_cbyersec_paper.pdf.

68. U.S. Department of Homeland Security, "SECURE (System Efficacy through Commercialization, Utilization, Relevance, and Evaluation) Program," n.d., http://www.dhs.gov/secure-system-efficacy-through-commercialization-utilization-relevance-and-evaluation-program.

69. Grant Gross, "State Department worker sentenced for passport snooping," networkworld.com, Jul 8, 2009, accessed September 4, 2012, http://www.networkworld.com/news/2009/070809-state-department-worker-sentenced-for.html?page=1; Grant Gross, "Sixth State Dept. Worker Pleads Guilty to Passport Snooping," pcworld.com, August 26, 2009, accessed September 4, 2012, http://www.pcworld.com/article/170864/sixth_state_dept_worker_pleads_guilty_to_passport_snooping.html; "Obama urges inquiry into passport snooping," cnn.com, March 21, 2008, September 4, 2012, http://www.cnn.com/2008/POLITICS/03/21/ obama.passport/ index.html; "Big-Name Passport Snooping Not Isolated," cbsnews.com, February 11, 2009, September 4, 2012, http://www.cbsnews.com/2100-250_162-3971357.html.

70. "MEMORANDUM OF AGREEMENT BETWEEN THE DEPARTMENT OF HOMELAND SECURITY AND THE DEPARTMENT OF DEFENSE REGARDING CYBERSECURITY," dhs.gov, September 2010, accessed September 4, 2012, http://www.dhs.gov/xlibrary/assets/20101013-dod-dhs-cyber-moa.pdf.

Chapter 4

Public-Private Partnerships and Information Sharing

Alhaji Umaru Mutallab walked into the U.S. Embassy in Abuja, Nigeria on November 19, 2009.[1] He was concerned about his son Umar Farouk Abdulmutallab's increasingly radical Islamic beliefs. Compounding Alhaji's worry, Umar had recently traveled to Yemen and abruptly cut off contact with his family, sending his father a text message that read, "I have found the true Islam. Don't try to contact me anymore."[2] Alhaji planned to go to Yemen to retrieve his son, but the Yemeni government would not grant Alhaji a visa.[3] Frustrated and out of options, Alhaji decided to warn the U.S. government about his son Umar and to ask for the U.S. government's help in tracking Umar down.[4] While at the embassy, Alhaji met with the U.S. Central Intelligence Agency's (CIA) chief of station—the top CIA official in Nigeria—and expressed his concerns about his son.[5]

The next day at the embassy, U.S. State Department and CIA personnel met to discuss the information that Alhaji had provided to the CIA chief of station. These U.S. government employees then wrote a set of reports about Alhaji's information, which they disseminated within the U.S. Intelligence Community (IC).[6] But despite these concrete steps to document Alhaji Umaru Mutallab's concerns about his son, and despite the possibility of Umar's links to Islamic extremists, Umar's name was not placed on any no-fly list or transportation watchlist.

Just over a month later on Christmas Day 2009, Alhaji's son, Umar Farouk Abdulmutallab, boarded Northwest Airlines flight 253 in Amsterdam, the Netherlands bound for Detroit, Michigan. 289 people were on the plane. Umar carried his own passport, in his own name, which contained an official U.S. visa—previously issued by the U.S. State Department—in 2008.[7] He had paid for his ticket in cash, and he did not check any luggage.[8] Umar had passed through multiple layers of airport security in Amsterdam, all the while concealing a mixture of high explosives in his underwear. He planned to detonate the explosives on flight 253 by using a syringe to inject a special liquid into them, which would set off a chemical reaction, triggering a violent explosion.[9] And as the plane approached Detroit, Umar injected the special liquid into the explosives inside his underwear. First there was a "pop" sound, like a firecracker.[10] But the explosives did not detonate properly. Instead, Umar's blanket, pants, and underwear caught fire.[11] A passenger on the flight leaped up to extinguish the flames, and then worked with crew members to restrain Umar so that the pilots could safely land the plane.[12]

Although in recent years there have been great advances in public-private sector information sharing for homeland security, the Underwear bomber plot demonstrates that the basic challenge of sharing information that is timely, accurate, and actionable persists. This chapter identifies and addresses several of the ongoing difficulties affiliated with information sharing between public and private sector partners and the subsequent impact of these difficulties on homeland security. As we will see, today public and private sector partners encounter challenges with inadequate trust between one another, difficulties in effectively filtering and processing a huge amount of incoming information, and problems with low quality of information. Public and private sector partners must deliberately seek to address these difficulties in order to bolster public-private sector information sharing.

The Underwear bomber plot occurred over eight years after the September 11th, 2001 terrorist attacks. Yet the parallels between the information sharing failures of 9/11 and the information sharing failures of the Underwear bomber plot are striking. The 9/11 Commission notes that in the lead-up to the 9/11 attacks, U.S. government agencies did not exchange bits of information in their possession, and these same bits of information, if properly integrated and analyzed, would have pointed toward an imminent terrorist attack upon the United States.[13] In advance of the Abdulmutallab bombing plot, multiple U.S. government agencies also had access to pieces of information which, when aggregated and analyzed, should have led them to place Abdulmutallab on a no-fly list. Yet that did not happen. Moreover, like the 9/11 attacks, U.S. government officials did not effectively communicate with private sector commercial airlines about the potential threat that certain individuals posed—in the former case, nineteen would-be hijackers, and in the latter case, Abdulmutallab himself.

There is, however, a fundamental difference between the information sharing failures in the Abdulmutallab case and the information sharing failures of 9/11. Unlike in 2001, when effective information sharing was more limited, today government is awash in duplicative, overlapping information sharing programs, tools, and initiatives. In order to alleviate the information sharing problems that failed to prevent the 9/11 attacks, the Information Sharing Environment (ISE) was created to streamline and facilitate information sharing across the federal government. And the ISE program has achieved significant success. For example, the ISE Program Manager notes that many of the 70+ fusion centers nationwide are sharing local-level suspicious activity reports with other local, state, and federal agencies.[14] The U.S. Department of

Homeland Security established its own office of Intelligence and Analysis, which took its place alongside the other 16 member agencies of the IC.[15] DHS now has plans to set up its own internal fusion center, with the goal of centralizing information from DHS's component agencies.[16] The National Counterterrorism Center (NCTC) was launched after 9/11 to centralize analysis of terrorism-related information from across the federal government.[17] And both public and private sector homeland security analysts are bombarded with information bulletins, alerts, memoranda, and reports each day. While on the surface it might appear that 9/11-era information sharing problems are solved, the Abdulmutallab case demonstrates that serious problems still exist.

In fact, in this chapter we argue that the efforts to correct the information sharing failures of 9/11 have not alleviated a trust deficit that exists between the public and private sectors. Moreover, the changes following September 11th have also inadvertently created new information sharing problems, including information overload for homeland security analysts and a decline in information quality. The challenge for public-private partnerships in homeland security now is to build cross-sector trust, control the flow of information, and manage information quality for decision-makers in government and business.

The chapter proceeds in four parts. The first part explains why information sharing is necessary for homeland security in general. In the second part, we describe how a lack of trust, information overload, and low-quality information hinder information sharing within government entities and between the public and private sectors. We then explain how public-private partnerships can help provide solutions to these difficulties by building trust between government and businesses, managing the information deluge, and improving information quality. The chapter concludes with a set of policy recommendations for government and businesses to address today's information sharing challenges.[18]

I. Why Information Sharing Is Necessary for Homeland Security

Information sharing is important for homeland security because public sector decision-makers can use this data to make more well-informed, and ostensibly better, decisions. And information sharing is more than just intelligence sharing. Schedules, bureaucratic processes and goals, individual agency and office plans, resource lists, and interpersonal communication all help policymakers to do their jobs more effectively. A lack of information exchange, or low-quality information exchange, can undermine national security by weakening precautions against conventional attack, terrorism, espionage, natural disasters, or other threats. For example, U.S. Immigration and Customs Enforcement needs to share information with U.S. Customs and Border Protection—both of which fall under the DHS umbrella—because their missions are complementary and they each deal with similar threats and challenges. The need for effective information sharing also transcends government departments. For instance, the Central Intelligence Agency (CIA) may need information on satellite orbits from the National Aeronautical and Space Administration (NASA) and National Geospatial-Intelligence Agency (NGA). In this way federal agencies collaborate through information exchange, which ultimately helps to achieve homeland security objectives.

Beyond information sharing among federal agencies and departments, homeland security data routinely passes horizontally among businesses and government agencies, as well as vertically among the local, state, and federal levels of government. In New York City, the NYPD Shield program exemplifies public-private sector information as well as vertical information sharing. NYPD Shield enlists local business owners to be the "eyes and ears" of the NYPD in identifying potential terrorist threats. The program encourages business owners and employees to report suspicious activity to the NYPD, because these private sector employees are familiar with what may be unusual or out of place in their facilities or neighborhoods.[19]

In exchange for their cooperation in the program, the NYPD gives business owners special access to NYPD intelligence or threat briefings, business owners can confer with local NYPD precinct counterterrorism coordinators, and they receive alert email messages from the NYPD.[20] Since New York City is under constant threat of terrorist attacks, the NYPD maintains a close working relationship with state-level agencies, including the New York State Police and New York State Division of Homeland Security and Emergency Services.[21] And both of these state-level agencies regularly communicate with federal law enforcement agencies like the Federal Bureau of Investigation (FBI). Thus it is entirely possible for a suspicious activity report from a Brooklyn police precinct to go through the NYPD, on to the state level of government, and then to the federal level of government. This type of vertical information sharing now occurs on a regular basis. But since 9/11, it is increasingly clear that vertical information sharing is not enough to achieve homeland security objectives. To protect the nation, government and businesses must exchange information with one another, too.

Government agencies and firms share information during disasters. Recent large-scale incidents in the United States illustrate the indispensable role of this public-private sector information sharing, for it facilitates effective disaster response coordination. As local, state, and federal agencies fanned out across New Orleans after Hurricane Katrina, Wal-Mart efficiently delivered tons of relief supplies to area residents. [22] But Wal-Mart also needed assistance in protecting its New Orleans–area stores from looters. As a result, Wal-Mart negotiated with local law enforcement officials, and agreed to provide them with supplies in exchange for protection from looters.[23] In this case information sharing between Wal-Mart and law enforcement officials helped to provide needed goods for first responders, and also helped Wal-Mart to be more effective in distributing relief supplies to disaster survivors.

After a powerful tornado struck Joplin, Missouri in 2011, Home Depot quickly re-opened its store there.[24] The store served as an important source of construction materials for emergency workers.[25] The Federal Emergency Management Agency (FEMA) and Home Depot shared information with one another about community post-disaster needs, and made arrangements to set up a FEMA information center inside the Joplin Home Depot store. The FEMA information center served to answer area residents' questions about rebuilding.[26] In this way, information exchange between FEMA and Home Depot met both public and private sector interests. FEMA provided information to area disaster survivors, helping to achieve its own organizational objectives. Home Depot benefited from locating the FEMA information center inside its store, because this co-location could draw more area residents to the store itself, potentially boosting sales. These examples demonstrate that when firms and government agencies share information, it enhances disaster relief efforts. This improved coordination can help to save lives and property in disaster-affected areas.

To be sure, information sharing for homeland security is happening within government and between businesses and government. Many of the fundamental information sharing problems that preceded 9/11 have been reduced or eliminated.[27] But new problems of low trust between the public and private sector, information overload, and low-quality information demonstrate that much important work remains.

II. Current Challenges with Information Sharing for Homeland Security

On April 15, 2013, several homemade bombs detonated near the finish line at the Boston Marathon, tragically killing three people and injuring over one hundred and fifty.[28] Within hours police officials had scoured surveillance videos to identify two suspects in the attacks—Tamerlan and Dzhokhar Tsarnaev, brothers and legal U.S. residents from the Boston area with ethnic ties to Chechnya.[29] In video from the scene, just prior to the explosions, Dzhokhar appeared to place a backpack on the ground in the area where one of the bombs detonated.[30] Tamerlan, wearing a ballcap and sunglasses, appeared alongside Dzokhar and was also carrying a backpack.[31] A huge manhunt began for the Tsarnaev brothers, culminating in two dramatic firefights with police that killed Tamerlan and severely injured Dzhokhar, who was later arrested.[32]

There are striking parallels between the information sharing failures of the Boston Marathon attack and other previous terrorist incidents, including the Underwear bomber case in 2009 and the Al-Qaeda attacks of 2001. The FBI was aware that Tamerlan Tsarnaev may have posed a threat, but Tamerlan's name never made it onto a "no-fly" list.[33] Moreover, despite having Tamerlan's name being entered into a federal terrorism database, no alert was triggered when Tamerlan flew from the United States to Russia and back in 2012.[34] The reason that there was no alert appears to be that Tamerlan's last name—Tsarnaev—was spelled differently on his flight manifest than in the terrorist database.[35] These information sharing failures, like those in the Underwear bomber case of 2009 and Al-Qaeda terrorist attacks of 2001, stem from a series of persistent challenges in homeland security information sharing. These challenges including a trust deficit, information overload, and low-quality information.

Lack of Trust between the Public and Private Sectors

The 9/11 Commission notes that the single biggest impediment to information sharing is human or systemic resistance to information sharing.[36] One of the biggest reasons for this resistance is a lack of trust.[37] Poor information sharing can damage trust. Similarly, damaged trust impedes information sharing. Without trust, communication becomes limited. This limited communication can delay important decisions, because both sectors cannot be certain that their efforts will be unified; they risk acting against one another's interests rather than working toward common objectives. Human lives, property, and the environment are ultimately put at risk because of this lack of trust between sectors.

The federal government has taken several steps to address the trust deficits that hampered information sharing prior to the 9/11 attacks. The ISE, which we discussed earlier, was created to build trusting relationships among government and non-government partners.[38] In its 2008 *Information Sharing Strategy*, DHS recognizes that it must cultivate trusting relationships with government agencies at all levels, as well as the private sector.[39] Today scholars outside government have also proposed new methods to improve trust between agencies so as to facilitate information sharing.[40]

But concerns about trust persist between the public and private sectors—and for good reason. Government may be concerned about disclosure of classified information—whether accidental or deliberate—and share lower-quality information with businesses to ameliorate these concerns. Similarly, businesses may be concerned about their own proprietary information being disclosed in public.[41] Trade secrets could leak to the media. Competitors could steal a firm's secrets. Confidential data could be introduced in court for civil or criminal matters. Government agencies could even seize upon discrepancies in company data, using them as a pretext to enforce certain business regulations. Given these concerns, the private sector may only share low-quality information with government, for doing so eliminates the chances of government disclosing trade secrets, competitors benefiting from leaked information, or firms having their own information used against them in civil or criminal litigation. Moreover, firms avoid being hauled into regulatory compliance hearings based upon information they provided to the government for homeland security purposes. While this reluctance to share information is understandable, it hampers homeland security efforts, because both the public and private sector are forced to operate with less than optimal amounts of data.

Information Overload

In light of the information sharing problems described above, the U.S. government has taken steps to boost homeland security information sharing. For example, DHS created the Homeland Security Data Network (HSDN) and Homeland Security Information Network (HSIN)—online portals for exchange of sensitive-but-unclassified and classified information alike.[42] SIPRNet, the Department of Defense's classified information sharing network, is now linked to HSDN, making classified defense information available to state-level fusion center analysts with security clearances.[43] Moreover, DHS produced Lessons Learned Information Sharing (llis.gov), an online repository for best practices in homeland security and emergency management.[44] The IC rolled out

Intellipedia—a classified intelligence sharing tool with the look and feel of the online encyclopedia Wikipedia—as well as A-Space, a networking and information exchange website for intelligence analysts.[45] Other tools that pre-date 9/11, such as the FBI's Law Enforcement Online (LEO), are still used by practitioners in the field.[46] Moreover, conventional methods of information exchange—telephone calls, emails, and meetings—are now easier through advancements in smartphones and online video conferencing.

Yet these efforts to improve information sharing, while beneficial in theory, may have actually created new information sharing problems. One study from 2009 suggests that analysts are frustrated—and overwhelmed—by the amount of information sharing that's happening now. For example, one of the study's respondents points out that there is not a clear consensus on what information sharing actually *is*: "[Information sharing means] *every little bit of information about everything that has to do with day-to-day crises to doom-and-gloom...all day, everyday, without filter.*"[47] Other practitioners note that the information being shared is vague, of little value, and often flows in only one direction, i.e. toward the federal government.[48] Moreover, the ever-important feedback loop, in which the information receiver conveys to the information sender how beneficial the information was, appears to be at best broken, at worst, non-existent.[49]

The Umar Farouk Abdulmutallab case highlights these ongoing problems of information overload in homeland security today. Multiple government entities—the CIA, U.S. State Department, and NCTC—had access to separate pieces of information about Abdulmutallab: a ticket paid for in cash, a warning to the CIA about links to Islamic extremists, and multiple reports entered into government databases.[50] Moreover, Northwest Airlines—a private sector entity—had basic information about Abdulmutallab's ticket purchase, lack of checked baggage, and passport number. With the benefit of hindsight, these data points should have stood out to homeland security analysts and prompted several U.S. government agencies to take actions that would have prevented Abdulmutallab from boarding flight 253. So what went wrong?

The U.S. Senate Select Committee on Intelligence (SSCI) studied the failed Underwear bombing, and the SCCI's findings show that information overload had a detrimental effect on intelligence analysis, leading to analytical oversights. The SSCI identified 14 distinct points of human, technical, or systemic failure that permitted Abdulmutallab to board the flight and attempt to bring it down. These data points are remarkable in that they echo many of the same types of intelligence failures from 9/11; information was not properly disseminated, there was a failure to "connect the dots," and Abdulmutallab's visa was not revoked. Perhaps most importantly, the SSCI found numerous instances of information overload. First, analysts across the IC were unable to handle multiple analytical priorities at once. At the time of the failed Underwear bombing, the IC was primarily focused on collecting and analyzing information about Al-Qaeda activities in Yemen, and not information about Al-Qaeda threats to the U.S. homeland. Second, there appeared to have been a backlog of unanalyzed intelligence about Abdulmutallab at the National Security Agency (NSA). In theory, had the NSA analyzed this backlog of intelligence about Abdulmutallab, then it might have provided stronger evidence for homeland security officials to place Abdulmutallab on a no-fly list. Third, the NCTC lacked the resources to process and integrate disparate pieces of intelligence about Abdulmutallab. Each of these findings suggests that there was too much information for IC analysts to process, and insufficient resources to do so effectively.[51]

The 2013 Boston Marathon bombing case appears to contain information sharing challenges that are similar to those in the

Underwear Bomber case. Tamerlan Tsarnaev, the Boston-area resident and suspected mastermind behind the Boston Marathon bombing, traveled to Russia in 2012 where he allegedly met with Islamist radicals and was surveilled by Russian security officials.[52] The Russian government warned the U.S. government about Tamerlan Tsarnaev's association with Islamist radicals, and requested further information on Tamerlan from the U.S. government.[53] Acting on the Russian government's request, FBI agents interviewed Tamerlan.[54] Following the interview, the FBI found no evidence of a crime—terrorism or otherwise—so it closed its investigation of Tamerlan. Although Tamerlan lived near Boston, and despite the fact that Boston Police and the FBI regularly coordinated as part of an area Joint Terrorist Task Force, the FBI did not share information about Tamerlan with Boston Police.[55]

In the aftermath of the Boston Marathon bombing, government officials quickly identified the breakdowns in information sharing that occurred prior to the Boston attack. On a Sunday morning news talk show, Senator Lindsay Graham noted:

> I think information sharing failed. The FBI investigated the older brother but never shared the information with [the] fusion cell in Boston so people in the Boston area could be on the lookout. When [Tamerlan] goes back to Russia in January 2012, the system pings at DHS, but DHS doesn't share the information with the FBI or the CIA...So it's a failure to share information and missing obvious warning signs.[56]

Representative Michael McCaul, Chair of the U.S. House Homeland Security Committee, commented that "We learned over a decade ago the danger in failing to connect the dots...[m]y fear is that the Boston bombers may have succeeded because our system failed."[57] And Boston Police Commissioner Edward Davis emphasized that "...when information is out there that affects the safety of my community, I need to know that [information]."[58] It is clear, therefore, that information sharing problems remain and stem in part from a trust deficit, information overload, and low-quality information.

Is the high volume of homeland security information sharing making people safer or not? Admittedly, it is difficult to prove a negative here; we cannot know how safe we would be if we were *not* taking these steps. But practitioners have suggested that, despite many positive steps that were taken to improve homeland security information sharing after 9/11, these changes are not achieving the successes that were hoped for.[59] Practitioners' perceptions of effectiveness matter a great deal. Because they are the ones who use this information, they are in the best position to evaluate the state of information sharing. If practitioners do not view these new information resources as helpful, they are less likely to use them.

Low-Quality Information

An increasingly widespread practitioner complaint about information sharing for homeland security is that the information itself is vague, dated, unreliable, and not actionable. This hinders analysts, because they are less able to make sense of the information, and it encumbers policymakers, who are presented with low-quality data that is not helpful for them in making decisions. In a 2009 study of homeland security officials, one practitioner framed the problem in blunt terms: *"There's a very fine line between information and s**t, and I think what we see a lot of times is that everybody's swapping s**t."*[60] This low-quality information problem holds true in many homeland security sub-disciplines, from law enforcement, to emergency management, to critical infrastructure protection, to cybersecurity.

Low-Quality Information in Law Enforcement. In policing there is an ongoing need for information sharing for criminal intelligence purposes; that is, developing information about criminals that can potentially be used later in prosecutions. Moreover, there is a general, everyday need for information to be shared about vehicles, individuals, properties, and so forth. Yet incomplete or duplicative information often makes its way into law enforcement databases, diluting the quality of information that can be shared.

For example, as we discussed above, the Russian government sent a request to the U.S. government for information on Tamerlan Tsarnaev in 2011. The FBI interviewed Tamerlan Tsarnaev in 2011, and it then notified the Russian government that it had turned up nothing derogatory about Tsarnaev. In folding up its investigation of Tsarnaev, the FBI entered his name into the Treasury Enforcement Communications System (TECS), which would trigger an alert to customs officials every time that he left the United States.[61]

Later in 2011 the Russian government asked the CIA for information about Tsarnaev. As part of this request, the Russian government provided the CIA with Tsarnaev's name—which the Russian government spelled "Tamerlan Tsarnayev"—as well as two possible birthdates for Tsarnaev. Like the FBI, the CIA also turned up nothing about him. In performing its own record checks, the CIA asked the NCTC to enter Tsarnaev's name into the Terrorist Identities Datamart Environment (TIDE), a database of persons with possible links to terrorism. TIDE is the "master list" from which other U.S. government terrorism watch lists, including the famous "no-fly" list, are constructed.[62]

The NCTC used the Russian government data provided to the CIA to build Tsarnaev's TIDE database entry. In TIDE, his name was spelled "Tamerlan Tsarnayev" (rather than Tsarnaev) and listed the two birthdates that the Russian government provided to the CIA. Unbeknownst to the CIA or the NCTC, both of these birthdates were incorrect.[63]

When Tsarnaev traveled to Russia in January 2012, his name was flagged in TECS, but not in TIDE. The reason for this discrepancy in database alerts is that his last name was spelled differently on his flight manifest—Tsarnaev—than the spelling in the TIDE database—Tsarnayev. Moreover, Tsarnaev's birthdate, as listed on his flight manifest, differed from both of the birthdates that appeared in TIDE. [64] Since both the name spelling and birthdate on his flight manifest differed significantly from the name spelling and birthdate in TIDE, Tsarnaev was able to travel to Russia without setting off significant alarm bells.

Tamerlan Tsarnaev's name can be spelled multiple ways because his name must be converted from the Cyrillic alphabet (i.e. тамерлан царнаев) to the Latin alphabet (i.e. Tamerlan Tsarnaev). This means that there is not one "correct" way to spell Tamerlan Tsarnaev. The broader rise in criminal intelligence about persons whose names do not use characters from the Latin alphabet (e.g. a, b, c, d) has proven challenging for law enforcement officials to navigate. For example, in Arabic, the name Mohammed is spelled in a consistent way: مُحَمَّد. By contrast, this name can be spelled any number of ways in English: Mohamed, Mohammed, Mohamad, Muhammad, and so on. Because of these differences in spelling, a police officer running a database check on "Mohammed" may turn up nothing at all, because "Mohammed" is actually listed in the database under "Muhammad" or "Mohamed"—a different spelling.[65] These inconsistent spellings can cause confusion both in data entry and data searches, because police officials may input or search for non-Latin character names in an inconsistent way.

The issue of sharing poor quality information now cuts across numerous homeland security-oriented law enforcement agencies.

Personally identifiable information (PII) refers to data that can be used to identify a distinct person. Examples of PII include birthdates, addresses, and social security numbers. The FBI is restricted in the types of PII it can share internally, let alone with other law enforcement agencies.[66] This means that the quality and specificity of information that the FBI shares internally and externally is less than ideal. U.S. Customs and Border Protection maintains 17 distinct databases for information on foreign nationals, making database checks cumbersome and information sharing difficult.[67] And in law enforcement agencies at all levels of government, there is still an underlying cultural resistance to sharing information, complicating this issue even more.[68]

Apart from this inter-governmental information sharing, there is frustration between the public and private sectors about the quality of law enforcement information currently being shared. Part of this frustration is rooted in professional prejudices. Some government law enforcement officials view private security officials as less trained, less qualified, and less competent than their public sector law enforcement colleagues.[69] Some private sector security officers feel police lack full understanding of private security officers' roles, are indifferent to private security officers, and have an elitist attitude toward private security officers.[70] While these perceptions are not necessarily shared by all police or all private security officials, they create tense conditions that are not conducive to sharing high quality information. On the contrary, they reinforce attitudes of mistrust, suspicion, and even hostility.

Public-private information sharing in law enforcement is also subject to cumbersome legal and financial restrictions that can undermine effective cooperation. Because classified government information cannot be shared with individuals who do not possess a federally issued security clearance, the number of private sector employees who can receive classified information is limited.[71]

Cross-sector information sharing is further inhibited by cost considerations. The average background investigation for a security clearance costs $1,230.00.[72] This fee is usually absorbed by the agency with which a firm is working. For example, if Company ABC is working with the Department of Defense, then the Department of Defense pays for Company ABC's employees to be investigated for a security clearance. Because of the costs involved with these background investigations, there is a natural tendency to limit the number of private sector employees who are issued security clearances; it saves money. While this is beneficial from a budgetary standpoint, it limits the number of private sector employees who can access classified government information, and therefore limits information sharing between the public and private sector.

Businesses are not necessarily quick to share law enforcement-related information with police, either. In the case of private security firms, there may be public relations tensions that inhibit information sharing. For example, if a private security firm detains a criminal, the firm may be reluctant to notify police immediately, because it wishes to claim credit for "catching the bad guy" in the public eye. The private security firm might take pains to get this information out into the open, because it boosts the firm's reputation as a reputable private security provider. If the private security firm were to turn the bad guy over to police immediately, then the police could claim credit for catching the bad guy, stealing the private security firm's public relations thunder. This would ruin an opportunity for the private security firm to market its success, and would sour the relationship between the private security firm and the police.

In the context of critical infrastructure protection, firms can also be reluctant to share sensitive information with law enforcement agencies. Firms within DHS's 16 critical infrastructure sectors can benefit from sharing information about their facilities and operations with police, because that information can be helpful for police during a crisis.[73] At the same time, however, no government agency is leak-proof. It is always possible for sensitive information about a private sector facility or equipment to enter the public domain. This type of disclosure can damage the firm's reputation or competitive advantage in the marketplace. Thus a company might only share superficial, basic information about its activities with police so as to avoid potentially damaging leaks.

Moreover, if firms seeking to avoid government regulations or industry requirements provide information on their activities to police, these firms can open themselves up to criminal investigations and prosecutions. This puts both businesses and police in an awkward position. Although it makes sense for firms to provide company information to police, they also share this information at their own peril. For police it is awkward because they have a vested interest in building a successful partnership with businesses, and these partnerships are built upon a foundation of trust. But if police discover that a firm is engaged in illegal activity, it cannot ignore that illegal activity—the police must enforce the law and stop the illegal activity. Yet enforcing the law violates the trust that the firm placed in the police. To prevent this sequence of events, firms may only provide "thin" information to police—that is, information that might be helpful for the police, but contains few useful details. This reinforces low-quality information sharing between the private sector and the public sector. Similar concerns about low-quality information sharing are now apparent in the emergency management community, as well.

Low-Quality Information in Emergency Management. Information sharing is at the very core of emergency management. Without it, effective coordination among individuals and organizations involved in disaster mitigation, preparedness, response, and recovery is impossible. But the quality of the information shared in the emergency management community is getting worse. For example, e-mailed information bulletins circulate widely among emergency management practitioners. Although these bulletins are often little more than news digests, they do help set agendas for emergency management organizations by repeatedly documenting certain threats over time, reinforcing pre-conceived notions of threat severity, and prompting organizations to take action.[74]

However, information in these bulletins often adds little value, and the bulletins are not organized in a way that is helpful for decision-makers. One study of multiple homeland security bulletins notes that they are often an amalgam of popular media stories from sources like *The Washington Post*, Bloomberg News, and MSNBC, along with other government-produced threat information.[75] Often these stories are displayed in an uncoordinated manner, and do not present a clear hierarchy of threat priorities.[76]

Although the threat information conveyed in these bulletins can be an important piece in developing a strategy to prepare for threats, bulletins can exaggerate certain threats while diminishing the importance of others, skewing emergency preparation measures and putting lives and property at risk. For example, an emergency management agency in rural Wyoming might receive numerous homeland security bulletins that continue to discuss terrorism, day after day. Terrorists usually attack in densely populated communities, so rural Wyoming is an unlikely place for a terrorist attack. But these bulletins can influence threat perception, and this has an effect on preparation measures. It might lead the agency to purchase things that it does not really need.

Skewed perceptions have contributed to some of the most outrageous post-9/11 emergency preparedness spending. Consider some examples: a rural county in Colorado purchased a $44,000 "mass fatality" trailer that sits unused; one community in Michigan bought 13 arctic blast snow-cone machines to prevent heat-related illnesses during emergencies; and the police department in Hartwell, Georgia (population 4,469) purchased multiple sets of night vision goggles.[77] To be clear, we are not suggesting that low-quality information sharing alone is driving these questionable purchases. However, low-quality information can influence threat perceptions, and these perceptions can lead to decisions to buy expensive and unnecessary equipment.

Electronic information sharing tools have proliferated since 9/11. Yet the effect of these tools in facilitating cooperation between the public and private sectors is unclear. For example, Lessons Learned Information Sharing (llis.gov) is a U.S. Department of Homeland Security website that serves as a repository for best practices related to homeland security and emergency management. The site is constructed as a kind of bulletin board; anyone with a user account can post documents from exercises, meeting notes, and similar types of material for the learning benefit of others. For example, in the wake of Hurricane Katrina, many communities were left with reduced access to clean drinking water because of flooding and contamination. Water had to be imported from one community to another to meet crucial needs. This process prompted a number of local governments in the Gulf to post information about their emergency water sharing activities on llis.gov. The National Rural Water Association (NRWA), a private sector organization, harvested these lessons for information. As a result, the NRWA developed written guidelines for water sharing networks and mutual-aid agreements between states and localities.[78] These guidelines are available for state and local water authorities to use in order to better prepare for emergencies. Thus the private sector (the NRWA) used lessons learned from the public sector (Gulf local governments) to benefit the public sector (other state and local governments). This case can be held up as a success story for high-quality information sharing in emergency management.

However, other evidence about information sharing tools paints a slightly different picture. A 2009 study of llis.gov users found that although the site seemed to increase awareness of homeland security threats, there was no significant correlation between frequency of information sharing and perceived ability to prevent homeland security emergencies. Nor was there a significant correlation between use of llis.gov and perceived organizational preparedness.[79] These findings suggest a gap between the actual sharing that takes place on sites like llis.gov and the effect of that sharing on homeland security activities. They imply that although information is being shared on sites like llis.gov, the quality of that information may not be of much use. One respondent framed the issue plainly: "I hope somebody someplace has more information that they're utilizing to protect the country because I'm not seeing a lot of stuff that's of great value."[80]

Low-Quality Information in Critical Infrastructure Protection. Some 85% of all critical infrastructure in the United States is owned or managed by the private sector.[81] Given this reality, government has little choice but to partner with businesses to protect critical infrastructure. It is logical to assume that because of this dependency, government and businesses would exchange information that is timely, relevant, and actionable on a frequent basis. While this is happening to a limited extent, many challenges remain unresolved related to information quality.

As stated earlier, certain government information is classified because releasing it to the public would damage U.S. national security. When the government classifies something, it attaches legal protections to that information, charging the holder of the information to safeguard it or face stiff legal penalties for disclosing it. In order to legally exchange classified information, both the sender and recipient of the information must have security clearances at or above the classification level of the information itself. Moreover, the recipient must have a need to know the information. [82] This compartmentalizes information, limiting any one person's knowledge of classified information beyond their immediate area of professional responsibility. These measures—security clearances and the "need to know"—have been in place for many years. But classified information also complicates the way information gets shared between the public and private sectors.

Many owners or operators of critical infrastructure companies and corporations do not have security clearances. As a result, when the government sends important information to these private sector employers, it must send an unclassified version of the information, rather than a classified version of the information. Often this unclassified version of the information omits certain details to protect information sources and intelligence-gathering methods. But these omissions limit the utility of the information. Without a source, a recipient cannot make independent judgments about how credible or non-credible a piece of information is. There are other issues that show how low-quality information sharing in critical infrastructure protection concerns more than just handling classified information.

Sharing information that is timely, relevant, and actionable costs time and money. Government officials must sift through databases and files to locate specific information that can benefit critical infrastructure owners and operators. If we consider information sharing to be a transaction, then the transaction cost of sharing high-quality information is greater than the transaction cost of sharing low-quality information, because high-quality information is always in short supply. If government officials act rationally (and we assume that they do) then they will gravitate toward lower cost information transactions.

Conditions are similar for the private sector. For example, businesses can easily generate information about sales revenue. This data is commonplace in any firm. But it is harder for a business to inventory each of its security cameras, conduct vulnerability assessments, or produce detailed facility maps. These tasks are less common, take time away from revenue-generating activities, and cost money—since labor and supplies to do these things are not free. But a detailed inventory of security cameras, vulnerability assessments, and facility maps are likely to be more useful for government than sales data. Thus there is a higher transaction cost associated with gathering data on security measures than gathering data on sales revenue. For both the public and private sectors, then, there is a high transaction cost in sharing high-quality information, and this means that government and businesses will naturally gravitate toward lower transaction costs, and therefore lower-quality information sharing.

Low-Quality Information in Cybersecurity. Cyber threats are exploding in number and scope. As in other areas of homeland security, the public and private sectors share information about these threats. And although substantial progress has been made in this area, low-quality information continues to circulate across the public-private sector divide in cybersecurity.

Information sharing agreements in cybersecurity are highly complex. [83] They extend horizontally across government, and vertically between local, state, and federal governments. Moreover, these agreements extend between the public and private sectors. [84] And while the complexity of an information sharing network does not necessarily equate with low-quality information sharing, threat information can fragment in a complex information sharing network. Fragmented information is incomplete information, and incomplete information is less useful for decision-makers. It is reasonable to assume that the tangled net of public and private sector entities sharing cybersecurity information can inadvertently generate fragmented, low-quality information.

Information sharing websites go a long way toward centralizing cybersecurity knowledge across government and the private sector. But at the same time, it is not clear that this centralized information is very useful for decision-makers.[85] Nor are the websites themselves immune to attack. In 2009 a hacker broke into HSIN.[86] During this incident, the hacker accessed the phone numbers and email addresses of state and federal employees, but he did not retrieve sensitive information like social security numbers.[87] This shows that information sharing websites may not be very useful, because they likely contain fragmented, low-quality information. And somewhat ironically, the websites used to share cybersecurity information are themselves vulnerable to cyber threats.

The public and private sectors are not meeting one another's expectations for sharing cybersecurity information, and this partly explains why low-quality information sharing occurs in this area. A 2010 Government Accountability Office (GAO) report points toward a number of the central problems that vex businesses and government working in cybersecurity. For example, the private sector expects government information on threats to be "usable, timely, and actionable," but this is still not happening, even with efforts to improve information sharing through tools like HSIN or professional organizations focused on cybersecurity issues. [88] Government believes that the depth and specificity of information that businesses share about cybersecurity is limited; this seems to stem from firms' reluctance to share sensitive and proprietary information with government.[89]

In sum, a lack of trust between the public and private sector impedes cross-sector information sharing for homeland security. There is an unmanageable tidal wave of homeland security information that hammers businesses and government daily. And the quality of that information is questionable. These issues point toward a series of new challenges for public-private partnerships in homeland security: building cross-sector trust over time, managing the flow of homeland security information, and improving the quality of shared information. Fortunately public-private partnerships are well-equipped to begin addressing these challen-ges.

III. Public-Private Partnership Solutions for Information Sharing in Homeland Security

Public-private partnerships offer a range of solutions to improve the state of homeland security information sharing. While these partnerships cannot solve every problem associated with information sharing in homeland security, they can increase cross-sector trust, help to manage the information deluge, and improve information quality. The following sections outline the opportunities for public-private partnerships in these areas.

Public-Private Partnerships Can Help Build Trust

The trust deficit between the public and private sector encumbers information sharing. It invites both sectors to view one another with mutual suspicion. This harms homeland security, because it limits the chances of cross-sector information sharing being helpful for either sector. So how can public-private partnerships increase cross-sector trust?

Trust forms through repeated contact between business and government representatives. This trust leads to professional relationships. These person-to-person relationships help to create trust between organizations. And groups like InfraGard and the CIPAC help facilitate this process. As Paul Byron Pattak, CEO of the InfraGard National Capital Members Region, explains:

> The first thing you have to do is create an environment where people are comfortable coming and meeting others. So before any [information sharing] happens, the relationships have to be established. And as we all know, we don't trust people immediately when we meet them. We need to get to know them a little bit better, we need to spend some time with them, maybe have lunch or dinner....so trust is built over time. But once you have it, there is so much you can do with the relationship.... Because we join [InfraGard] individually as members, we're really good at helping forge those relationships. And people come to InfraGard and get the opportunity to meet people that you are unlikely to meet in other contexts.[90]

Pattak's remarks underline the way in which personal relationships can translate into inter-organizational trust. This inter-organizational trust enhances effectiveness in sharing information. With greater trust, the public sector will be more likely to share sensitive or classified information with the private sector, not only because private sector officials hold the requisite clearances to safeguard classified information (a formal indicator of trust) but also because of individual relationships between public and private sector representatives (an informal indicator of trust).

An additional way public-private partnerships can increase cross-sector trust is by constructing service level agreements (SLAs) in contracts and honoring them. This is a business-focused approach to set expectations between public-private partners. An SLA sets specific, measurable metrics for vendor performance, whether that vendor is delivering a product or a service. These metrics often come with incentives for excellent performance, or penalties for poor performance. For example, an SLA might stipulate the time for delivery of a desktop computer, from order submission to installation, at 48 hours. Using this example, if a desktop computer is ordered, delivered, and installed in less than 48 hours, the vendor might receive a small bonus payment. If the desktop computer is not delivered in 48 hours, by contrast, the vendor might compensate government by paying a penalty for failing to meet the SLA.

SLAs manage public and private sector expectations in contracts, building trust over time. Both parties know that good work is rewarded, and shoddy work is not rewarded. A certain "gray area" of work is eliminated through this arrangement, too. That is, without SLAs, if a product or service is not delivered correctly or on time, there is no recourse or compensation for government—just a "gray area" of frustration and violated expectations. And firms have no incentive to work more efficiently, other than meeting the minimum requirements of contracts with government. But with SLAs, government knows that it can be compensated for the contract not being fulfilled according to its expectations. From the government's perspective, SLAs eliminate this "gray area" of unfulfilled expectations. From the private sector's perspective, SLAs offer incentives to do better work more efficiently, which can increase the firm's bottom line even more. SLAs manage public and private sector expectations, and they diminish the chance of expectations being violated by either government or businesses. And with fewer violations of expectations, trust increases over time.

Public-Private Partnerships Can Help to Manage the Information Deluge

There is a natural limit to the amount of information a given homeland security analyst can process. It does not really matter that the most advanced technology is being applied to information sharing problems in homeland security; the true problem here is that while computers' ability to process information grows constantly, a human being's ability to process information remains unchanged. In the midst of the present information sharing tidal wave, public and private sector homeland security analysts are encouraged to review as many sources of information as possible, because (the thinking goes) this leads to higher quality analyses. This places homeland security analysts in an impossible position, where they have to sort through an unmanageably high level of information and continue to produce high quality analyses.[91] Yet public-private partnerships offer a number of important solutions to help manage the flow of homeland security information.

Technological innovations, coupled with enhanced operator skills to use new technologies, are perhaps the most obvious solutions for managing the homeland security information deluge. Firms, collaborating with government, can develop software to filter and prioritize information for individual analysts. This helps to ensure that analysts review and study information that is most relevant to them. By managing the flow of information in this way, public-private partnerships help analysts. And analysts can do more with less, because the information they review has been reduced to manageable levels. When the flood of information slows, analysts can focus more upon analysis itself, rather than filtering through information so that they can begin analysis. This ultimately benefits decision-makers that are consumers of intelligence products.

Programmatic innovation, too, can help to manage the high volume of information. For example, the FBI's InfraGard program is heavily populated by law enforcement personnel, especially FBI employees. InfraGard meetings typically include significant informal interaction between police and private sector representatives. And these low-level interactions serve an important agenda-setting function which helps to manage the flow of information.[92] In informal conversations and formal presentations at InfraGard meetings, certain topics come up regularly: terrorism, surveillance of nuclear power plants, synthetic drugs, and so forth. These conversations help to set organizational agendas, because they reinforce the importance of certain homeland security concerns over others, and they demonstrate that those concerns are shared by numerous public and private sector organizations. This agenda-setting effect helps to manage the information flood, because it prompts analysts to focus more on higher priority issues that are discussed than lower priority issues that are not discussed.

Business process analysis is a favorite tool of the private sector, because it helps to identify and eliminate inefficiencies, leading to cost savings for firms. Process improvements can also help to manage the homeland security information flood. Private sector consultants can help review government homeland security information sharing processes and identify areas of weakness or waste within them. By implementing process changes, government's information sharing efforts become more effective and can help to reduce the information deluge to reasonable levels. And consultants benefit by being paid for their expertise. Thus public-private partnerships can help to manage the information sharing flood in an effective, mutually beneficial way.

Public-Private Partnerships Can Improve Information Quality

Alliances between businesses and government can improve the quality of homeland security information. This can happen in ways that are practically identical to those benefits conferred in managing the information flow: via technology, programming, and process analysis.

The same software used to filter the volume of information seen by homeland security analysts can also be used to enhance the quality of the information. For example, a new tool developed by IBM addresses poor data quality in police databases.[93] This tool—a software application—searches for entries in databases that appear to be duplicative and flags them for further investigation. This helps the police to identify fragmented or low-quality data and to improve the data so that it is more useful in practice. Eliminating duplicate or fragmented database entries improves data consistency, and data consistency helps analysts.

Programming innovations also help to improve information quality. For example, the DHS CIPAC focuses on sharing threat information to enhance critical infrastructure protection.[94] Moreover, the CIPAC is further sub-divided into sector-specific working groups. These groups address issues germane to each of the 16 critical infrastructure sectors that DHS identifies.[95] Because of the substantial level of cross-sector communication and collaboration involved in the CIPAC, the group provides an agenda-setting function that manages the volume of information being shared, as well as the quality of the information being shared. By filtering out low-priority topics in CIPAC discussions, public and private sector leaders are better able to set information sharing agendas within their own organizations, and they can make more informed decisions about the amount and type of information they share with other organizations. Because of this, analysts are fed higher quality information. And this means that analyses are better than they would be otherwise.

Business process analysis can improve the quality of information being shared. A business process analysis of multiple intelligence agencies, for example, might find that they are all producing redundant reports about the same topic, and that they are all sharing those redundant reports with other agencies.

Private sector consultants can spot and change this behavior. This not only saves taxpayer dollars by eliminating duplication of effort, but it also helps to reduce the amount of information analysts must sort through. This increases the quality of information being shared, and it makes the information sharing process more effective for both government and businesses.

IV. Recommendations for Future Information Sharing

Low cross-sector trust, the persistent flood of homeland security information, and the abundance of low-quality information all challenge public-private partnerships in homeland security. But public-private partnerships offer a number of avenues to improve homeland security information sharing over the long haul, too. By building trust over time, managing the information deluge, and improving the quality of information, public-private partnerships can be a catalyst for better information sharing in homeland security. To bolster homeland security information sharing using public-private partnerships, four specific policy recommendations follow below. While these recommendations cannot address every challenge in homeland security information sharing, they are concrete steps for government agencies and businesses to begin improving their information sharing practices:

- **Learn to measure trust.** Most data on cross-sector trust tends to be qualitative and descriptive. Quantitative data on precisely how much public and private sector entities do or do not trust one another could be useful for scholars in assessing trust levels over time and identifying effective ways to improve cross-sector trust. For example, using surveys containing Likert scales, which can assign numerical values to trust levels, public and private sector officials can more accurately gauge how the entities in a given partnership view each other.[96] Where partners desire to improve their partnership, private sector polling firms could provide valuable assistance in administering these surveys. Insights from these surveys can be used to improve public-private partnerships in general.

This survey data could also open the door to future "action research." Action research involves scholars actively working with practitioners in order to test theories or bring about a desired outcome, rather than serving as passive, disinterested observers.[97] Scholars can help homeland security practitioners to improve their operations by offering a fresh, outside perspective and enabling practitioners to see their work practices in a new light. In action research that focuses upon homeland security information sharing, scholars could serve as active facilitators in public-private sector trust-building fora and collaborative projects.[98] Conducting action research in this way, and publishing the results of this research, could be valuable for homeland security scholars and practitioners alike.

- **Software algorithms can help manage the information overload.** The private sector can help government intelligence analysts to deal with information overload by developing innovative software algorithms to assist in processing and sorting through information. In much the same way that a particular Google search term can retrieve precisely the information that a computer user is searching for, well-designed intelligence analysis software can help analysts to separate useful information from less-useful information. These algorithms can be integrated into existing IC databases, making it easier to connect disparate pieces of information, look up names with multiple possible spellings, or discern patterns that point toward suspicious activity.

Additionally, these same algorithms can help to integrate separate IC databases, making it possible for analysts to conduct a single search that covers numerous databases at once. These kinds of software algorithms can help to ensure that information gathered by one IC member agency can be accessed by all IC member agencies, helping analysts to "connect the dots." While tools like software algorithms cannot be a cure-all for the problem of information overload, they *can* make it easier for intelligence analysts to make sense of the information overload and ultimately help homeland security policymakers to make more well-informed decisions.

- **Determine how much information is too much information.** The general consensus among researchers is that homeland security analysts are drowning in data. In business management literature there is a concept called "span of control" that refers to the number of persons one individual can effectively supervise.[99] There is a similar "span of control" limit for the amount of information one individual can effectively process and analyze in an hour, a day, or a week.[100] Using data on the amount of information that homeland security analysts can effectively process, homeland security managers can develop specific targets that designate how much information a given analyst can receive and analyze at any given time.

  Furthermore, as discussed above, software algorithms can help to manage this information deluge. But beyond managing the information flood, software algorithms offer a second, related benefit: these algorithms can also bolster individual analysts' effectiveness. When software algorithms steer analysts toward useful, high-quality information, that same high-quality information influences their analyses. Using high-quality raw data can lead to sharper, more insightful intelligence analyses.

These improved analyses signal an increase in analysts' efficiency and effectiveness. Well-designed software algorithms help to keep analysts from drowning in data and also help them to be better analysts.

- **Improve analysis through peer review.** Some information sharing tools such as Intellipedia permit IC analysts to peer review information, enhancing the credibility of a particular piece of analysis and its author.[101] Amazon.com and EBay.com, two of the world's largest online shopping websites, use similar ratings systems for buyers to evaluate sellers. Pandora.com, an Internet radio website, permits listeners to rate each song they hear. With this information, Pandora.com uniquely tailors each listener's experience according to her own musical preferences; a listener can reject certain genres or artists while embracing others. Could homeland security information circulated via email or other information sharing networks employ a similar rating system? And could the rating system be designed so that high-priority, high-quality analyses "bubble up," while redundant or vague analyses get filtered out? Scholars and practitioners can benefit from exploring this idea further.

Information sharing will continue to be vital in homeland security for the foreseeable future. Public-private partnerships are essential to making this information sharing effective. In building cross-sector trust, managing the information flood, and honing the quality of information, public-private partnerships hold great promise for the future of homeland security.

Notes

1. U.S. Immigration and Customs Enforcement, "Underwear Bomber Umar Farouk Abdulmutallab sentenced to life" [Press Release], February 16, 2012, accessed October 5, 2012, http://www.ice.gov/news/releases/1202/120216detroit.htm.

2. Barbara Van Woerkem, Peter Kenyon, Ofeibea Quist-Arcton, Dina Temple-Raston, Priscilla Villareal, "Timeline: From Student to Radical," npr.org, n.d., accessed October 5, 2012, http://www.npr.org/templates/story/story.php?storyId=123768455

3. Sarah Childress, Jay Solomon, and Stephen Fidler, "Suspect's Privileged Existence Took a Radical Turn," *The Wall Street Journal*, December 29, 2009, accessed October 5, 2012, http://online.wsj.com/article/SB126187511080506063.html.

4. Woerkem et al., "Timeline."

5. Ibid.

6. Senate Select Committee on Intelligence, "Attempted Terrorist Attack on Northwest Airlines Flight 253," May 24, 2010, accessed October 5, 2012, http://www.intelligence.senate.gov/pdfs/111199.pdf, 2; Mark Hosenball, "What the CIA Did and Didn't Know About Alleged Underpants Bomber," *The Daily Beast*, December 30, 2009, accessed October 5, 2012, http://www.thedailybeast.com/newsweek/blogs/declassified/2009/12/30/what-the-cia-did-and-didn-t-know-about-alleged-underpants-bomber.html.

7. Sarah Netter, "Jasper Schuringa Yanked Flaming Syringe Out of Abdulmutallab's Pants," abcnews.com, December 28, 2009, accessed October 5, 2012, http://abcnews.go.com/GMA/northwest-flight-253-hero-yanked-flaming-syringe-abdulmutallab-pants/story?id=9432099#.UFH_d5gVoro.

8. Peter Baker and Scott Shane, "Obama Seeks to Reassure U.S. After Bombing Attempt," *The New York Times*, December 28, 2009, accessed October 5, 2012, http://www.nytimes.com/2009/12/29/us/29terror.html.

9. U.S. Immigration and Customs Enforcement, "Underwear Bomber Umar Farouk Abdulmutallab sentenced to life."

10. "Passenger says he helped thwart terror attack," cnn.com, December 26, 2009, accessed October 5, 2012, http://articles.cnn.com/2009-12-26/justice/airliner.attack.schuringa_1_umar-farouk-abdulmutallab-plane-northwest-airlines-flight?_s=PM:CRIME.

11. Tom Leonard, "Hero tackled alleged Northwest plane bomber as flames came from him on flight to Detroit," *The Telegraph*, December 26, 2009, accessed October 5, 2012, http://www.telegraph.co.uk/news/worldnews/

northamerica/usa/6890990/Hero-tackled-alleged-Northwest-plane-bomber-as-flames-came-from-him-on-flight-to-Detroit.html.

12. Ibid.

13. Barbara A. Grewe, "Legal Barriers to Information Sharing: The Erection of a Wall Between Intelligence and Law Enforcement Organizations," National Commission on Terrorist Attacks Upon the United States: Staff Monograph, August 20, 2004, accessed October 9, 2012, http://www.fas.org/irp/eprint/wall.pdf; National Commission on Terrorist Attacks Upon the United States, "How To Do It: A Different Way Of Organizing The Government," 2004, accessed October 9, 2012, http://govinfo.library.unt.edu/911/report/911Report_Ch13.htm; U.S. Department of Homeland Security, *Implementing 9/11 Commission Recommendations: Progress Report 2011*, 2011, accessed October 9, 2012, http://www.dhs.gov/xlibrary/assets/implementing-9-11-commission-report-progress-2011.pdf, 11–12; CBS/AP, "Costly post-9/11 info sharing program slammed," cbsnews.com, October 3, 2012, accessed October 9, 2012, http://www.cbsnews.com/8301-201_162-57524994/costly-post-9-11-info-sharing-program-slammed/.

14. Jolie Lee, "Agencies get better at 'whole of government' info sharing," federalnewsradio.com, August 30, 2012, accessed October 5, 2012, http://www.federalnewsradio.com/490/3014484/Agencies-get-better-at-whole-of-government-info-sharing.

15. U.S. Intelligence Community, "Our Strength Lies In Who We Are," intelligence.gov, n.d., accessed October 9, 2012, http://www.intelligence.gov/about-the-intelligence-community/member-agencies/.

16. Kashmir Hill, "The Department of Homeland Security Wants All The Information It Has On You Accessible From One Place," forbes.com, November 29, 2011, accessed October 5, 2012, http://www.forbes.com/sites/kashmirhill/2011/11/29/department-of-homeland-security-wants-all-the-information-it-has-on-you-accessible-from-one-place/.

17. National Counterterrorism Center, "About the National Counterterrorism Center," n.d., accessed October 5, 2012, http://www.nctc.gov/about_us/about_nctc.html.

18. Portions of this chapter appear in Austen D. Givens and Nathan E. Busch, "Information Sharing in Homeland Security: The Role of Public-Private Partnerships," *Homeland Security Review* 7, no. 2 (Summer 2013).

19. New York Police Department, "NYPD Shield: About," 2006, accessed October 5, 2012, http://www.nypdshield.org/public/about.aspx.

20. Ibid.

21. *The Washington Post*, "Top Secret America: New York," 2012, retrieved October 5, 2012, http://projects.washingtonpost.com/top-secret-america/ states/new-york/.

22. Michael Barbaro and Justin Gillis, "Wal-Mart at Forefront of Hurricane Relief," *The Washington Post*, September 6, 2005, accessed October 5, 2012, http://www.washingtonpost.com/wp-dyn/content/article/2005/09/05/ AR2005090501598.html; Steven Horwitz, "Wal-Mart to the Rescue: Private Enterprise's Response to Hurricane Katrina," June 2008, accessed March 6, 2013, http://myslu.stlawu.edu/~shorwitz/Papers/Wal-Mart_to_the_Rescue. pdf.

23. Ami J. Abou-bakr, *Managing Disasters through Public-Private Partnerships* (Washington, DC: Georgetown University Press, 2013), 24.

24. For a more extended discussion of the Joplin tornado, see Chapter 6.

25. Craig Allen, "As Joplin, Missouri Rebuilds, a Home Depot Store Reopens," homedepot.com, January 11, 2012, accessed October 5, 2012, http://ext. homedepot.com/community/blog/tag/joplin/.

26. Roger McKinney, "RESOURCE: FEMA specialists on hand at Home Depot," *The Joplin Globe*, July 1, 2011, accessed March 6, 2013, http://www. joplinglobe.com/tornadoresources/x652255506/FEMA-specialists-on-hand-at-Home-Depot.

27. U.S. Department of Homeland Security, *Implementing 9/11 Commission Recommendations: Progress Report 2011*, 3–6.

28. Rhonda Schwartz and Brian Ross, "Feds Race to Trace Boston Marathon Pressure Cooker Bomb," abcnews.com, April 17, 2013, accessed May 28, 2013, http://abcnews.go.com/Blotter/feds-race-trace-boston-marathon-pressure-cooker-bomb/story?id=18976352#.UaStTWQ4W7s.

29. Jocelyne Cesari, "Tamerlan and Dzhokhar Tsarnaev: The terrorists next door?" *The Washington Post*, April 29, 2013, accessed May 28, 2013, http://www.washingtonpost.com/blogs/on-faith/wp/2013/04/29/tamerlan-and-dzhokhar-tsarnaev-the-terrorists-next-door/.

30. Ken Dilanian, "Boston bombings: Video said to show suspect setting backpack down," *Los Angeles Times*, April 21, 2013, accessed May 28, 2013, http://articles.latimes.com/2013/apr/21/nation/la-na-nn-boston-bombings-video-backpack-20130421.

31. Elliot C. McLaughlin, "FBI Chronology: Brothers used similar bombs in marathon, police showdown," cnn.com, April 23, 2013, accessed May 28, 2013, http://www.cnn.com/2013/04/22/us/criminal-complaint-boston-marathon.

32. John Dawsey, Evan Perez, Devlin Barrett and Jennifer Levitz, "Manhunt Ends With Capture of Boston Bombing Suspect," *The Wall Street Journal*, May 8, 2013, accessed May 28, 2013, http://online.wsj.com/article/ SB10001424127887324493704578432030609754740.html.

33. Federal Bureau of Investigation, "2011 Request for Information on Tamerlan Tsarnaev from Foreign Government," April 19, 2013, accessed May 28, 2013, http://www.fbi.gov/news/pressrel/press-releases/2011-request-for-information-on-tamerlan-tsarnaev-from-foreign-government.

34. Scott Shane and David M. Herszhenhorn, "Agents Pore Over Suspect's Trip to Russia," *The New York Times*, April 28, 2013, accessed May 28, 2013, http://www.nytimes.com/2013/04/29/us/tamerlan-tsarnaevs-contacts-on-russian-trip-draw-scrutiny.html?pagewanted=all.

35. Eric Schmitt and Michael S. Schmidt, "2 U.S. Agencies Added Bomb Suspect to Watch Lists," *The New York Times*, April 24, 2013, accessed May 28, 2013, http://www.nytimes.com/2013/04/25/us/tamerlan-tsarnaev-bomb-suspect-was-on-watch-lists.html.

36. National Commission on Terrorist Attacks Upon the United States, *The 9/11 Commission Report*, 2004, accessed March 6, 2013, http://www.9-11commission.gov/report/911Report.pdf, 433.

37. U.S. Department of Homeland Security, *Department of Homeland Security Information Sharing Strategy*, April 18, 2008, accessed March 6, 2013, http://www.dhs.gov/xlibrary/assets/dhs_information_sharing_strategy.pdf, 6; Peter J. Denning, "Hastily Formed Networks," *Communications of the ACM* 49, no. 4 (April 2006): 18–19; Naim Kapucu, "Non-Profit Response to Catastrophic Disasters," *Disaster Prevention and Management* 16, no. 4 (2007): 551–561; Eugene Bardach, *Getting Agencies to Work Together: The Practice and Theory of Managerial Craftsmanship* (Washington, DC: Brookings Institution Press, 1998), 252–253; William L. Waugh, Jr., "Terrorism, Homeland Security, and the National Emergency Management Network," *Public Organization Review* 3, no. 4 (December 2003): 373–385.

38. The White House, *National Strategy for Information Sharing*, October 2007, accessed March 6, 2013, http://www.fas.org/sgp/library/infoshare.pdf, 10.

39. U.S. Department of Homeland Security, *Department of Homeland Security Information Sharing Strategy*, 2.

40. Joseph W. Pfeifer, "Network Fusion: Information and Intelligence Sharing for a Networked World," *Homeland Security Affairs* 8 (October 2012): 11.

41. Nathan E. Busch and Austen D. Givens, "Public-Private Partnerships in Homeland Security: Opportunities and Challenges," *Homeland Security Af-*

fairs 8, Art. 18 (October 2012): 13.

42. Joseph Straw, "Intelligence Sharing Improves," *Security Management*, n.d., accessed October 5, 2012, http://www.securitymanagement.com/article/intelligence-sharing-improves.

43. U.S. Department of Homeland Security, "DHS Announces New Information-Sharing Tool to Help Fusion Centers Combat Terrorism " [Press Release], September 14, 2009, accessed October 9, 2012, http://www.dhs.gov/news/2009/09/14/new-information-sharing-tool-fusion-centers-announced.

44. Federal Emergency Management Agency, Lessons Learned Information Sharing (llis.gov), n.d., accessed October 9, 2012, https://www.llis.dhs.gov/index.do.

45. Central Intelligence Agency, "Intellipedia Celebrates Third Anniversary with a Successful Challenge," April 29, 2009, accessed October 9, 2012, https://www.cia.gov/news-information/featured-story-archive/intellipedia-celebrates-third-anniversary.html; Joab Jackson, "A-Space melds social media and intelligence gathering," gcn.com, November 20, 2009, accessed October 9, 2012, http://gcn.com/articles/2009/11/30/a-space-dia-intell-sharing-wiki.aspx.

46. Federal Bureau of Investigation, Law Enforcement Online (leo.gov), n.d., accessed October 9, 2012, http://www.leo.gov/.

47. Hamilton Bean, "Exploring the Relationship between Homeland Security Information Sharing & Local Emergency Preparedness," *Homeland Security Affairs* 5, no. 2 (May 2009): 9, italics in the original.

48. Ibid., 8.

49. Henry H. Willis, Genevieve Lester, and Gregory F. Treverton, "Information Sharing for Infrastructure Risk Management: Barriers and Solutions," *Intelligence and National Security* 24, no. 3 (June 2009): 362–363.

50. Senate Select Committee on Intelligence, "Attempted Terrorist Attack on Northwest Airlines Flight 253," 2.

51. Ibid., 2–9.

52. Scott Shane and David M. Herszhenhorn, "Agents Pore Over Suspect's Trip to Russia," *The New York Times*, April 28, 2013, accessed May 28, 2013, http://www.nytimes.com/2013/04/29/us/tamerlan-tsarnaevs-contacts-on-russian-trip-draw-scrutiny.html?pagewanted=all.

53. Scott Shane and Michael S. Schmidt, "F.B.I. Did Not Tell Police in Boston of Russian Tip," *The New York Times*, May 9, 2013, accessed May 28, 2013,

http://www.nytimes.com/2013/05/10/us/boston-police-werent-told-fbi-got-warning-on-tsarnaev.html.

54. Federal Bureau of Investigation, "2011 Request for Information on Tamerlan Tsarnaev from Foreign Government."

55. Ibid.

56. CBS, "Face the Nation transcripts April 28, 2013: Syria and Boston, Graham, McCaskill, and Chambliss," April 28, 2013, accessed May 30, 2013, http://www.cbsnews.com/8301-3460_162-57581787/face-the-nation-transcripts-april-28-2013-syria-and-boston-graham-mccaskill-and-chambliss/.

57. Ibid.

58. Shane and Schmidt, "F.B.I. Did Not Tell Police in Boston of Russian Tip."

59. Bean, "Exploring the Relationship."

60. Ibid., 9, asterisks ours.

61. Eric Schmitt and Michael S. Schmidt, "2 U.S. Agencies Added Bomb Suspect to Watch Lists," *The New York Times*, April 24, 2013, accessed May 28, 2013, http://www.nytimes.com/2013/04/25/us/tamerlan-tsarnaev-bomb-suspect-was-on-watch-lists.html.

62. Ibid.

63. Ibid.

64. Ibid.

65. Converting names from one alphabet to another alphabet is called transliteration. The issue of transliteration in national security databases is receiving increasing attention. See David Holmes, Samsun Kashfi, and Syed Uzair Aqeel, "Transliterated Arabic Name Search," Proceedings of the Third IASTED International Conference: Communications, Internet, and Information Technology, November 2004, accessed October 9, 2012, http://uzair.nairang.org/wp-content/uploads/2006/10/433-175.pdf;   Mark Arehart, "Indexing Methods for Faster and More Effective Person Name Search," Proceedings of the 2010 Language Resources Evaluation Conference, 2010, accessed October 9, 2012, http://www.lrec-conf.org/proceedings/lrec2010/pdf/166_Paper.pdf.

66. Peter L. Gomez, "ENHANCING FBI TERRORISM AND HOMELAND SECURITY INFORMATION SHARING WITH STATE, LOCAL, AND TRIBAL AGENCIES" (master's thesis, Naval Postgraduate School, September 2010, 2.

67. U.S. Department of Homeland Security Office of the Inspector General, *Information Sharing on Foreign Nationals: Border Security (Redacted)*, February 2012, OIG-12-39, 2.

68. Willis, Lester, and Treverton, "Information Sharing," 348.

69. International Association of Chiefs of Police, *National Policy Summit: Building Private/Public Policing Partnerships to Prevent and Respond to Terrorism and Public Disorder—Vital Issues and Policy Recommendations*, 2004, accessed October 9, 2012, https://www.theiacp.org/LinkClick.aspx?fileticket=UVc2ImxcWpQ%3D&tabid=938, 7.

70. Ibid.

71. Richard A. Best Jr., "Intelligence Information: Need-to-Know vs. Need-to-Share," Congressional Research Service, June 6, 2011, retrieved September 21, 2012, http://www.fas.org/sgp/crs/intel/R41848.pdf, 3.

72. William Henderson, "How Much Does It Really Cost to Get a Security Clearance?, clearancejobs.com, August 7, 2011, accessed October 9, 2012, http://www.clearancejobs.com/cleared-news/381/how-much-does-it-really-cost-to-get-a-security-clearance.

73. Presidential Policy Directive (PPD) 21 reduced the number of federally recognized critical infrastructure sectors from 18 to 16. See The White House, "Presidential Policy Directive—Critical Infrastructure Protection and Resilience," February 12, 2013, accessed March 7, 2013, http://www.whitehouse.gov/the-press-office/2013/02/12/presidential-policy-directive-critical-infrastructure-security-and-resil; U.S. Department of Homeland Security, "Critical Infrastructure Sectors," n.d., accessed March 6, 2013, http://www.dhs.gov/critical-infrastructure-sectors.

74. Hamilton Bean and Lisa Keränen, "The Role of Homeland Security Information Bulletins Within Emergency Management Organizations: A Case Study of Enactment," *Journal of Homeland Security and Emergency Management* 4, no. 2 (June 2007): 9.

75. Ibid.

76. Ibid.

77. David Olinger and Jennifer Brown, "Colorado's homeland security spending has been all over the map," *The Denver Post*, September 4, 2011, accessed October 9, 2012, http://www.denverpost.com/911/ci_18805920; "Montcalm County gets homeland security snow cone machine," wzzm13.com, December 5, 2011, accessed October 9, 2012, http://www.wzzm13.com/news/article/188877/14/Montcalm-County-gets-homeland-security-snow-cone-machine.

78. Katherine J. Worboys, "Recent Research from *Lessons Learned Information Sharing*: The Importance of Partnerships in the Rural Water Response to Hurricane Katrina," *Journal of Environmental Health* 69, no. 2 (September 2006): 31–33.

79. Bean, "Exploring the Relationship," 7.

80. Ibid., 12.

81. U.S. Department of Homeland Security, "Critical Infrastructure Sector Partnerships," n.d., accessed October 9, 2012, http://www.dhs.gov/critical-infrastructure-sector-partnerships.

82. Richard A. Best Jr., "Intelligence Information: Need-to-Know vs. Need-to-Share," Congressional Research Service, Report No. R41848, June 6, 2011, retrieved September 21, 2012, http://www.fas.org/sgp/crs/intel/R41848.pdf, 1–13.

83. Rachel Nyswander Thomas, "Securing Cyberspace Through Public Private Partnership: A Comparative Analysis of Partnership Models" (master's thesis, Georgetown University, 2012).

84. Ibid.

85. Bean, "Exploring the Relationship."

86. Ben Bain, "Information-sharing platform hacked," *Federal Computer Week*, May 13, 2009, accessed October 9, 2012, http://fcw.com/articles/2009/05/13/web-dhs-hsin-intrusion-hack.aspx.

87. Ibid.

88. U.S. Government Accountability Office, "CRITICAL INFRASTRUCTURE PROTECTION: Key Private and Public Cyber Expectations Need to Be Consistently Addressed," July 2010, GAO-10-628, 13.

89. Ibid., 22.

90. "Public-Private Sector Information Sharing-Paul Byron Pattak," Symposium on Homeland Security, 26.16–27.10, posted by Christopher Newport University Center for American Studies, July 20, 2012, http://www.symposiumonhomelandsecurity.com/Panel3.html.

91. Nathan Alexander Sales, "Mending Walls: Information Sharing After the USA PATRIOT Act," *Texas Law Review* 88, no. 7 (June 2010): 1804.

92. This is similar to the agenda-setting function of homeland security bulletins. See Bean and Keränen, "The Role of Homeland Security Information Bulletins," 9–10.

93. Darryl Plecas, Amanda V. McCormick, Jason Levine, Patrick Neal, and Irwin M. Cohen, "Evidence-based information sharing solution between law

enforcement agencies," *Policing: An International Journal of Police Strategies and Management* 34, no. 1 (2011): 120–134.

94. U.S. Department of Homeland Security, "Critical Infrastructure Partnership Advisory Council," n.d., accessed October 9, 2012, http://www.dhs.gov/critical-infrastructure-partnership-advisory-council.

95. U.S. Department of Homeland Security, "Critical Infrastructure Sectors," n.d., accessed April 19, 2013, http://www.dhs.gov/critical-infrastructure-sectors.

96. For an example of how Likert scales have been used to measure trust, see John K. Butler Jr., "Toward understanding and measuring conditions of trust: Evolution of a conditions of trust inventory," *Journal of Management* 17, no. 3 (September 1991): 643–663.

97. Jean McNiff and Jack Whitehead, *Action Research in Organisations* (London: Routledge), 2001, 3–4; Jack Whitehead and Jean McNiff, *Action Research: Living Theory* (Thousand Oaks, CA: Sage Publications, Inc.), 2006, 13.

98. For a recent example of how action research can be applied to homeland security, see Stig Johnsen and Mona Veen, "Risk assessment and resilience of critical communication infrastructure in railways," *Cognition, Technology & Work* 15, no. 1 (March 2013): 95–107.

99. For a classic treatment of this concept, see Michael Keren and David Lehari, "The Optimum Span of Control in a Pure Hierarchy," *Management Science* 25, no. 11 (November 1979): 1162–1172.

100. Marten van Someren, Niels Netten, Vanessa Evers, Henriette Cramer, Robert de Hoog, and Guido Bruinsma, "A trainable information distribution system to support crisis management," *Proceedings of the Second International ISCRAM conference* (Brussels, Belgium), April 2005.

101. Frank Ahrens, "A Wikipedia of Secrets," *The Washington Post*, November 5, 2006, accessed September 28, 2012, http://www.washingtonpost.com/wp-dyn/content/article/2006/11/03/AR2006110302015.html; Nancy M. Dixon and Laura A. McNamara, "Our Experience With Intellipedia: An Ethnographic Study at the Defense Intelligence Agency," Defense Intelligence Agency Laboratory Project, February 5, 2008, accessed September 28, 2012, http://www.au.af.mil/au/awc/awcgate/sandia/dixon_mcnamara_intellipedia.pdf.

Chapter 5

Integrating Public-Private Capabilities at U.S. Ports of Entry

At 9:20 am on May 18, 2010, a small boat loaded with explosives rammed into the massive container ship M/V Singapore at the Port of Oakland, California. The explosives detonated upon impact and set the ship on fire.[1] Another vessel—the M/V Goodship—was simultaneously docking at the Port of Oakland and struck an underwater Improvised Explosive Device (IED), damaging its steering system and causing the ship to run aground.[2] The damaged M/V Goodship could not be moved, blocking the entrance to the port.[3] By 11:00 am, emergency management officials had activated the California Emergency Operations Center (EOC) to begin coordinating their response to these attacks.[4] This catastrophic breach of port security would require close public-private sector cooperation over the next 48 hours to recover from these attacks.

The California Emergency Management Agency's Golden Guardian 2010 full-scale exercise—which simulated the terrorist attacks described above—brought together a wide range of government and business maritime port security stakeholders.[5] The purpose of the exercise was to assess the ability of different government agencies and business entities to respond to and recover from terrorist attacks in multiple Bay Area maritime ports.[6] This is for good reason, as neither public nor private sector entities fully control maritime ports. Rather, responsibilities for security, shipping, and operations are shared among government and business officials.

Sharing these responsibilities effectively is important, because breaches of maritime port security have significant safety and economic implications. Explosions can kill or maim people; the human cost of terrorism is tremendously high.[7] And when maritime port security is compromised, port officials can slow or halt traffic into and out of the port in order to deal with the security breach. This impacts the delivery of goods on container ships, which can result in monetary losses for buyers and sellers of those goods. Slowing or stopping maritime port traffic can create a tremendous backlog of ships and trucks involved in moving cargo from point to point. This backlog can have a ripple effect on the U.S. economy as a whole. In October 2002, the government contractor Booz Allen Hamilton facilitated a hypothetical emergency response exercise involving a number of radiological bombs entering the United States through several maritime ports. This exercise included participants from the White House Office of Homeland Security (predecessor to the Department of Homeland Security), Department of Defense, U.S. Coast Guard, and other federal agencies. After the exercise ended, the participants observed that under this hypothetical scenario, there would be a 92 day backlog of cargo entering U.S. ports, triggering economic losses of approximately $58 billion.[8] Given the serious implications of security breaches in maritime ports, effective public-private sector coordination is essential for achieving resilience in maritime port security.

These issues are not limited to maritime ports alone. At America's airports and border crossings, public-private partnerships are also transforming how security is implemented in practice. From passenger screening procedures at LaGuardia International Airport in New York City to surveillance cameras along the southern border in Laredo, Texas, alliances between government and businesses prove indispensable to achieving homeland security objectives.

To date, much of the literature on port of entry security focuses on narrow issues.[9] For example, many scholars examine industry and government best practices in border security, while others analyze organizational management challenges along the border.[10] Most studies of maritime port security emphasize container screening procedures, which require public-private sector collaboration.[11] A handful of other researchers discuss information sharing challenges in maritime ports, economic impacts of terrorist attacks in maritime ports, and legal issues in maritime ports.[12] A few scholars have looked at persistent threats to airport security, as well as the need for new private sector security innovations to protect against those threats.[13] But so far, there has not been an examination of public-private partnerships in port of entry security as a whole.

This chapter argues that public-private partnerships are now having a substantial impact on security across all of America's ports of entry, and that this creates potential for new advances in cross-sector collaboration, as well as multiple challenges that will need to be overcome. We first examine the status of public-private partnerships in U.S. maritime ports, U.S. airports, and along the U.S. northern and southern borders. In discussing each of these areas, we highlight many of the challenges that these public-private partnerships face. We also explore a number of promising opportunities for further developing these partnerships. The chapter then highlights a number of shared security challenges that are apparent in each type of port of entry. We conclude the chapter by offering a few predictions about the future of public-private partnerships in port of entry security and describing the need for further research in this area.

I. Public-Private Partnerships in Maritime Port Security

About 75% of all goods that enter and exit the United States go through maritime ports.[14] These goods include virtually everything that we use for daily living, from sink faucets, to cars, to computers, to sports equipment, to food products. Given maritime ports' tremendous importance for daily living, as well as the American economy as a whole, effectively protecting maritime ports is a top homeland security priority. To this end, government and businesses partner together to ensure the safety of shipping activities in and out of America's maritime ports.

The U.S. Coast Guard (USCG) maintains a "96-hour rule" for ships bound for U.S. maritime ports. This rule states that any cargo ship bound for the United States is required to send a list of its crew members, passengers, cargo, and voyage history to the USCG's National Vessel Movement Center 96 hours before arriving at a U.S. maritime port.[15] After Coast Guard officials receive this information, they work with other government agencies to vet the names of the crew members and passengers to determine if any of them might pose a threat. This is done by cross-checking the names of crew members and passengers against databases of known persons of interest, such as terrorist watchlists.[16]

Public-private partnerships figure prominently in the implementation of the USCG's 96-hour rule. For example, the USCG contracted with Microsoft to produce a special electronic ship information form for shippers to use. A ship's crew could fill in the form offline, while still at sea, and then transmit the form to the USCG once they are able to connect to the Internet.[17] While on its face this might seem like a relatively low-tech innovation, it is substantially more efficient than the previously used manual system. Prior to this partnership between Microsoft and the USCG, the National Vessel Movement Center would receive "hand-written faxes, telephone calls, and e-mails with Microsoft Excel database spreadsheets attached" that contained information about a ship's crew, passengers, cargo, and voyage history.[18] These bits of information then had to be manually typed into USCG databases by Coast Guard employees. This manual data entry was a resource-draining, time-consuming, error-prone process.[19] The Microsoft solution provides ships' crew members with a simple, efficient way to deliver needed information to the USCG to enhance maritime port security.

Similarly, U.S. Customs and Border Protection (CBP) maintains a 24-hour rule for ships bound for U.S. ports. This 24-hour rule states that 24 hours prior to cargo being loaded onto a ship heading for the United States, the shipping company must provide CBP with a detailed cargo description and a list of addresses where the cargo will be delivered upon arrival.[20] If the shipping company does not provide this information to CBP, then CBP can issue a "do not load" order for the inbound cargo. This means that the cargo will not be removed from the ship once in port—the cargo must remain on the ship. In this way, CBP can penalize the shipping company for not complying with the 24-hour rule. Like the 96-hour rule, cargo description information provides CBP with data that can be checked and vetted against multiple databases. And this vetting process can help to catch and stop illegal or dangerous goods from entering the United States.

Logisuite, a software company, produces a product that makes complying with the 24-hour rule easier. This product, called Automated Manifest System (AMS) Ocean, standardizes the electronic transmission of data between shipping companies and CBP.[21] By doing this, electronic data flows more readily between shipping companies and CBP. In turn, this eases compliance with the 24-hour rule, because CBP officials can expect to receive data from shipping companies in a form that is useful for CBP. In this way, a public-private partnership eases the burden of maritime port security on both government and businesses.

Public-private partnerships also extend to security along the docks at maritime ports. The Transportation Security Administration's (TSA) Transportation Worker Identification Credential (TWIC) is a form of public-private partnership designed to enhance the physical security of ports, as well as the ships docked in those ports.[22] There is a continual need for many workers, such as longshoremen and truckers, to have unescorted access to different areas of maritime ports.[23] But like all workers in positions of public trust, there is concern that a criminal or terrorist could make his way into one of these positions, compromising maritime port security.

To prevent these kinds of security breaches, TSA's TWIC program actively vets workers who need unescorted access to areas inside maritime ports.[24] TSA fingerprints, photographs, and investigates the backgrounds of workers requiring unescorted access within maritime ports.[25] Once the TWIC vetting process is complete, workers are issued a TWIC identification card by TSA.[26] These TWIC identification cards are "smart cards," meaning they contain a special computer chip that holds authentication data about the card holder. The cards also have a magnetic stripe, like those seen on credit cards, and an optical bar code.[27] This public-private partnership between the TSA and firms involved in maritime port operations provides a valuable hedge against maritime port security breaches. It is also worth noting that TSA contracted with a private firm, Lockheed Martin, to collect information from maritime port workers for the TWIC program and to issue the TWIC cards to workers, as well.[28]

Public-private sector information sharing is essential to effective maritime port security. Since 9/11, much progress has been made in this area. Beth Rooney, who manages maritime port security for the Port Authority of New York and New Jersey, notes that:

> [T]here's no competition among ports when it comes to security...There's nothing that's proprietary about these best practices. If something happens, it will affect us worldwide, so the collaboration and cooperation [among port security stakeholders] is intense.[29]

Today, maritime port security officials from around the world, representing both the public and private sectors, routinely visit other maritime ports in other cities to share information and to learn how to improve their own security procedures.[30] Moreover, the DHS transportation system sector—which is recognized as one of the 16 critical infrastructure sectors in the United States— includes 361 maritime ports on its list of critical transportation system assets.[31] This means that maritime ports garner a significant amount of attention from federal policymakers, and there is recognition among these policymakers that public-private partnerships are indispensable to maritime port security.[32]

There are a number of formal groups to facilitate maritime port security information exchange between businesses and government. Information Sharing and Analysis Centers (ISACs) are organizations composed of critical infrastructure sector officials that examine all hazards—meaning potential threats—and analyze these hazards' possible impact on their respective assets.[33] One ISAC, called the Maritime Security Council, is composed of public and private sector maritime port officials from around the world. Other members include representatives from cruise lines and import/export firms.[34] The Maritime Security Council produces research reports, publishes policy articles, and holds regular meetings among its stakeholders.[35]

Maritime port security information is also shared via National Maritime Security Advisory Committees (NMSACs). These public-private sector groups are facilitated by the U.S. Coast Guard and provide a means for stakeholders in specific maritime ports—as opposed to regional or national maritime port security stakeholders—to come together to exchange information.[36] For example, stakeholders in the maritime ports of Los Angeles, California; Houston, Texas; New Orleans, Louisiana; and Norfolk, Virginia all have these committees.[37] Like ISACs, NMSACs can help facilitate the information sharing process among maritime port security stakeholders. In turn, this can bolster maritime port security as a whole.

Despite these positive developments, there remain numerous challenges that will need to be addressed over the long run for public-private partnerships to become as effective as possible in maritime port security. The next section discusses some of the persistent challenges facing government and businesses in maritime port security.

Challenges for Public-Private Partnerships in Maritime Port Security

Rigorous maritime port security requires continuous engagement from public and private sector stakeholders. And in recent years, there has been excellent progress in this regard. But lingering challenges in maritime port security include aligning international security standards, balancing the need for security and commerce, fighting corruption, and developing emergency response plans for maritime ports. Some of these challenges primarily impact public sector entities, while others mostly affect businesses. But the majority of these challenges simultaneously affect both sectors. It will be important for businesses and government to continue to address these issues in the coming years.

Governments involved in maritime port security face a fundamental challenge: there are no uniform security standards for cargo shipments worldwide. This means that maritime port security officials cannot expect every container of cargo to have been protected in a robust way from its point of departure to its destination. CBP launched the Container Security Initiative (CSI) in 2002 to help mitigate this issue.[38] Under the CSI, CBP officials inspect potentially high-risk cargo overseas, prior to its being shipped to the United States.[39] These containers are screened at their foreign point of departure for weapons of mass destruction (WMDs) or other hazardous materials. In this way, officials can inspect suspicious cargo before it departs for the United States and stop the cargo before it could potentially pose a threat to the United States. One study, published in 2007, found that while the CSI is helpful, it still leaves a number of high-risk countries' maritime ports unaffected, and it leaves open the possibility that terrorists could sneak WMDs onto a container ship in one of those unmonitored maritime ports.[40] Moreover, the CSI relies on data from shippers overseas, which may or may not be accurate. All of this suggests that there is no "silver bullet" to aligning international cargo security standards. Instead, a layered and collaborative approach to cargo security is likely best.[41]

A second public sector challenge in maritime port security is corruption, a little-discussed but ever-present threat. To date, much of the documented concern about corruption in maritime port security tends to focus on foreign maritime ports, rather than U.S. maritime ports.[42] Yet whether one is discussing foreign or domestic maritime port security, reducing the possibility of corruption requires close public-private cooperation. Governments abroad can pressure private sector firms to vet their maritime port workers. Better vetting of workers reduces the possibility of hiring employees who are vulnerable to bribery. Moreover, these same governments can request and receive U.S. government training in background investigation techniques. In the United States, the TWIC program helps to evaluate the trustworthiness of private sector workers with unescorted access to certain areas of maritime ports. While this is not an end-all solution for corruption, it does provide a means for firms to weed out employees that could be vulnerable to corruption.

Businesses involved in maritime port security need detailed contingency plans. What happens when a maritime port must close for security reasons? Where do the ships bound for that port go next? What happens to those ships' cargo once the ships arrive at an alternate-site maritime port? How does the alternate site maritime port contend with the surge of screening and off-loading required during this situation? In a 2009 study, Grillot, Cruise, and d'Erman found that although many maritime ports claim to have these sorts of contingency plans in place, a significant number of maritime ports do not.[43] This means that in the event of a maritime port closing, ships must improvise, and make their own way to another maritime port without any kind of advance preparation.[44] The economic ramifications of a maritime port closing for security reasons are significant. When a ship is delayed because it is re-routed, perishable cargo (e.g. fruits, vegetables, flowers) can spoil, costing firms money. Shipment delays can impede timely delivery of products, frustrating potential customers. And maritime port workers, who rely on the maritime port for their own wages, are forced into the difficult position of waiting for the temporarily closed maritime port to re-open.

The public and private sectors face a number of shared challenges in maritime port security, as well. Since 75% of all goods entering the United States come through maritime ports, slowing or halting those imports can negatively impact the American economy and national quality-of-life.[45] To their credit, businesses and government continue to seek the elusive balance between free-flowing commerce and security in America's maritime ports. For example, new screening technologies help save time and money by expediting cargo inspection. One such device acts like a giant truck-mounted X-ray machine. Security officials can drive this device past a cargo container, providing them with a detailed picture of a cargo container's contents. If the device identifies a suspicious item inside the container, then security officials can open and physically inspect the container.[46] This is helpful because without this screening technology, officials would have to rely on a traditional inspection method that can prove less reliable—physically inspecting cargo containers based upon intelligence information. When these physical searches do not pan out, security officials waste valuable time and energy that could be spent elsewhere. There are monetary costs, too. Opening containers for inspection can be expensive for maritime port operations.[47]

As we have noted elsewhere in this book, information sharing in homeland security as a whole can be problematic. Businesses recognize that sharing information with government can be beneficial, and government understands that it should share information with businesses. But mutual mistrust can prevent information sharing. As maritime port security stakeholders, firms worry that proprietary information entrusted to government officials could leak out to competitors and the public. This, in turn, can put a business at a competitive disadvantage.[48] But at the same time, both businesses and government officials appear to view the advance transmission of shipping manifests as a sensible, effective security measure.[49]

A second information sharing problem relates to the sheer number of stakeholders in maritime ports. A 2007 study of the Port of Long Beach, California notes that the port has over fifteen different law enforcement agencies with differing areas of responsibility.[50] It is logistically difficult for officials in each of these law enforcement agencies to develop relationships with one another and also develop relationships with private sector maritime port security stakeholders like shipping company representatives and longshoremen who work at the port itself. The same study notes that the overwhelming majority of maritime port security stakeholders in Long Beach say they need more public-private collaboration to prevent maritime port security breaches.[51] As the study's author suggests, a "virtual solution"—a fusion center for maritime port information that is electronic, rather than a physical facility—may help to fill the information sharing gaps among these different stakeholders.[52] And private sector experts, working alongside their government counterparts, can collaborate to produce this type of virtual fusion center—again demonstrating the importance of public-private partnerships in maritime port security.

These challenges in maritime port security all underscore the need for public-private partnerships; maritime ports require ongoing cross-sector collaboration in order to function normally. Businesses and government also have a number of opportunities to meaningfully address these maritime port security challenges, which we discuss in the next section.

Opportunities for Public-Private Partnerships in Port Security

Public-private partnerships can enhance maritime port security through better information sharing, partnerships with foreign business organizations, development of non-lethal technologies to deter piracy and terrorism, and creation of contingency plans for use of alternate maritime ports during emergencies. While this list of opportunities in maritime port security is not comprehensive, it does indicate the many ways in which government and businesses can collaborate to address ongoing challenges in maritime port security.

In discussing public-private partnerships for maritime port security, we generally refer to partnerships between U.S. government agencies and U.S. businesses. But government projects like the CSI demand a certain level of cooperation from overseas governments and businesses, too. Moreover, the USCG's 96-hour rule and CBP's 24-hour rule are fundamental examples of public-private partnerships whose reach extends beyond U.S. borders. There are additional opportunities to deepen public-private partnerships for maritime port security by reaching out to foreign chambers of commerce. U.S. government and business officials can develop relationships with industry and government leaders abroad. By doing this, U.S. government and business officials can promote business activity, and they can help to influence security policies at maritime ports overseas by encouraging compliance with USCG and CBP shipping regulations. These actions help to facilitate the movement of cargo into and out of ports, and they also enhance maritime port security in the United States.

Piracy is a source of continuing concern for businesses and governments involved in maritime port security. Somali pirates, often operating off the horn of Africa, frequently hold ships and their crews hostage for ransom money. [53] Recently pirates have also hijacked ships that are physically close to maritime ports, and in at least one case, hijacked a ship that was *already docked* at a port.[54] Terrorism also worries maritime port security officials. In 2000, terrorists rammed a small boat filled with explosives into the U.S.S. Cole, which was docked at a port in the Middle East.[55] This tragic attack killed 17 U.S. sailors.[56] Public-private partnerships can help to thwart these threats through security training, security personnel, and new non-lethal technologies.

Governments are often responsible for managing the consequences of pirate attacks—collecting intelligence about the attack,
developing a hostage rescue plan, and criminally prosecuting
pirates after the attack. Yet at the same time, private shipping
companies—not government agencies—are usually the victims of
pirate attacks. This confluence of public and private sector interests in stopping piracy means that both government and businesses benefit when shipping companies receive anti-piracy training. A
number of firms have begun offering anti-maritime piracy training,
including Tactical Intelligence International, APPDS Maritime
Security Ltd., Trojan Securities International, and International
Maritime Security Network LLC.[57] Firms like these can train ships'
crews in protection techniques, and they can also conduct vulnerability assessments of the ships themselves, identifying potential
points of entry for pirates who wish to board the ship.

When these security companies provide shipping firms with
information about the shipping firms' vulnerabilities, the shipping
firms can then take action to close security gaps onboard their
vessels. With this training in anti-piracy techniques and tactics,
ships' crews become less vulnerable to piracy attacks. This reduced
vulnerability to piracy saves shipping firms money; it helps firms
to avoid delayed cargo delivery due to a vessel being hijacked.
Government also indirectly benefits from this arrangement,
because it does not have to provide the anti-piracy training to
shipping companies, which would require government time and
resources. Not having to provide training saves government money.
Moreover, when shipping companies know how to prevent piracy,
this knowledge means that government can conserve its own
resources by not having to collect intelligence on pirate attack
victims, not having to develop a hostage rescue plan, and not
having to go through the expense of criminally trying pirates after
a pirate attack. In this sense, private security firms that offer anti-

piracy vulnerability assessments and training can benefit government and shipping companies alike.

Another way that private maritime security firms assist government is through deploying security personnel onboard ships. Firms like Tactical Intelligence International and International Maritime Security Network LLC offer shipping companies highly trained security personnel. [58] These personnel travel onboard shipping vessels alongside the ship's crew. By riding onboard ships in this way, these private security firms can provide shipping companies with an extra layer of physical protection from piracy and terrorism. If terrorists or pirates approach the ship, these security personnel can use any number of weapons or techniques to deter or stop them. This arrangement increases maritime port security, for it better protects ships while at sea and as ships dock in maritime ports.

Private firms also produce technology that ships can use to stop piracy and terrorism. For example, LRAD Corporation developed a non-lethal technology called the Long Range Acoustic Device (LRAD).[59] The LRAD looks like a large, thick plate mounted on top of a metal box. This tool can concentrate sound waves in a focused beam, much like how a laser concentrates light waves in a focused beam. This beam of sound can be trained on specific targets from hundreds of yards away. The LRAD can be used to project audible warning messages toward small boats approaching ships. The device can also be used as a non-lethal weapon. The volume of the LRAD can be raised to the decibel level of a jet engine. When used in this way, and trained on one or more persons, the LRAD's sound beam becomes so intolerably painful to human ears that the targeted person or persons have no choice but to drop what they are doing to cover and protect their ears from the penetrating sound waves. In this way, the LRAD is a helpful tool to thwart pirate and terrorist attacks.

For example, if a small boat full of Somali pirates was approaching a ship at a maritime port in Africa, the ship's crew could train its LRAD on the pirates' boat. The pain from the LRAD would be so intense that the pirates would be forced to stop and turn back, effectively thwarting the attack. Similarly, a boat with one or more terrorists heading toward a ship could be slowed—if not halted entirely—using the LRAD. Since the LRAD is non-lethal, it also avoids the risk of an accidentally fatal misidentification of suspected adversaries.

A second example of innovative non-lethal technology for maritime port security is the Active Denial System (ADS), which looks like a square-shaped satellite dish and is produced by the well-known defense firm Raytheon after some 15 years of testing and research with DOD. [60] The ADS is typically vehicle-mounted, but could be mounted on ships, as well. The ADS concentrates high-frequency radio waves on a target. The sensation caused by the ADS is like the rush of heat one feels after opening a kitchen oven. [61] It causes a near-immediate reflex reaction to pain that prompts the target to jump out of the way to escape the pain. [62] Yet the pain does not cause lasting damage to the human body and fades soon after the target walks out of the ADS beam. [63]

Like the LRAD scenario described above, the ADS can be used onboard ships to thwart pirate and terrorist attacks, and in much the same way—by focusing the ADS beam on the suspected pirate or terrorist himself. Both the LRAD and the ADS demonstrate how innovative public-private partnerships can benefit maritime port security. The LRAD and ADS are produced by private firms, yet their creation was many years in the making, requiring extensive research, testing, and consultation with government officials. Today, the LRAD and ADS provide non-lethal solutions to avert pirate and terrorist attacks. These innovations have the potential to make maritime ports safer. Future public-private collaboration to develop other non-lethal technologies can contribute in a substantial way to bolstering maritime port security.

The apparent lack of contingency plans for using alternate maritime ports during emergencies has significant implications for homeland security. From both an economic and quality-of-life perspective, not delivering goods on time can have far-reaching negative consequences. Through public-private partnerships, maritime port security stakeholders can collaborate to develop these contingency plans. For example, the Area Maritime Security Committees facilitated by the USCG provide a potential forum for developing these plans for maritime ports nationwide. Ongoing communication between different Area Maritime Security Committees—for example, Houston and New Orleans, Oakland and Los Angeles, Miami and Norfolk—can help to create plans that capture a wide range of stakeholder interests and provide workable solutions. And by leading this effort from the ground-up, maritime port security stakeholders can potentially avoid burdensome government regulation over the long run.

It is clear that public-private partnerships impact maritime port security today in a substantial way. From screening workers at maritime ports to examining cargo overseas, alliances between businesses and government help to protect this area of U.S. critical infrastructure. And the future of maritime port security depends on excellent public-private sector collaboration, whether in developing relationships with overseas professional organizations, creating non-lethal technologies, or planning for worst-case scenarios. Public-private partnerships have also had a substantial impact in America's airports, which we discuss in the next section.

II. Public-Private Partnerships in Airport Security

When Hurricane Sandy struck the northeastern United States in November 2012, few could have anticipated its far-reaching impacts on air travel. Airlines cancelled some 20,000 flights. [64] LaGuardia International Airport and John F. Kennedy International Airport in New York City closed for days because portions of their runways flooded. [65] The halted airline service in the northeast had a ripple effect across the world, causing hundreds of flight cancellations in other major cities. [66] The disaster underscored the significant reach of air travel in modern society. And Hurricane Sandy demonstrated the importance of private airline companies' coordination with government agencies during large-scale emergencies.

Disruptions to airports can impact quality of life and economic activity in substantial ways. Security at America's airports, therefore, is a high priority for homeland security officials in the public and private sectors. Working together in partnerships, businesses and government now secure U.S. airports in innovative ways that are a significant departure from even just a few years ago. This arrangement has been advantageous for homeland security— airports and airlines are now safer than ever before. Yet over the coming years, businesses and government will also have to work together closely to navigate a number of emerging challenges and to capitalize on several excellent opportunities to bolster their effectiveness.

Since 2001, the technologies used to screen baggage and passengers at airports have developed in remarkable ways. Perhaps the most striking and controversial of these technologies is the millimeter wave scanner, popularly known as a "body scanner." These scanners are produced by a small number of companies, including General Electric and L-3 Communications. [67] They are able to produce a full image of a human being that highlights suspicious objects beneath that person's clothing. This means that after a suspicious object is identified, a Transportation Security Officer (TSO) must investigate the suspicious object. This can be done using a range of techniques, from follow-up use of a hand-held magnetometer to a physical pat-down of the person by a TSO. This follow-up investigation either confirms that the object is benign and therefore permitted onboard a plane, or leads to a deeper investigation of the person being screened. On the whole, the public-private partnership between TSA and firms like General Electric and L-3 has produced a highly effective passenger security screening tool that makes airlines and the flying public safer.

At the same time, however, there have been significant privacy concerns associated with the use of millimeter wave scanners. Since they can produce a full body image of the person being scanned, civil libertarians and citizens have been skeptical about how TSA handles these images.[68] To address these privacy concerns, in October 2012 TSA announced that it was removing the full body image scanners from several major airports—LaGuardia and JFK in New York, O'Hare in Chicago, Los Angeles International, Logan in Boston, as well as Charlotte, North Carolina and Orlando, Florida—and re-assigning them to smaller airports.[69] And the full body image scanners in these major airports will be replaced with new millimeter wave scanners that produce a cartoon-like outline of the person being screened, rather than a full image of the person being screened.[70] While the overall effectiveness of these new millimeter wave scanners remains to be seen, this shift in technology does help address many of the personal privacy concerns associated with millimeter wave scanners. Since smaller airports now use the full image body scanners, rather than these major airports, fewer passengers overall will be screened using the full image body scanners.

Just as port security authorities rely on manifests of ships' crews and cargo to screen ships effectively, airport security officials rely on manifests of passenger names to screen planes effectively. Through public-private partnerships, government and airline companies are better able to assure the security of the flying public through use of these lists. For example, federal law requires that all international flights bound for the United States transmit a list of all crew members and passengers to CBP prior to the flight landing in the United States.[71] The information for each crew member and passenger includes full names, dates of birth, and passport information.[72] The thinking behind this law is that CBP can check the crew and passenger information against other databases that contain threat-related information, such as terrorist watchlists or federal arrest warrant databases. By doing this, CBP identifies crew members or passengers who should be intercepted—and possibly questioned or detained—upon arrival in the United States. Working together in this way, airline companies and the federal government are better able to protect U.S. citizens against terrorists or other criminals entering the country by air. However, it is also worth noting that this system is not ideal. The truth is that CBP can receive these lists of crew and passengers while a plane is actually airborne and heading for the United States. This does nothing to prevent someone on that plane from doing harm to its passengers while it is in flight. Ideally, this system would stop potentially threatening passengers from boarding U.S.-bound flights in the first place.

There is a period following every flight's arrival in which an airplane is cleaned, inspected, and readied for its next voyage. Part of this process involves carefully checking the plane for suspicious objects or other contraband that could pose a risk to the safety of the crew and passengers. In recent years firms have begun performing these duties. For example, Global Elite Group, a New

York-based firm, handles this inspection process at JFK International Airport in New York.[73] Global Elite Group employees are supposed to check overhead bins, seat back pockets, floors, and lavatories for items that could be threatening or illegal.[74] If one of these types of objects is discovered, then the firm's employees can alert TSA and airport police to further investigate the item. This type of public-private partnership works because it frees up TSA employees and airport police to address other pressing security concerns. At the same time, it permits Global Elite Group to operate as a flexible, scalable asset for TSA. Moreover, given that airline security will remain a high priority for businesses and government for the foreseeable future, this kind of service will likely be in demand over the long haul.

Immediately following the terrorist attacks of September 11th, 2001, the Federal Aviation Administration (FAA) grounded all flights in U.S. airspace.[75] The decision was completely unprecedented and required rapid, large-scale coordination between airlines and government air traffic controllers.[76] If already airborne, pilots were instructed to land as soon as possible. JetBlue landed one of its planes at the airport in tiny Stewart, New York.[77] Southwest Airlines landed flights at Denver International Airport—an airport that it normally does not use.[78] While the 9/11 terrorist attacks were a great national tragedy, federal aviation officials and airlines learned a great deal about rapid, wide-scale communication because of the attacks. And eight years later, these valuable lessons learned from 9/11 would become relevant again—this time after a failed terrorist attack.

As we discussed in Chapter 4, on Christmas Day 2009, Umar Farouk Abdulmutallab tried to detonate explosives hidden in his underwear onboard a Northwest Airlines flight bound for Detroit, Michigan.[79] Abdulmutallab's explosives failed to detonate properly, and he was tackled and restrained by passengers and crew members. Immediately following the incident, DHS officials began communicating specific warnings and instructions to airlines and airports nationwide. This series of actions prompted Secretary of Homeland Security Janet Napolitano to note:

> [O]ne thing I'd like to point out is that the system worked. Everybody played an important role here. The passengers and crew of the flight took appropriate action. Within literally an hour to 90 minutes of the incident occurring, all 128 flights in the air had been notified to take some special measures in light of what had occurred on the Northwest Airlines flight. We instituted new measures on the ground and at screening areas, both here in the United States and in Europe, where this flight originated.[80]

Napolitano's remarks in this interview that "the system worked" were immediately and rightly criticized.[81] Obviously the system did *not* work, because Abdulmutallab was able to board a U.S.-bound flight with a bomb in his underwear. Nonetheless, Napolitano did correctly identify some of the ways in which the information sharing mechanisms put in place after 9/11 were effective after Abdulmutallab's failed terrorist attack.

Public-private partnerships have a significant impact on airport security in recent years. But for these partnerships to be as effective as possible, they will now have to confront a number of important challenges, as well.

Challenges for Public-Private Partnerships in Airport Security

Businesses and government face a host of shared challenges in airport security today, including deploying detection technology, building administrative software, and employing security personnel. While this list of challenges is not comprehensive, it provides a general sense of the scope of issues that businesses and government must address in airport security.

Public agencies and private firms must ensure that new screening technologies achieve what they are supposed to achieve. The millimeter wave scanner controversy, in particular, underscores the importance of balancing new security innovations against the need for passenger privacy. It is reasonable to suggest that the TSA did not expect significant public backlash against the body scanner technology. But a widely publicized-yet-unsuccessful national protest against the body scanners just before Thanksgiving Day 2010 shows that the scanners touched a nerve among travelers.[82]

These events underline the importance of proof-of-concept testing in airport screening technology. Both TSA and the private sector must collaborate to produce new innovations like the cartoon-image body scanners. Not only must the technology work as it is intended to work, but for financial and personal privacy reasons, there needs to be some degree of buy-in from the flying public, too. Without this public buy-in, the TSA—and the firm producing the technology—both risk a financial loss due to ineffective or controversial equipment being rejected by the flying public as unreasonably intrusive or ineffective.

The public and private sectors will also need to confront persistent software concerns in aviation. Around Christmas Day 2004, the airline Comair's flight scheduling software failed, prompting Comair to cancel all 1,100 of its flights.[83] The incident badly damaged Comair's public reputation and resulted in a $20 million loss.[84] On a larger scale, experts have warned for years that the FAA's flight tracking software is out-of-date and urgently needs to be upgraded.[85] To address this concern, the FAA is beginning to replace the older flight tracking software with new flight tracking software. But data security concerns hamper this replacement process; consultants and industry leaders note that the new software is vulnerable to hacking, which could potentially put the flying public at risk.[86]

These software-related concerns demonstrate the importance of cross-sector collaboration in airport security. Aviation industry software must simultaneously meet the needs of government aviation officials, airline companies, and the flying public. To accomplish this, public-private partnerships will be essential for successful outcomes. Cross-sector collaboration can help to ensure that government aviation officials clearly communicate their own software requirements to the firms producing the software. Additionally, a feedback loop between the aviation industry, government aviation officials, and software companies can work to refine and enhance these software applications over time. By closely working together, the public and private sectors can increase the overall efficiency and effectiveness of aviation industry software, making the public safer as a result.

In recent years there has been public discussion of potentially re-privatizing airport security functions.[87] Prior to 9/11, most airport security screeners *were* private sector employees. During the flurry of post-9/11 governmental re-organization, Congress passed the Air Transportation Security Act of 2001, which established the TSA and handed primary responsibility for airport security to government rather than businesses.[88] Then, in 2004, TSA created the Screening Partnership Program (SPP), which provides a means for individual airports to request private sector security screening personnel, rather than TSA personnel.[89] Under the SPP, private sector security firms must adhere to TSA standards for baggage screening, and contractors must meet certain federal hiring standards.[90] In this way, TSA retains a kind of supervisory role over private sector security screeners in airports.

This discussion of potentially re-privatizing airport security is significant, because there is a subtle-yet-persistent tension between government security objectives and businesses' profit-oriented objectives. Some thirty employees from Global Elite Group at JFK International Airport, which we discussed earlier in this chapter, recently filed a formal complaint with the TSA.[91] The complaint states that the employees are often rushed to complete security inspections on planes because of pressure to keep the planes moving in and out of the airport on time. As a result, the employees claim, their inspections are not meeting the TSA's requirements for post-flight security inspections.[92] This case demonstrates that while public-private partnerships can have clear benefits for airport security, there are also many challenges that will have to be worked through for them to achieve their full potential. Yet at the same time, a number of emerging trends hold great promise for public-private partnerships in airport security. We explore a few of these trends in the next section.

Opportunities for Public-Private Partnerships in Airport Security

While the challenges above demonstrate how businesses and government will need to collaborate to improve airport security, public-private partnerships can help create new screening technologies, build new administrative software, and close security loopholes. While public-private partnerships in these areas will not solve all airport security challenges, they can certainly improve airport security conditions beyond the status quo.

The need for continual innovation in airport security underscores why public-private partnerships are so essential in this area of homeland security. But as the body scanner controversy makes clear, rolling out new technologies can be financially risky, and it can potentially damage relationships with the general public, as well. Two new DHS initiatives that we discussed previously in this book—SECURE and FutureTECH—are a unique type of public-private partnership that potentially holds great promise for airport security.

The SECURE initiative pairs industry officials with DHS representatives.[93] Working together, these members of the public and private sector collaborate on research and development projects. These projects are designed to meet DHS's immediate and short-term future needs. This represents a significant break from previous models of research and development activity. In the past, firms put up their own money to finance new innovations, and then tried to sell those prototypes to government without active assistance from government. This new collaborative approach, by contrast, helps to ensure that government requirements for a new innovation are correctly incorporated from product design through product completion. In this way, there is potential for fewer iterations in the production cycle, which shortens the time it takes for industry to produce a new technology. This is beneficial for the private sector, for it helps to ensure that government will accept businesses' prototypes. It is also beneficial for government, because it speeds up deployment of new homeland security technologies. FutureTECH, the SECURE initiative's sister program, takes a similar collaborative approach to developing homeland security technologies that will be needed in the medium and long-term future.[94]

These research and development initiatives are relevant to airport security because they can produce new screening technologies that are used in airports. At the time of this writing, the most advanced passenger screening technology used in airports is the millimeter wave scanner. Yet like all screening technologies, it is not a complete solution to airline security. Rather, it is a tool that can assist in screening airline passengers. SECURE and Future-TECH would seem to be ideal programs in which to generate new screening technologies that carefully balance the interests of the public sector, private sector, and the general public.

The Comair flight cancellation fiasco underlines the airline industry's vulnerability to software failures. These failures can take multiple forms: data breaches, where information that should remain confidential is disclosed in an unauthorized way; software failures, where specific software applications do not work as they are designed to work; and hardware failures, where physical computer equipment fails. Given these pressing issues, and the airline industry's ever-increasing dependence on computer systems, the public and private sector can work together to enhance software and hardware security. The government has a vested interest in the smooth functioning of airline software and hardware, since the airline industry forms part of the transportation sector, and DHS considers the transportation sector to be one piece of U.S. critical infrastructure. [95] At the same time, businesses in the aviation industry have a strong profit motive to keep data secure, and to make sure that software and hardware are working as they are designed to work.

A combination of government incentives for industry, such as tax breaks for companies that achieve certain data security benchmarks, as well as regulation, such as resiliency standards for airline hardware and software products, stand to benefit both the public and private sector in this regard. Government benefits from reliable and secure data, hardware, and software in the airline industry. Firms also benefit from high data security standards, by achieving a measure of resilience that they did not previously enjoy.

As discussed above, public-private partnerships can also help to shore up the nation's aging air traffic control system. Industry and government leaders scrutinize the FAA's National Airspace System, which air traffic controllers use to track flights across the country.[96] There is widespread agreement that this software is reaching a breaking point, having not been appropriately updated in years, despite the fact that the airline industry has exploded in size and complexity.[97] To address this issue, there is a movement toward using new open architecture software for the National Airspace System. This type of software is highly customizable, rather than standardized. In theory, individual airports can tailor the software to their own unique needs. Yet this flexibility also means that the software is more open to exploitation for nefarious purposes. Thus there is a tension between the need to modernize the National Airspace System and, at the same time, to ensure that the system remains secure from malicious cyberattacks and data breaches.

Public-private partnerships are essential to achieving this balance. Government can provide helpful input into this process by outlining specific security requirements for software to control the National Airspace System. At the same time, the private sector can respond to those security needs in a few ways. First, software producers can work to meet—and even exceed—those government-defined security standards. Second, airlines themselves can provide input into the process of updating the software, based upon their own commercial needs. Third, having produced versions of this new software, firms can work with government to trial the software—in the software industry this is called "beta testing"—to confirm that it meets expectations. In light of these points of confluence between government and private sector interests, it is clear that government and businesses offer one another a great deal in potentially improving the National Airspace System.

The Umar Farouk Abdulmutallab case demonstrates that there are still important gaps in aviation security. The fact that Abdulmutallab paid in cash for his flight and that he did not check any luggage is suspicious on its face.[98] So it is striking that despite

the advanced screening technology and heightened security awareness that exists in the aviation industry today, Northwest Airlines
did not flag Abdulmutallab for further investigation prior to his
departure from the Netherlands for Detroit. Moreover, Abdulmutallab possessed a valid U.S. entry visa, but the U.S. State Department did not cancel the visa, even though Abdulmutallab's
father alerted the U.S. government about his son's possible involvement with extremists.[99] These facts suggest that more robust
algorithms are needed to flag suspicious passenger behaviors
before they board planes.

Public-private partnerships can play an important role in
strengthening these algorithms. While governmental standards for
aviation security are uneven worldwide, there remain certain
security benchmarks that airlines must meet in order to fly to the
United States. In light of this, the U.S. government can require
international airline companies to use certain types of software
algorithms to identify passengers who may pose a threat based
upon their purchasing behavior. Software firms, for their part, can
work with U.S. government officials to develop the algorithms that
should be used in the software. Ideally, behaviors like cash payments for international flights can be cross-checked against other
passenger data to identify potentially suspicious individuals.
Additionally, DHS and the U.S. State Department can do a better
job of flagging visas that are potentially problematic. And again,
private sector software can play a vital role here. Certain fields in
one U.S. State Department visa database can connect to other
DHS databases. In this way, if a U.S. State Department official
"red flags" a visa in one database, DHS is alerted to that fact in
another database.

To be clear, we do not believe that any of these opportunities
for public-private partnerships will somehow resolve all the challenges of aviation security. America's adversaries have proven

remarkably adaptable and persistent in seeking to disrupt the aviation industry and thereby harm national security. But we do think that these opportunities underscore how important public-private partnerships are in airport security today. Moreover, these opportunities forecast the substantial role that public-private partnerships will play in airport security in the years ahead.

III. Public-Private Partnerships in Border Security

Drug-related violence in Mexico is at an all-time high. There are scores of media accounts of citizens being beheaded and dismembered.[100] Entire groups of police officers have been shot and killed while on duty. Mexican journalists have been murdered for their reporting.[101] And there is widespread corruption among Mexican government officials. In 2010, for example, Mexico's Secretary of Public Safety estimated that some $100 million in bribes were being paid monthly to municipal police officers across the country.[102] This combination of factors—high levels of violent crime, systematic intimidation of journalists, and corruption of public officials—has created an intractable security problem in Mexico. This has begun to stoke fears of violence spilling over the border into the United States, and indeed, this violence has begun to make itself felt along the southern border. In short, the border security mission is now broader than ever, but the resources available to achieve this mission remain limited.[103]

In light of today's persistent border security challenges, public-private partnerships stand to benefit border security initiatives in numerous ways, from enhancing cross-sector information sharing, to use of new cargo screening technologies, to developing relationships with foreign business organizations. And while public-private partnerships will undoubtedly face many challenges in border security over the next few years, government and businesses will enjoy a range of new opportunities to expand and deepen these partnerships, as well.

Cross-border violence is an increasing concern in southern border communities. In at least one case, Texas public safety officers engaged in a firefight with drug cartel members, literally shooting across the U.S.-Mexico border.[104] And many government officials from communities along the southern border publically call for additional resources, including personnel and equipment, to be deployed along the border to enhance security.[105] But this is not to suggest that violence along the southern border is necessarily widespread, either. Publically available analyses indicate that the *perception* of increased violence along the border may be stronger than the *actual* presence of increased violence along the border.[106] Nonetheless, the threat of cross-border violence remains and will continue to be a high priority for homeland security policymakers for the foreseeable future.

To address these concerns of spillover violence along the border, the Secure Border Initiative (SBINet), which we first discussed in Chapter 1, sought to implement a series of detection technologies along unmanned areas of the border. These technologies, which included radar and sophisticated cameras, were designed to detect illegal border crossings in unmanned areas and to alert CBP officers to the location of these illegal border crossings.[107] In this way, private sector technology was supposed to enhance CBP's surveillance capabilities and enable CBP officers to spread their presence across greater swaths of territory. DHS ultimately scuttled SBINet due to underperforming technology and cost overruns. [108] Nevertheless, SBINet shows that partnerships between the public and private sectors can be used to address complex border security challenges.

A related border security concern is that international terrorists may attempt to cross the southern border illegally to enter the

United States. The thinking goes that if significant quantities of drugs and thousands of persons are able to enter the United States undetected each year, then it is not difficult to imagine terrorists with a WMD making their way across the border in the same manner.[109] Given that large portions of the southern border remain porous, this is not an unreasonable assumption. Moreover, the northern border is also vulnerable to illegal smuggling. In 2007, investigators from the U.S. Government Accountability Office (GAO) easily moved fake radioactive material inside a gym bag across an unguarded portion of the U.S.-Canadian border.[110] The GAO investigation demonstrated that while national attention tends to emphasize security along the southern border, there are vulnerabilities along the northern border, as well.

Public-private partnerships can play a significant role in combatting illegal border crossings and smuggling. For example, cargo screening technologies make it harder for vehicles to move across the border carrying contraband material. In May 2011, CBP officials used a large X-ray machine to locate over 500 illegal migrants packed into two tractor trailers.[111] Massachusetts-based American Science & Engineering produces this large-scale scanning technology.[112] The firm also produces similar types of screening tools to screen cargo in maritime ports. [113] Using these technologies, government officials can better perform screening and interdiction duties. Firms benefit through sales relationships with government. Government feedback on how technologies are performing strengthens research and development activities.

Cross-border information sharing, too, proves helpful in facilitating cargo screening and building relationships between firms and government authorities. As of 2004, CBP requires firms to provide advance information about the cargo they are transporting across U.S. borders into the United States. [114] Moreover, CBP's Free and Secure Trade (FAST) program provides truckers with a credential to enter the United States that certifies their trustworthiness.[115] In theory, having this credential expedites the cargo screening process, permitting a trucker to move his cargo to its final destination faster. Putting these requirements in place is initially burdensome on firms, because it requires an extra layer of paperwork and attention in order to transport goods into the United States. But it is ultimately beneficial for both government and businesses. The U.S. government can be more aware of who and what is actually being moved across the border. This enhances homeland security. And through this awareness, shipping can be expedited, ultimately benefitting firms and their customers.

Public-private partnerships can facilitate the transport of licit goods, while also helping to stop the illegal movement of persons and contraband. But given the security environment in Mexico, public-private partnerships will have to navigate a number of pressing challenges in order to achieve their full potential. At the same time, businesses and government can also capitalize on a number of rich opportunities in the years ahead.

Challenges for Public-Private Partnerships in Border Security

A wide range of challenges now impact public-private partnerships in border security. Among the most pressing of these challenges are balancing the role of federal, local, and state governments, closing gaps along the borders, combatting corruption, and developing new detection technologies. Some of these challenges affect the public sector more directly, while others affect the private sector in a more pronounced way. But because of the need for continual cooperation between businesses and government in border security, all of these challenges ultimately affect both sectors.

Corruption in border security is mostly a public sector concern, since it is CBP officials—not business representatives—that are ultimately accountable for securing the border itself. There is little public discussion of corruption among border security officers, yet it can and does occur. Thomas M. Frost, DHS Assistant Inspector General for Investigations, noted in 2010 that in 2009, some 576 CBP employees were investigated for corruption.[116] Corruption rots border security efforts by undermining the ability of government to block illegal shipments of goods and persons. But no matter how rigorous the background investigations of CBP officials working along the border, or how closely CBP employees are monitored, it is reasonable to expect that corruption will remain a problem for the foreseeable future.

Shrinking budgets are a problem for all government agencies in the midst of the ongoing global financial crisis. CBP is no exception. In recent public remarks, CBP Acting Deputy Administrator Thomas S. Winkowski noted that CBP is going to face a difficult budgetary outlook for the next few years.[117] One challenge for CBP will be to continue to achieve excellent results in stopping the flow of goods and persons entering the United States illegally, while at the same time not being able to hire many more personnel or procure a great deal more equipment. CBP will have to do more with less.

Cross-border underground tunnels and ultralight unmanned aircraft are an increasing problem in border security. Some of the underground tunnels are remarkably sophisticated and feature air conditioning, lighting, and even fixed tracks for carts to be moved from one end of the tunnel to the other.[118] Smugglers use the tunnels to move goods and persons under the border undetected.[119] Moreover, in fiscal year 2011, CBP confirmed 101 ultralight aircraft events.[120] Smugglers use these ultralight unmanned aircraft to move drugs across the border under cover of darkness.[121]

These aircraft provide numerous advantages for smugglers: they are relatively inexpensive to produce; they are generally too small for a helicopter to intercept; and they don't put a smuggler at risk of capture.[122]

Businesses face a number of challenges in border security, as well. Firms may also find themselves juggling their client relationships among local, state, and federal government entities along the border. No business can devote 100% of its time and attention to a single customer, so it is reasonable to assume that firms will have to carefully balance the need for revenue against the need to keep all of their customers happy. Moreover, businesses may be invited to participate in local, state, and federal committees that address border security issues. In the context of these committees, government representatives can provide firms information about their agencies' ongoing requirements, as well as feedback on how firms' products and services are delivering (or not delivering) results as expected. This helps firms to deliver better products and services, which helps to build long-term business relationships with government. It also gives firms a window onto emerging threats, which can help them to develop new tools to secure the borders.

In discussions of border security, the U.S.-Mexico border usually receives a great deal more attention than the U.S.-Canada border. Yet it's clear that many of the same security risks that exist along the southern border are equally present along unprotected portions of the northern border. There are numerous remote openings for smugglers to move drugs and persons into the United States from Canada. And the GAO has demonstrated that these same routes could be used to move WMD precursor materials, as well. Given the security risks that exist along the northern border, public-private partnerships may play a significant and increasing role in protecting the northern border. Privately produced detection technologies can be installed in strategic locations along the northern border.[123] CBP can use these same technologies to supplement the work of CBP personnel, expanding security coverage of the northern border—especially in areas where there is little to no CBP presence to begin with. This presents an opportunity for firms to deepen relationships with the federal government by selling products that can stand up to below-freezing conditions along the northern border. Additionally, private sector consultants can provide vulnerability assessments for remote areas along the northern border. CBP can use these vulnerability assessments to develop plans that optimize distribution of border surveillance technology. Through the use of consultants and via sales of new technology, government benefits from better border security, and firms benefit from their business relationships with government.

Shared public and private sector challenges in border security, too, require close attention from businesses and government. Given that the local, state, and federal governments are engaged in border security operations, firms may sell detection products to agencies at each level of government. This, in and of itself, is a novel development. Major industry contractors like Boeing, Raytheon, and Booz Allen Hamilton are accustomed to doing business with the federal government for homeland security purposes. But what is new is the prospect of these and other large firms engaging in contracts with states and localities. Given the groundswell of support in border communities for increased border security, the prospect of firms like these doing business with non-federal government entities is very realistic. This will present a challenge for firms accustomed to dealing with federal clients, and it will also represent a shift for localities and states, because localities and states may not have much experience interacting with large vendors. There will be a degree of adaptation necessary for contractors, too, in learning how to do business with state and local governments.

SBINet, which we discussed earlier in this chapter, illustrates how public-private partnerships can sometimes break down. The network of sensors, cameras, and radar that made up SBINet did not deliver as expected. The equipment malfunctioned frequently. The failed SBINet provides an excellent case study of the kinds of challenges that can impact public-private partnerships in border security. In this case, poor communication between the vendor and customer, lack of effective oversight mechanisms, and faulty equipment combined to produce a less-than-desirable outcome. Challenges like this will likely occur again in the context of border security efforts, and it will require excellent cooperation between government and businesses to navigate them successfully.

There are many challenges facing border security today, and we have only discussed a few of them here. But these same issues also present a number of excellent opportunities for public-private partnerships to strengthen border security.

Opportunities for Public-Private Partnerships in Border Security

There are numerous opportunities for public-private partnerships to enhance border security today, and many of these same opportunities are directly connected to the challenges we outline above. Information sharing agreements, as well as development of new detection technologies, stand out as areas for government and businesses to collaborate in a productive, mutually beneficial manner.

Firms can now help to facilitate information sharing in an informal way that is useful for government agencies. It is plausible that different government representatives may look to their vendors to learn about what other levels of government are doing in border security. For example, let us assume that a locality in

Arizona purchases a set of night vision goggles from a vendor. That locality's representative may casually ask the vendor if he or she has recently sold those same goggles to other localities, states, or CBP. In this way, firms can be an informal communication bridge between different levels of government involved in border security. They serve as a source of information about ongoing border security activities for all levels of government.

Firms can also formally partner with local and state authorities to share information for border security purposes. This is a relatively new development, because historically the federal government has led border security efforts, with local and state governments not taking as significant a role in border security as they are today. Regardless of whether this information sharing between firms and local and state governments occurs informally, through one-to-one relationships with government officials, or via formal mechanisms like committees or non-governmental organizations, it seems clear that the rising role of local and state involvement in border security means that localities and states will need to include businesses when they share border security-related information. This can help firms gain greater insight into the border security challenges being faced by local and state governments. It also means that local and state governments can informally propose solutions for the private sector to develop, whether in providing products or services. Thus information sharing between firms and local and state governments proves beneficial to both businesses and government.

Opportunities exist for increased U.S. government ties with foreign business organizations, as well. Chambers of commerce promote business activity, so it makes sense for homeland security officials to have strong working relationships with Mexican and Canadian chambers of commerce. By developing professional relationships with Mexican and Canadian chambers of commerce,

U.S. government officials can learn more about trusted Mexican and Canadian business entities, as well as those whose reputations might be suspect, meaning that they might engage in smuggling operations. This type of information is valuable because it can support border security operations—it is intelligence that can make more efficient use of limited border security resources. Through information exchange with chambers of commerce, the U.S. government can informally recognize Mexican and Canadian firms for excellent or suspect business practices. In other words, a senior CBP official, reviewing a list of incoming trucks at a border crossing in Texas, might recognize a firm on the list as "suspect," prompting him to alert a subordinate officer to give the truck extra scrutiny. At the same time, a company that is known and trusted might prompt the same official to alert his subordinate to only give that truck a "standard" screening, rather than an extra level of scrutiny. This kind of intelligence-driven screening can help to give trusted firms an easier experience importing goods into the United States, and it can also assist government officials in identifying shipments that need to be searched more thoroughly. It is a mutually beneficial arrangement that flows from developing a public-private partnership between U.S. government entities and private sector chambers of commerce outside the United States.

New challenges to border security, including underground tunnels and ultralight aircraft, underline the need for new privately developed detection technologies in border security. Putting aside the mechanical failures of detection equipment in SBINet, there are excellent opportunities for firms to create innovative solutions for these new challenges. At the 2012 Symposium on Homeland Security at Christopher Newport University, CBP Acting Deputy Administrator Thomas S. Winkowski noted:

We should certainly be sitting down with industry on a whole host of issues....tunnel detection, I think, is a huge area....who's got that technology out there in tunnel detection? Well, really nobody [has that technology] including some of the best in the military that we've worked with.[124]

Turning to the issue of unmanned ultralight aircraft, Winkowski highlighted part of the technological challenges that CBP faces:

[CBP has] the best technology in the world....[yet if] we have some guy who decides to take a lawnmower engine and attach it to some [airplane] frame and [puts] 300 pounds of marijuana on [it]....it flies right over us.[125]

Firms have a clear opportunity to partner with government to develop tunnel detection technologies, as well as tools to stop ultralight aircraft from crossing the border. This helps firms continue to generate revenue while trimming costs, and it assists government in achieving the border security mission.

Public-private partnerships have an important role in border security today, and they will continue to play an important role in the years ahead. Whether these partnerships facilitate information sharing, provide innovative detection technology, or deliver consulting services to government stakeholders, government and businesses can work together to strengthen border security.

IV. Conclusions and Suggestions for Further Research

Surveying the challenges in maritime port security, airport security, and border security today, a number of common themes emerge. Public-private partnerships can contribute in a significant way to enhancing border security in each of these areas, and this will affect the future of border security as a whole.

Since 9/11 there is widespread recognition that information needs to be shared more effectively across government and the private sector. Ports have numerous stakeholders, often featuring multiple law enforcement agencies with overlapping areas of jurisdiction. Airports are similar, often being operated by quasi-governmental business entities and staffed by a mixture of public and private sector employees. Border crossings require heavy interaction between government officials, business representatives, and members of the general public. Public-private partnerships can enhance information sharing across all of these areas. Where there are large numbers of stakeholders operating in a single location, local web or intranet-based information sharing solutions may be helpful and cost-effective in enhancing situational awareness. Across maritime ports, airports, and border crossings, a combination of formal information sharing agreements, like committees or working groups, as well as technologies, such as shared databases, can also enhance overall awareness of threats and help to direct homeland security limited resources in an efficient way. Public and private sector participation in these formal groups and development of new information sharing technologies can benefit all stakeholders in port of entry security.

Cargo, passenger, and vehicle screening technologies have changed a great deal since 9/11. Firms and government are developing new technologies today that will ultimately replace those that are currently in use. The new "cartoon image" millimeter wave scanners discussed earlier in this chapter may strike the right balance between meeting security needs and protecting passenger privacy—for now. But as terrorists and other nefarious actors devise new ways to beat the scanners, the public and private sectors will have to deploy new types of screening devices to outflank the bad guys. For example, it may be that radiation detection technology for cargo containers on ships, which used to give "false positives" on items as benign as kitty litter, becomes more sophisticated and useful for customs officials in maritime ports.[126] Similarly, backscatter scanners, like those that CBP uses to screen the contents of tractor trailers, may become obsolete as smugglers find new ways to mask their cargo. There will be a continuing need for better detection and screening technologies in America's ports of entry, and by working together, the public and private sector can build, test, and deploy these technologies in an efficient and effective way.

The development of ultralight unmanned aircraft that can fly over the heads of CBP officers, as well as near-miss terror attacks like the case of Umar Farouk Abdulmutallab, show that there is an ongoing need to adapt quickly to security threats. In the former example, drug cartels have found a low-cost solution to beat the world's most sophisticated detection technology. Abdulmutallab hid explosives in his underwear—a place he knew that airport security officers would not check. These examples demonstrate that drug cartels and terrorists are constantly adjusting their tactics to take advantage of security vulnerabilities.

Public-private partnerships help to build capacity for rapid adaptation to threats. Firms offer government a flexible, scalable workforce that can be deployed, shifted, expanded, or contracted as threats evolve. Moreover, businesses can quickly re-allocate physical capital—things like detection equipment, computers, and uniforms—in a highly efficient way. Partnering with the private sector, government is freed from these functions to focus on other security-related priorities. This speeds up government's ability to react to evolving threats. And firms benefit, because these types of activities also mean added revenue for the firms themselves.

Future research into public-private partnerships at America's ports of entry should continue to explore the sometimes blurry line between business and government security functions. For example, if a foreign-flagged ship is docked in a U.S. maritime port, and a terrorist manages to sneak aboard and detonates a bomb, who is primarily responsible for investigating the security breach? Is it the Federal Bureau of Investigation (FBI), which has primary responsibility for investigating terrorist attacks in the United States? Do the TSA and USCG play a role? If so, what is that role? And is the foreign shipping company liable for damage to the maritime port itself? These questions invite careful inquiry and may have important legal implications for business and government agencies working at ports of entry.

Information sharing for homeland security has improved a great deal since 9/11, but cross-sector information sharing remains problematic. As public-private partnerships evolve, sharing information may actually become harder. For example, if most TSA functions in airports are re-assigned to private security firms, it is not clear that TSA would share the same type of detailed intelligence information with those private security officers that they would with government security officers. Since the private security firm is a non-governmental entity, TSA may have a lingering resistance to sharing information with the private security firm's employees. The few airports that now use mostly private sector security screeners under TSA's Screening Partnership Program (SPP) could be excellent case studies in how cross-sector information sharing can change under these circumstances.

Finally, the failed SBINet project, as well as the public outcry over the original full body image millimeter wave scanners, shows that improperly tested technology can prove to be a great waste of taxpayer money. It is not enough for screening or detection technology to be innovative and useful—the people who would use the technology must provide input into its design, and at some level, the general public must buy into the technology, as well. To be successful, officials involved in proof of concept testing for new technology in America's ports of entry must keep these principles in mind. Researchers can examine how security officials and the public react to new screening technologies. Scholars can use this data to develop a working list of best practices for deploying new security technology at ports of entry.

Securing America's ports of entry remains a daunting task. But through public-private partnerships, American ports of entry are safer. Whether by sea, air, or land, the goods and persons entering and exiting the United States are better controlled and monitored through public-private partnerships. This is helpful from an economic perspective, because it means that commerce can flow more freely, and it is helpful from a security perspective, because it means that persons and goods that should not enter the United States do not enter the United States. In this way, public-private partnerships can help to achieve the broader homeland security mission, by effectively balancing the free flow of persons and goods with the need for constant vigilance against outside threats.

Notes

1. California Emergency Management Agency, *Golden Guardian 2010: After Action Report Executive Summary*, n.d., accessed October 29, 2012, http://www.calema.ca.gov/TrainingandExercises/Documents/GG%202010% 20AAR%20Executive%20Summary.pdf, 8.
2. Ibid.
3. Ibid.
4. California Emergency Management Agency, *Golden Guardian 2010: After Action Report Executive Summary*, 9.
5. Ibid., 4–5.
6. Ibid.
7. For example, Stephen Flynn, *The Edge of Disaster* (New York, NY: Random House, Inc., 2007), 20–36. Flynn describes the threat posed by Liquefied Natural Gas (LNG) tankers in Boston Harbor.

8. Organisation for Economic Co-Operation and Development, *SECURITY IN MARITIME TRANSPORT: RISK FACTORS AND ECONOMIC IMPACT*, July 2003, accessed December 3, 2012, http://www.oecd.org/sti/transport/maritimetransport/18521672.pdf/, 22.

9. In this chapter the term "port of entry" refers generally to maritime ports, airports, and border crossings.

10. Edwin Alden and Bryan Roberts, "Are U.S. Borders Secure?" *Foreign Affairs* 90, no. 4 (July 2011): 19–26; Todd Steinmetz, "Mitigating the Exploitation of U.S. Borders by Jihadists and Criminal Organizations," *Journal of Strategic Security* 4, no. 3 (Fall 2011): 29–48; Richard J. Kilroy, Jr., Abelardo Rodriguez Sumano, and Todd S. Hataley, "Toward a New Trilateral Strategic Security Relationship: United States, Canada, and Mexico," *Journal of Strategic Security* 3, no. 1 (March 2010): 51–64; Michael P. Wigginton and Carl J. Jensen, "The Texas Border Sheriff's Coalition: an Analysis of Policing Along the U.S.-Mexican Border," *The Homeland Security Review* 6, no. 1 (Winter 2012): 35–59.

11. Jon D. Haveman, Ethan M. Jennings, Howard J. Shatz, and Greg C. Wright, "The Container Security Initiative and Ocean Container Threats," *Journal of Homeland Security and Emergency Management* 4, no. 1 (March 2007): 1–19; Suzette R. Grillot, Rebecca J. Cruise, and Valerie J. D'Erman, "National and Global Efforts to Enhance Containerized Freight Security," *Journal of Homeland Security and Emergency Management* 6, no. 1 (January 2009): 1–31; Niyazi Bakir and Detlof Von Winterfeldt, "Is Better Nuclear Weapon Detection Capability Justified?" *Journal of Homeland Security and Emergency Management* 8, no. 1 (January 2011): 1–18; Marc Thibault, Mary R. Brooks, and Kenneth J. Button, "The Response of the U.S. Maritime Industry to the New Container Security Initiatives," *Transportation Journal* (Winter 2006): 5–15. A notable exception is Michael McNicholas, *Maritime Security* (Burlington, MA: Elsevier, Inc., 2008), which provides a comprehensive treatment of maritime port security, rather than focusing on narrow topics within maritime port security.

12. Candice L. Wright, "BRIDGING THE GAP IN PORT SECURITY; NETWORK-CENTRIC THEORY APPLIED TO PUBLIC/PRIVATE COLLABORATION," (master's thesis, Naval Postgraduate School, 2007); Ji Young Park, "The Economic Impacts of Dirty Bomb Attacks on the Los Angeles and Long Beach Ports: Applying the Supply-Driven National Interstate Economic Model," *Journal of Homeland Security and Emergency Management* 5, no. 1 (January 2008): 1–20; Katie Smith Matison, "What's In The

Box? An overview of domestic and international developments in port security and safe carriage of containerized cargo," *Journal of Transportation Law, Logistics & Policy* 76, no. 3 (Third Quarter, 2009): 329–349.

13. Joseph S. Szyliowicz, "Aviation Security: Promise or Reality?" *Studies in Conflict and Terrorism* 27 (June 2004): 47–63; Mark G. Stewart and John Mueller, "Cost-Benefit Analysis of Advanced Imaging Technology Full Body Scanners for Airline Passenger Security Screening," *Journal of Homeland Security and Emergency Management* 8, no. 1 (January 2011): 1–18.

14. Thibault, Brooks, and Button, "New Container Security Initiatives," 6.

15. Liza Porteus Viana, "Best Practices Half a World Away," *HSToday*, March 2009, 20–24; Antony Pate, Bruce Taylor, and Bruce Kubu, *Protecting America's Ports: Promising Practices*, Police Executive Research Forum, November 20, 2007, 46.

16. Ibid.

17. Microsoft, "U.S. Coast Guard Expects to Save $1 Million Annually With Data Transmission Solution," n.d., accessed December 6, 2012, http://www.judyb.com/coastguardcs.doc, 1–5.

18. Ibid., 2.

19. Ibid, 2–3.

20. Pate, Taylor, and Kubu, *Protecting America's Ports*, 45–46.

21. Logisuite Corporation, "Automated Manifest System," 2012, accessed December 6, 2012, http://www.logisuite.com/automated-manifest-system/.

22. Transportation Security Administration, "Transportation Worker Identification Credential," November 20, 2012, accessed December 6, 2012, http://www.tsa.gov/stakeholders/transportation-worker-identification-credential-twic%C2%AE.

23. Transportation Security Administration, "Program Information: Transportation Worker Identification Credential," October 15, 2012, accessed December 6, 2012, http://www.tsa.gov/stakeholders/program-information.

24. Transportation Security Administration, "Transportation Worker Identification Credential."

25. Transportation Security Administration, "Program Information: Transportation Worker Identification Credential."

26. Certain criminal convictions, such as murder, treason, conspiracy to commit terrorism, and improper transport of hazardous materials, can disqualify a candidate from obtaining a TWIC card. See Transportation Security Administration, "Frequently Asked Questions: Transportation Worker

Identification Credential," November 20, 2012, accessed December 6, 2012, http://www.tsa.gov/stakeholders/frequently-asked-questions-0.

27. Transportation Security Administration, "Frequently Asked Questions: Transportation Worker Identification Credential."

28. Calvin Biesecker, "Lockheed Martin Snares $70 Million TWIC Contract," securityinfowatch.com, February 5, 2007, accessed December 6, 2012, http://www.securityinfowatch.com/news/10558983/lockheed-martin-snares-70-million-twic-contract.

29. Viana, "Best Practices," 21.

30. Ibid., 20–24; Port of Yokohama, "Port Security Officer of the Port of Oakland Visit (sic) the Port of Yokohama," 2012, accessed December 6, 2012, http://www.city.yokohama.lg.jp/kowan/english/interexchange/2012/2012060 4.html.

31. U.S. Department of Homeland Security, "Transportation Systems Sector: Critical Infrastructure," n.d., accessed December 6, 2012, http://www.dhs. gov/transportation-systems-sector.

32. U.S. Department of Homeland Security, "National Infrastructure Protection Plan: Maritime Transportation Mode," 2011, accessed December 6, 2012, http://www.dhs.gov/xlibrary/assets/nppd/nppd-ip-maritime-snapshot-2011.pdf.

33. National Council of ISACs, "About Us," 2012, accessed December 6, 2012, http://www.isaccouncil.org/index.php?option=com_content&view=article&id =87&Itemid=194.

34. Maritime Security Council, 2011, accessed December 6, 2012, http://www. maritimesecurity.org/.

35. Maritime Security Council, "MSC Programs," 2009, accessed December 6, 2012, http://www.maritimesecurity.org/program.html; Maritime Security Council, "MSC Leaders Speak at Global Futures Forum," September 2012, accessed December 6, 2012, http://www.maritimesecurity.org/Press%20 Releases/Global%20Futures%20Forum%20Release.10.3.2012.pdf.

36. U.S. Coast Guard, "National Maritime Security Advisory Committee," 2012, accessed December 6, 2012, https://homeport.uscg.mil/mycg/portal/ep/ browse.do?channelId=-26462&channelPage=%2Fep%2Fchannel%2 Fdefault.jsp&pageTypeId=13489.

37. The Port of Los Angeles, "Homeland Security," 2012, accessed December 6, 2012, http://www.portoflosangeles.org/security/homeland_security.asp; U.S. Department of Homeland Security, "Maritime Security in the Port of Houston," June 16, 2010, accessed December 6, 2012, http://www.asishouston.

org/ChapterNews/Speakers/061610_USCG_Speaker_Peresentation.pdf; Port of New Orleans, "Harbor Police Department," March 11, 2005, accessed December 6, 2012, http://www.portno.com/ hpdhistory.htm; Hampton Roads Planning District Commission, "Emergency Management Committees," 2008, accessed December 6, 2012, http://www.hrpdc.org/ EMERMGMT/EM_Committees.asp.

38. Haveman, Jennings, Shatz, and Wright, "Container Security Initiative," 1.

39. Ibid.

40. Ibid., 13.

41. McNicholas, *Maritime Security*, 296.

42. For example, Nick McKenzie and Richard Baker, "Crime groups rife at ports, inquiry finds*," The Sydney Morning Herald*, May 25, 2012, accessed December 6, 2012, http://www.smh.com.au/national/crime-groups-rife-at-ports-inquiry-finds-20120524-1z7yp.html; "Port security officers urged to stay away from corruption," *Jamaica Observer*, July 31, 2008, accessed December 6, 2012, http://www.jamaicaobserver.com/news/138448_Port-security-officers-urged-to-stay-away-from-corruption; Sandra Sequiera and Simeon Djankov, "Trade costs and corruption in ports," *Port Technology International*, March 8, 2012, accessed December 11, 2012, http://www.porttechnology.org/images/uploads/technical_papers/PTI-121.pdf.

43. Grillot, Cruise, and D'Erman, "National and Global Efforts," 14.

44. Ibid.

45. Thibault, Brooks, and Button, "New Container Security Initiatives," 6.

46. Elaine Rundle, "Port Security Improves With Nonintrusive Cargo Inspection and Secure Port Access," *Emergency Management*, July 28, 2009, accessed December 11, 2012, http://www.emergencymgmt.com/infrastructure/ Port-Security-Improves-With.html.

47. Nitin Bakshi, Stephen E. Flynn, and Noah Gans, "Estimating the Operational Impact of Container Inspections at International Ports," *Management Science* 57, no. 1 (January 2011): 1–20.

48. Grillot, Cruise, and D'Erman, "National and Global Efforts," 9.

49. Ibid., 8–9.

50. Wright, "BRIDGING THE GAP IN PORT SECURITY," 2.

51. Ibid., 24.

52. Ibid., 48–49.

53. Associated Press, "Somali pirates free 4 South Korean crewmen from 19 months of captivity after ransom was paid," December 2, 2012, accessed December 7, 2012, http://www.foxnews.com/world/2012/12/02/somali-

pirates-free-4-south-korean-crewmen-from-1-months-captivity-after-ransom/l; Reuters, "Somali pirates jailed for attack on Italian oil tanker," December 4, 2012, accessed December 7, 2012, http://uk.reuters.com/article/2012/12/04/uk-italy-pirates-idUKBRE8B30KZ20121204.

54. British Broadcasting Corporation, "Nigerian navy frees hijacked Singapore-owned oil tanker," September 5, 2012, accessed December 7, 2012, http://www.bbc.co.uk/news/world-africa-19486746; Reuters, "Somali pirates hijack Indian ship with 21 crew off Oman," August 20, 2011, accessed December 7, 2012, http://www.reuters.com/article/2011/08/20/us-india-hijack-idUSTRE77J1DY20110820; Safety4Sea, "Cargo ship hijacked at port," November 1, 2012, accessed December 11, 2012, http://www.safety4sea.com/page/13783/4/cargo-ship-hijacked-at-port.

55. Michael Isikoff, "U.S. failure to retaliate for USS Cole attack rankled then—and now," msnbc.com, October 12, 2010, accessed December 7, 2012, http://www.msnbc.msn.com/id/39622062/ns/us_news-security/t/us-failure-retaliate-uss-cole-attack-rankled-then-now/#.ULzK_5gVoro.

56. Ibid.

57. Tactical Intelligence International, "Maritime Security," n.d., accessed December 7, 2012, http://www.tacticalintel.com/maritime-security.html; APPDS Maritime Security Ltd., "Anti-piracy training courses," n.d., accessed December 7, 2012, http://www.appds-maritime-security.com/en/appds-maritime-services/anti-piracy-training-courses-en; Trojan Securities, "Maritime Security," 2012, accessed December 7, 2012, http://www.trojansecurities.com/trojan-maritime-security.html; International Maritime Security Network LLC, 2011, accessed December 7, 2012, http://www.imsn.us/.

58. Tactical Intelligence International; International Maritime Security Network LLC.

59. LRAD Corporation, "LRAD/Product Overview," n.d. accessed December 7, 2012, http://www.lradx.com/site/content/view/15/110/.

60. Raytheon, "Raytheon Produces Active Denial and Other Directed Energy Solutions," 2008, accessed December 7, 2012, http://www.raytheon.com/newsroom/feature/ads_03-08/; Sandia Corporation, "Team Investigates Active Denial System for security applications," June 30, 2005, accessed August 12, 2013, https://share.sandia.gov/news/resources/releases/2005/def-nonprolif-sec/active-denial.html.

61. U.S. Department of Defense, "Active Denial System Frequently Asked Questions," n.d., accessed December 7, 2012, http://jnlwp.defense.gov/pressroom/faq_p2.html.

62. Ibid.

63. Ibid.

64. Karen Jacobs, "Airlines look to resume full flight schedules in New York area," Reuters, November 2, 2012, accessed December 7, 2012, http://www.reuters.com/article/2012/11/02/uk-storm-sandy-airlines-idUSLNE8A100R20121102.

65. Hugo Martin, "La Guardia opens for limited service; flight cancellations drop," *Los Angeles Times*, November 1, 2012, accessed December 7, 2012, http://www.latimes.com/business/money/la-fi-mo-la-guardia-sandy-20121101,0,7495287.story.

66. Jim Avila, "Sandy Grounds More Than 10,000 Flights, Train Traffic Derailed," abcnews.com, October 29, 2012, accessed December 7, 2012, http://abcnews.go.com/Travel/sandy-grounds-13000-flights-train-traffic-derailed/story?id=17587109#.UJPjsJgVoro.

67. Joseph Straw, "New Views On Airport Screening," n.d., securitymanagement.com, accessed December 7, 2012, http://www.securitymanagement.com/article/new-views-airport-screening-004586?page=0%2C1; Tek84 Engineering Group, "Body Scanner," n.d., accessed December 7, 2012, http://www.tek84.com/bodyscanner.html.

68. American Civil Liberties Union, "ACLU Backgrounder on Body Scanners and 'Virtual Strip Searches'," January 8, 2012, accessed December 7, 2012, http://www.aclu.org/technology-and-liberty/aclu-backgrounder-body-scanners-and-virtual-strip-searches; CBS Dallas-Ft. Worth, "Female Passengers Say They're Targeted By TSA," February 3, 2012, accessed December 7, 2012, http://dfw.cbslocal.com/2012/02/03/female-passengers-say-theyre-targeted-by-tsa/.

69. CBS News, "TSA quietly removing some full body scanners," October 25, 2012, accessed December 7, 2012, http://www.cbsnews.com/8301-201_162-57540714/tsa-quietly-removing-some-full-body-scanners/.

70. Ibid.

71. *Passenger Manifests, U.S. Code* 49 (2001), § 44909, accessed December 7, 2012, http://www.law.cornell.edu/uscode/text/49/44909.

72. Ibid.

73 Sarah Maslin Nir, "Workers at J.F.K. Say Security Inspections Are Rushed," *The New York Times*, September 26, 2012, accessed December 7,

2012, http://www.nytimes.com/2012/09/27/nyregion/post-flight-airline-security-workers-say-they-are-rushed.html.

74. Ibid.

75. Sally Donnelly, "The Day the FAA Stopped the World," *Time*, September 14, 2001, accessed December 7, 2012, http://www.time.com/time/nation/article/0,8599,174912,00.html.

76. Ibid.

77. Ibid.

78. Ibid.

79. British Broadcasting Corporation, "Profile: Umar Farouk Abdulmutallab," October 12, 2011, accessed December 7, 2012, http://www.bbc.co.uk/news/world-us-canada-11545509.

80. CNN, "STATE OF THE UNION WITH JOHN KING: Interview with Janet Napolitano (Transcript)," cnn.com, December 27, 2009, accessed December 7, 2012, http://transcripts.cnn.com/TRANSCRIPTS/0912/27/sotu. 01.html. Napolitano was later sharply criticized for the using the words "the system worked" in this interview. Some interpreted these comments to mean that Napolitano believed the security screening procedures for international flights were effective in the Abdulmutallab case—which is obviously untrue. Her full comments, which we quote here, provide greater context for what Napolitano meant by "the system worked."

81. Peter Baker, "A Phrase Sets Off Sniping After a Crisis," *The New York Times*, December 29, 2009, accessed December 10, 2012, http://www.nytimes.com/2009/12/30/us/politics/30baker.html?_r=0.

82. Scott Mayerowitz, "TSA Opt Out Day: Thanksgiving Travelers Quiet So Far," abcnews.com, November 24, 2010, accessed December 7, 2012, http://abcnews.go.com/Travel/tsa-opt-day-thanksgiving-travelers-sound-off-pat/story?id=12228442#.UL4ZPoX6iHk.

83. Associated Press, "US Airways, Comair struggle to recover from holiday woes," December 27, 2004, accessed December 7, 2012, http://www.msnbc.msn.com/id/6754453/ns/business-us_business/t/us-airways-comair-struggleto-recover-holiday-woes/#.UJpmEuMSXNc; Stephanie Overby, "Comair's Christmas Disaster: Bound to Fail," CIO.com, May 1, 2005, accessed December 7, 2012, http://www.cio.com/article/112103/Comair_s_Christmas_Disaster_Bound_To_Fail?page=1&taxonomyId=3206.

84. Overby, "Comair's Christmas Disaster."

85. Edward Cone, "Crash Landing Ahead?" informationweek.com, January 12, 1998, accessed December 7, 2012, http://www.informationweek.com/664/64iufaa.htm.

86. Joan Lowy, "FAA's New Air Traffic System Hits Turbulence," Associated Press, October 5, 2011, accessed December 7, 2012, http://travel.usatoday. com/flights/story/2011-10-05/FAAs-new-air-traffic-system-hits-turbulence/50669726/1; John Foley, "FAA's New Flight Control System Has Security Holes: Researcher," informationweek.com, July 26, 2012, accessed December 7, 2012, http://www.informationweek.com/security/government/faas-new-flight-control-system-has-secur/240004424; Matt Thurber, "Hackers, FAA Disagree Over ADS-B Vulnerability," AINonline. com, August 21, 2012, accessed December 7, 2012, http://www.ainonline. com/aviation-news/ainalerts/2012-08-21/hackers-faa-disagree-over-ads-b-vulnerability.

87. Keith Laing, "TSA approves private screeners for Orlando airport," *The Hill*, June 11, 2012, accessed December 7, 2012, http://thehill.com/blogs/transportation-report/tsa/232093-tsa-approves-private-screeners-for-orlando-airport.

88. *Aviation and Transportation Security Act of 2001*, Public Law 107-71, accessed December 7, 2012, http://www.gpo.gov/fdsys/pkg/PLAW-107 publ71/html/PLAW-107publ71.htm.

89. Transportation Security Administration, "Screening Partnership Program," November 21, 2012, accessed December 7, 2012, http://www.tsa.gov/stakeholders/screening-partnership-program.

90. Ibid.

91. Nir, "Workers at J.F.K.."

92. Ibid.

93. U.S. Department of Homeland Security, "SECURE (System Efficacy through Commercialization, Utilization, Relevance, and Evaluation) Program," dhs.gov, n.d., accessed December 7, 2012, http://www.dhs.gov/secure-system-efficacy-through-commercialization-utilization-relevance-and-evaluation-program.

94. U.S. Department of Homeland Security, "FutureTECH," n.d., accessed December 7, 2012, http://www.dhs.gov/futuretech.

95. U.S. Department of Homeland Security, "Transportation Systems Sector: Critical Infrastructure."

96. Szyliowicz, "Aviation Security," 48–49.

97. Ibid., 47–63.

98. Mark Memmott, "Paying Cash For A Ticket Not Necessarily A 'Red Flag' About Abdulmutallab," NPR.org, January 6, 2010, accessed December 7, 2012, http://www.npr.org/blogs/thetwo-way/2010/01/abdulmutallab_detroit_

terror _f.html. Memmott points out that it is fairly common for flights to be paid for in cash in Africa, as many passengers have to convert their local currency and do not have credit cards. But this does not explain fully why Northwest Airlines did not flag Abdulmutallab as a potentially suspicious passenger, especially given that Abdulmutallab both paid in cash for his international flight and was also not checking luggage.

99. Elise Labott and Jill Doughtery, "State Department failed to confirm terror suspect's visa," cnn.com, January 8, 2010, accessed December 7, 2012, http://www.cnn.com/2010/POLITICS/01/08/terror.suspect.visa/index.html; John F. Burns, "Britain Rejected Visa Renewal for Suspect," *The New York Times*, December 28, 2009, accessed December 7, 2012, http://www.nytimes.com/2009/12/29/world/europe/29london.html.

100. Associated Press, "Investigating Beheadings, 12 Officers Slain in Mexico," *The New York Times*, March 19, 2012, accessed December 7, 2012, http://www.nytimes.com/2012/03/20/world/americas/investigating-beheadings-12-officers-slain-in-mexico.html; Elyssa Pachico, "Rise in beheadings in Mexico—sign of splintering drug gangs?" *The Christian Science Monitor*, November 4, 2012, accessed December 7, 2012, http://www.csmonitor.com/World/Americas/Latin-America-Monitor/2012/1104/Rise-in-beheadings-in-Mexico-sign-of-splintering-drug-gangs.

101. Alma Guillermopuerto, "Mexico: Risking Life for Truth," *The New York Review of Books*, November 22, 2012, accessed December 7, 2012, http://www.nybooks.com/articles/archives/2012/nov/22/mexico-risking-life-truth/?pagination=false.

102. Steinmetz, "Mitigating the Exploitation of U.S. Borders," 31–32.

103. Wigginton and Jensen, "Texas Border Sheriff's Coalition," 35–59.

104. Patrick Manning, "Cross-Border Drug Violence Rages as Obama Mulls Pulling Troops," Fox News Latino, December 19, 2011, accessed December 7, 2012, http://latino.foxnews.com/latino/politics/2011/12/19/cross-border-drug-violence-rages-as-obama-mulls-pulling-troops/.

105. Alejandro Martinez-Cabrera, "U.S. warns Mexican cartels on cross-border violence," Reuters, January 31, 2011, accessed December 7, 2012, http://www.reuters.com/article/2011/01/31/us-usa-mexico-napolitano-idUSTRE70U5TB20110131.

106. Ibid.; Alan Gomez, Jack Gillum, and Kevin Johnson, "U.S. border cities prove havens for Mexico's drug violence," *USA Today*, July 18, 2011, accessed December 7, 2012, http://usatoday30.usatoday.com/news/washington/2011-07-15-border-violence-main_n.htm.

107. Alice Lipowicz, "Boeing's SBINet contract gets the axe," Washington Technology, January 14, 2011, http://washingtontechnology.com/articles/2011/01/14/dhs-cancels-rest-of-sbinet-and-plans-mix-of-new-technologies-at-border.aspx.

108. Ibid.

109. Steinmetz, "Mitigating the Exploitation of U.S. Borders," 34–35.

110. Kevin Bohn, "Report: Security on U.S.-Canada border fails terror test," cnn.com, September 28, 2007, accessed December 7, 2012, http://www.cnn.com/2007/US/09/27/border.security/.

111. J. David Goodman, "X-Ray Scan Reveals 513 Migrants In 2 Trucks," The Lede Blog, The New York Times, May 18, 2011, accessed December 7, 2012, http://thelede.blogs.nytimes.com/2011/05/18/x-ray-scan-reveals-513-mexican-migrants-in-2-trucks/.

112. AS&E, 2012, accessed December 7, 2012, http://as-e.com/.

113. Ibid.

114. U.S. Customs and Border Protection, "Things commercial carriers (i.e. truckers) should know before transporting cargo from Canada or Mexico into the United States," November 1, 2012, accessed December 7, 2012, https://help.cbp.gov/app/answers/detail/a_id/615/~/things-commercial-carriers-%28i.e.-truckers%29-should-know-before-transporting.

115. Ibid.

116. Statement of Thomas M. Frost, "Border Related Corruption," Trends in Organized Crime 13 (September 2010): 179–180. Numerous ethical conflicts have arisen among DHS component agencies investigating corruption allegations. Frost himself was placed on administrative leave in March 2012 in connection with allegedly falsified investigation documents. See Andrew Becker, "Homeland Security IG in conflict with agencies on corruption probes," The Washington Post, March 30, 2010, accessed December 7, 2012, http://www.washingtonpost.com/wp-dyn/content/article/2010/03/29/AR2010032903207.html; see also Andrew Becker, "Homeland Security Office Accused of Faking Reports on Internal Investigations," The Huffington Post, April 6, 2012, accessed December 7, 2012, http://www.huffingtonpost.com/andrew-becker/homeland-security-office-_b_1408532.html.

117. Thomas S. Winkowski, Day 2 Keynote Speech at the Symposium on Homeland Security at Christopher Newport University, July 20, 2012, http://www.symposiumonhomelandsecurity.com/Day2PostLunchKeynote.html.

118. "Border Security Threats to the Homeland: DHS' Response to Innovative Tactics and Techniques," Hearing of the House Committee on Homeland Security, Subcommittee on Border and Maritime Security, 112th Cong., 2nd Sess. (2012) (written testimony of U.S. Customs and Border Protection Office of Intelligence and Investigative Liaison Assistant Commissioner Donna Buccella), June 15, 2012, accessed December 7, 2012, http://www.dhs.gov/news/2012/06/15/written-testimony-us-customs-border-protection-house-homeland-security-subcommittee.

119. Ibid.

120. Ibid.

121. Ibid.

122. Ibid.

123. Alice Lipowicz, "New border strategy to incorporate SBINet-like capabilities," Government Computer News, March 18, 2011, accessed December 7, 2012, http://gcn.com/articles/2011/03/15/dhs-buying-sbinetlike-system-for-border-despite-uncertainties-gao-says.aspx.

124. Winkowski, "Keynote Speech," 38.00–40.12.

125. Ibid.

126. Bakir and von Winterfeldt, "Is Better Nuclear Weapon Detection Capability Justified?"

Chapter 6

Public-Private Sector Collaboration
in Disaster Recovery

On May 22, 2011, one of the most powerful tornadoes in American history ripped through Joplin, Missouri.[1] With winds in excess of 200 miles per hour, the tornado destroyed everything in its path, tragically killing 158, wounding over 1,000, and damaging up to 30 percent of the city—some 8,000 buildings in total.[2] Emergency response efforts began immediately, and with each passing hour, the scale of the disaster became increasingly clear. The principal of Joplin High School remarked to a reporter, "You see pictures of World War II, the devastation and all that with the bombing. That's really what it looked like...I couldn't even make out the side of the building. It was total devastation in my view. I just couldn't believe what I saw."[3] Missouri Governor Jay Nixon underlined the scope of the state's recovery efforts: "As a state, we are deploying every agency and resource available to keep Missouri families safe, search for the missing, provide emergency medical care, and begin to recover."[4] And among the many organizations that began recovery operations, businesses immediately assumed substantial and broad-ranging roles to help restore Joplin to a sense of normalcy.[5]

Home Depot and Wal-Mart each pledged $1 million to assist with disaster relief.[6] Moreover, Home Depot partnered with Delta Airlines to fly in 200 volunteers from Atlanta, Georgia–area businesses.[7] Home Depot also delivered goods to assist in relief efforts in addition to clean-up supplies from Georgia Pacific, as well as food and beverages from Chik-fil-A and the Coca-Cola

Company.[8] The Empire District Electric Company, which services Joplin, teamed up with neighboring power companies to restore electricity and natural gas service to Joplin residents.[9] The mobile phone company Sprint provided cell phones and satellite phones to local emergency officials.[10] Numerous firms deployed to the Missouri Emergency Operations Center (EOC) to help coordinate response and recovery efforts.[11] A Texas-based development firm, Wallace Bajjali Development Partners, began consulting with the Joplin City Council to attract private sector investors for residential and commercial re-construction projects.[12] Government and businesses worked together effectively to begin the rebuilding process in Joplin.

What occurred in Joplin is increasingly common nationwide. Public-private partnerships help communities become more resilient in the face of natural and man-made disasters. These partnerships are part of a broader trend in emergency management that emphasizes the importance of building resilient communities. Resilience is a relatively new concept in U.S. emergency management which acknowledges that natural and man-made disasters will occur, and that all segments of society should be prepared in order to bounce back quickly from these disasters.[13] This emphasis upon resilience represents an evolution in U.S. emergency management as a whole. Although government has long emphasized the importance of emergency preparedness in communities—that is, measures taken before disaster strikes—historically, government has not emphasized resilience as a desirable quality for communities.

As we first discussed in Chapter 2, there is also widespread recognition among practitioners that public-private partnerships are an integral part of strengthening resilience, because they can help to increase efficiency and effectiveness in emergency management.[14] In this sense, public-private partnerships and resilience are now closely linked to one another in emergency management. The Federal Emergency Management Agency (FEMA) embraces this connection between public-private partnerships and resilience. In an illustration of its commitment to cultivating public-private partnerships for emergency management, FEMA sponsored a widely attended 2011 professional conference at the U.S. Chamber of Commerce entitled "Building Resilience through Public Private Partnerships."[15] Additionally, FEMA Administrator Craig Fugate regularly emphasizes the importance of public-private partnerships in emergency management, such as in this 2011 Congressional testimony:

> The private sector, from Fortune 500 companies to your local grocery store, is an essential member of the team....Growing strong working relationships between emergency managers and the private sector is a good business decision for everyone—it helps us better serve survivors, rebuild our communities and boost local economies.[16]

Whether in preparation for natural disasters or terrorist attacks, resilience-oriented public-private partnerships are now an essential part of U.S. emergency management. Furthermore, numerous opportunities are emerging for these partnerships to grow and thrive. This trend is a generally positive development. At the same time, however, resilience-oriented public-private partnerships also face a number of shared challenges that will need to be worked through in the coming years if public-private partnerships are to realize their potential for improving resiliency.

This chapter examines the current status of public-private partnerships in emergency management, as well as the emerging opportunities and challenges that need to be addressed for these partnerships to achieve their full potential. It begins with a systematic overview of the strategic, operational, and tactical effects of public-private partnerships in emergency management today and describes how these effects can increase societal resilience. Next, the chapter describes several of the emerging opportunities and challenges that these partnerships will have to work through in the coming years. The chapter concludes with a set of policy recommendations to enhance the efficiency and effectiveness of public-private partnerships in emergency management.

I. Defining and Clarifying Public-Private Partnerships in Emergency Management

In emergency management public-private partnerships can take many forms, including service contracts and information dissemination partnerships. [17] Government emergency management agencies focus on the need for public-private partnerships, as well as the potential advantages of these partnerships. [18] Academic research in fields related to emergency management, such as critical infrastructure protection and public administration, addresses the evolving role of public-private partnerships.[19] Moreover, debate on the private sector's role within other emergency management-related fields, such as public health and hazard mitigation, demonstrates increasing awareness of how businesses impact traditionally government functions.[20]

But there has been comparatively little examination of public-private partnerships for emergency management in the academic literature, and even less on their role in achieving resiliency. The one notable exception to this lack of debate involves the current discussion surrounding the federal framework for public-private partnerships in emergency management and the argument that this framework is not sustainable over the long run.[21] This chapter, however, contends that public-private partnerships now have substantial strategic, operational, and tactical impacts on emergency management and that these impacts can increase societal resilience despite facing a number of challenges in the years ahead.

To understand the effects of these partnerships, it is useful to begin with the U.S. Department of Homeland Security's 2009 *Integrated Planning Strategy* (IPS), which divides organizational planning into three distinct, though interrelated, tiers. The first tier, strategic planning, involves decisionmakers providing "overall high-level guidance for planners."[22] The second tier, operational planning, translates strategic plans into concrete actions and sequences of events.[23] The third tier, tactical planning, concerns the coordination of resources in relation to one another and in relation to natural or man-made hazards.[24] Using these tiers as a framework of analysis, we can see that public-private partnerships can have a substantial effect on these three organizational levels— strategic, operational, and tactical—and thus have a substantial impact on emergency management as a whole.

Strategic Effects of Public-Private Partnerships in Re-Shaping Emergency Management

Public-private partnerships can alter the strategic focus of emergency management agencies. For instance, when government views the private sector as a full partner in its efforts to mitigate, prepare for, respond to, and recover from disasters, this also means that the private sector is expected to assume a level of accountability and responsibility before, during, and after emergencies. The private sector can handle virtually any task related to emergency management, such as issuing warnings, facilitating evacuation, or organizing food service. As a result, government may find that it no longer needs to perform certain services it would typically provide to the public, because private sector entities now fill those functions. For strategic planning purposes, this means that government leaders can worry less about certain functions.

Negotiating contracts for goods and services before emergencies can streamline the strategic planning efforts for both businesses and governments. For example, when a business drafts its own strategic plan, it is helpful to know that it can expect financial returns from selling goods or services to government during disasters. For the business, this means that even if demand for products and services dries up immediately after a disaster, the government will be a customer that can be counted upon immediately after a disaster. Moreover, when government can count on firms to provide it with certain goods or services during disasters, this enables government to focus on other strategic planning priorities, as it reduces the number of resource procurement decisions that the government must make in the midst of a crisis.

Operational Effects of Public-Private Partnerships in Re-Shaping Emergency Management

Public-private partnerships can smooth the operations of emergency management agencies during normal, non-emergency circumstances. A government agency can potentially achieve its objectives more efficiently via public-private partnerships than by relying solely on its own resources and capabilities to achieve its objectives.[25] This has a positive effect on operational efficiency in emergency management. It means that the government agency can respond faster to community needs.

Public-private partnerships can also make emergency management operations more flexible. Private sector consultants can be quickly hired for project-oriented purposes, and they can be discharged once the project is complete or kept on board in order to provide consulting services on other projects. In this way, private sector consultants provide a scalable asset that can be used to supplement government workers on specific emergency management projects in need of attention. The reason for this organizational flexibility is that the private sector does not require the same level of internal administrative oversight that public agencies require.[26] If a large emergency management agency with multiple divisions needs a team of private sector consultants to move from one division to another, then private sector consultants can jump across divisions faster and more efficiently than government employees, because they require less paperwork to be completed in order to move laterally within an organization.[27] The speed with which these private sector consultants can be shifted from one division to another is ultimately advantageous for the emergency management agency.

Tactical Effects of Public-Private Partnerships in Re-Shaping Emergency Management

Public-private partnerships play a significant role in tactical response to emergencies and thus contribute in a powerful way to strengthening resilience. After Hurricane Katrina struck the Gulf coast in 2005, Wal-Mart played a vital part in distributing relief supplies to Gulf residents.[28] During the 2010 Deepwater Horizon oil spill firms such as Nalco, which manufactures oil dispersants, worked closely with government to help with clean-up efforts.[29] As we noted at the beginning of this chapter, businesses are helping to bring needed redevelopment investments back to Joplin, Missouri after a devastating tornado. Since Hurricane Sandy leveled significant portions of the New Jersey shoreline and New York City's outer boroughs in late 2012, there is a flurry of renewed focus on how public-private partnerships can help the communities affected by Sandy to recover faster.[30] It is clear that both businesses and government need to be involved in tactical decision-making during and after disasters. Better synchronizing public and private sector contributions will result in greater community resilience.

How Public-Private Partnerships Strengthen Community Resilience

Partnerships between firms and government are re-shaping emergency management strategy, operations, and tactics. These effects combine to strengthen community resilience in the face of disasters in multiple ways. Strategically, when firms and government partner together, this arrangement can re-shape the focus of government agencies involved in emergency management. Public-private partnerships reduce the burdens placed upon government to provide certain goods and services over time, permitting the public sector to focus on other important strategic priorities. Operationally, cross-sector partnerships enable government agencies to move internal resources rapidly, making the system more responsive to changing community needs. Tactically, public-private partnerships play a substantial role in responding to and recovering from disasters. These partnerships can help to deliver needed goods and services to affected communities with greater efficiency. In aggregate, these strategic, operational, and tactical changes help communities to bounce back faster from disasters.

II. Opportunities for Public-Private Partnerships in Emergency Management

As public-private partnerships continue to influence emergency management nationwide, businesses and government have a number of opportunities to expand and deepen their cooperation with one another. This cooperation enhances resilience by helping to synchronize the actions of public sector agencies and private firms in emergency management. Working in a more coordinated fashion also reduces duplication of effort, improving efficiency and helping to return communities affected by disasters to a state of normalcy faster than either government or businesses acting independently. The next section focuses on three ways that businesses and government can enhance their partnerships for emergency management: by defining expectations for partnerships, preserving partnerships forged during emergencies, and expanding the role of firms in shaping public policy.

Defining Expectations Can Increase the Value of Public-Private Partnerships in Emergency Management

There is now an excellent opportunity for public and private sector actors to define their expectations for public-private partnerships more clearly. Recent research on public-private partnerships for emergency management suggests that if businesses and government take the time to clearly define what a partnership is—that is, spelling out the desires of both public and private sector actors in the partnership—then this reduces the chances of either party violating the other's expectations.[31] If both government and businesses take advantage of the opportunity to better define these expectations, they can create a stronger structural framework for the partnership that expands and deepens over time.

In recent years, despite an emerging consensus among scholars and practitioners about the *need* for public-private partnerships in emergency management, there is still no clear agreement on what public-private partnerships actually *are*. Ami J. Abou-bakr at King's College London notes that poorly defined public-private partnerships help to explain why many public-private partnerships fall short of expectations.[32] Moreover, Thomson, Perry, and Miller point out that despite the proliferation of organizational networks today, it is difficult to measure collaboration because there is no consensus on what collaboration is or how to measure it.[33] Provan and Kenis define three distinct types of network governance—that is, program administration by multiple organizations—yet these are only a few of the potential models for public-private sector collaboration in emergency management.[34] Robinson and Gaddis identify multiple forms of collaboration using post-disaster surveys, and they suggest that opportunity costs should be considered in measuring collaboration among organizations.[35] Of particular note, according to Robinson and Gaddis:

> There is a sense that 'parallel play' represented by mere communication, information provision, or contact is not enough [to constitute collaboration]—*even if it is frequent*.[36]

We agree that it can be difficult to distinguish between genuine partnership and "parallel play," particularly when the level of interaction between a public and private entity is relatively low. But at the same time, *frequent* communication, information sharing, and inter-organizational contact certainly qualifies as a partnership, because these are indicators of a convergence in organizational objectives, just as fever, sneezing, and weakness are indicators of human illness. To label these organizational behaviors as "parallel play" overlooks the many forms and degrees of public-private partnerships, and it implies that only certain kinds of high-opportunity-cost activities should qualify as partnerships. Labeling frequent interaction between public and private entities as "parallel play" misses the mark—this *is* a form of partnership, even if it does not come at great cost for participants in the partnership.

Despite our disagreement with Robinson and Gaddis, we acknowledge that public and private sector participants need to define clearly what they want and expect from a partnership. When expectations for public-private partnerships are not well-defined by partnership participants, the potential for inter-organizational conflict grows. No partner can be entirely sure that the other partners understand its needs. Resentment between organizations' employees can increase. Trust, which is essential for effective partnerships, erodes. All of these possibilities can rot a public-private partnership from within. And in the extreme, they can end the partnership altogether. To avoid this possibility, public and private sector partners can look to an excellent example of how expectations can be clearly established in a public-private partnership: the New York Police Department's (NYPD) *Shield* program.

The NYPD *Shield* program brings together public and private sector entities to facilitate information sharing for security purposes.[37] For instance, if a New York City business owner wishes to become part of the program, he can apply to be a member of NYPD *Shield* online.[38] Notably, the NYPD *Shield* website clearly states the benefits of the program for business owners, and it sets expectations for business owners that participate in the program:

> NYPD SHIELD is a two-way street; the key to success is for information to flow in two directions. Private sector personnel are well situated to serve as eyes and ears of the NYPD. We ask your assistance in the fight against terrorism by reporting suspicious behavior as soon as possible.
>
> In addition, we recognize that our private sector partners are uniquely qualified to assist NYPD personnel during counterterrorism deployments. Your personnel know your buildings, blocks and neighborhoods from a different perspective. You know what belongs and what is out of place. We urge you and your staff to speak with the police officers you see on the street, particularly those assigned to posts in the vicinity of sensitive

and critical locations. Sharing your perspective can help us be more effective.[39]

By stating clearly what its expectations are up front, the NYPD can count on NYPD *Shield* program members being better informed and thus being better able to provide information to the NYPD on suspicious activity. This reduces the potential for business owners to notify the NYPD of extraneous or less-than-useful information, which saves NYPD personnel time and money. For business owners, this creates a clearer sense of what is required of them, which can improve efficiency and reduce the time burden required of them to report suspicious activity. In return for their cooperation in the NYPD *Shield* program, the NYPD provides program participants with certain benefits, which it also lists clearly on the *Shield* program website:

- In-person intelligence and threat briefings conducted by Counterterrorism Bureau and Intelligence Division personnel;
- Informal conferrals with Patrol Borough Counterterrorism Coordinators;
- NYPD Website postings;
- Shield Alert e-mail messages.[40]

By identifying the benefits of participating in the *Shield* program, the NYPD lets business owners know what they can get out of the partnership. This reduces the potential for business owners to become resentful of the NYPD, because business owners know exactly what they can expect (and not expect) from the NYPD in return for their participation in the *Shield* program.

By establishing clear expectations and responsibilities for *Shield* program participants, the NYPD laid the groundwork for a highly successful program. As a result, the *Shield* program has been recognized as a model for public-private partnerships and has been adopted by additional law enforcement agencies.[41] In 2011, the program was awarded the Matthew Simeone Award by the security professional organization ASIS for demonstrating "an innovative approach to successful problem resolution, effective executive leadership and a willingness of all partners to share information."[42] Other public-private partnerships could potentially benefit from the NYPD *Shield* program's clear and systematic approach.

Preserving and Enhancing Partnerships Formed During Emergencies Can Increase Resilience

Sometimes an emergency will require public and private sector organizations to immediately collaborate, even when they have no previous history of collaboration. Peter J. Denning at the Naval Postgraduate School calls this type of near-instant collaboration a "hastily-formed network," which is a form of public-private partnership.[43] There is potential for these hastily-formed networks to continue, even after an emergency ends. This can increase societal resilience, because it forms lasting ties between key community stakeholders in emergency management. But without a concerted effort to sustain hastily-formed networks, it is not reasonable to expect them to continue. Businesses and government agencies should embrace the chance to sustain hastily-formed partnerships, because this can ultimately benefit both sectors in the long run. To effectively sustain hastily-formed networks will require both parties to carefully analyze the incentives, penalties, and social factors that contribute to the partnership itself.

Incentives in hastily-formed networks can include a combination of financial and non-financial factors. A business may find that, because of its work with a public sector organization, it is able to accomplish more—and even profit—from ongoing collaboration with government. In this case, from a financial perspective, it makes great sense for the business to continue to partner with government. A government agency could find that developing a more stable relationship with a business can provide the government agency with needed resources and expertise. These types of services can sometimes come at a lower cost, and with greater efficiency, than if public sector employees performed them. Given these circumstances, a government agency might recognize that there is value in partnering with a business, and this recognition provides the government agency with just the "push" that it needs to sustain a hastily-formed network with a private sector counterpart.

Viewed another way, the penalties associated with *not* sustaining a hastily-formed network can also be compelling for public and private sector entities. For example, a disaster that suddenly requires a government agency and a business to work together could prompt both to recognize that they *must* continue to work together. It may well have been a failure to work together that led to the disaster in the first place. If this is the case, then the disaster itself can be viewed as one consequence of the government agency and the business not collaborating.

The 9/11 terrorist attacks are an extreme recent example of this type of consequence. Government agencies responsible for counterterrorism largely failed to share timely, accurate, useful information with one another leading up to the 9/11 terrorist attacks. [44] This failure to share information was a significant contributing factor in al-Qaeda's ability to pull off the 9/11 attacks successfully. [45] In the wake of the attacks, the 9/11 Commission underlined that the government needed to share information more effectively to avoid similar terrorist attacks in the future. [46] Partly as a result of the 9/11 Commission's findings, the federal government created the Information Sharing Environment (ISE). The ISE is an initiative to help facilitate better information sharing among government agencies, as well as between government agencies and private sector partners.[47] Moreover, in 2008, DHS noted in its own *Information Sharing Strategy* that it needs to develop better information sharing relationships with government agencies and businesses.[48] Both the creation of the ISE and DHS's *Information Sharing Strategy* serve to improve public-private sector information sharing and cooperation. U.S. counterterrorism agencies recognize that they run the risk of a horrific consequence for not sharing information: terrorists killing people and destroying property. And as a result, they have made great strides in sharing information since 2001. While the 9/11 attacks are a more extreme example of what can happen when organizations do not share information effectively, they also show how hastily-formed networks can continue well after the emergency that created them ends.

There is a third set of variables associated with sustained cooperation that can be called social factors. In most of the literature on cooperation among individuals and organizations, there is a focus upon incentives and penalties for behavior. Recently, however, a new set of motivations emerges in the literature: social factors that are associated with self-motivated cooperation. Tom R. Tyler, a psychologist at Yale University, notes that variables like clear and fair-minded organizational policies and procedures, as well as more personal variables, like transparent, rule-based decision-making, soliciting input from employees, and demonstrating how employee input has contributed to decision-making, all have a role in motivating people to cooperate with one another.[49] Tyler's insights can be applied to sustaining hastily-formed partnerships between the public and private sectors. They suggest that partnerships that have clearly defined expectations, that are rooted in values like honesty, respect, empathy, and trust, and that reach joint decisions using predictable guidelines and facts have a better chance of sustained success. The parties to these partnerships—organizational leaders and line-level employees alike—are more likely to act for the good of the partnership itself under these circumstances and will do so in a way that is largely self-motivated, rather than driven by incentives or penalties.[50]

Potential Marketing Opportunities for Firms

If a business is involved in a partnership with government for emergency management purposes, there is a certain amount of marketing caché from which it can benefit. In the case of Wal-Mart during Hurricane Katrina, the firm's actions to assist Gulf communities affected by the storm helped to shape and soften perceptions of the firm itself. Wal-Mart has long come under scrutiny for questionable labor practices and the perception of its "squeezing out" local businesses from communities.[51] But Wal-Mart's actions in Hurricane Katrina ran counter to those perceptions. Instead, the public saw a firm that was out in the community, delivering relief supplies where they were needed and providing valuable assistance to those affected by the storm. By making itself visible during Hurricane Katrina, Wal-Mart not only provided invaluable assistance to affected communities, but it also enjoyed marketing benefits from national media exposure. It was a win-win-win for Wal-Mart, government, and Katrina survivors.

Wal-Mart's experience points toward a broader opportunity for firms that engage in public-private partnerships for emergency management. The marketing value of being involved in public-private partnerships, and truly making a difference via these partnerships, can increase positive public perceptions of a firm—even long after an emergency ends. This shift in perception can lead to increased sales and favorable media attention over the long run. In this sense, public-private partnerships in emergency management not only help communities affected by disasters, but they are also a smart business decision.

Opportunities for Businesses to Influence Governmental Policy

Given the widespread influence of firms on emergency management today, it also makes sense for businesses to play a role in shaping public policy. When businesses and government collaborate to make public policy, this can provide both the public and private sectors with distinct benefits, and make the policies themselves more effective than they might have been absent this collaboration.

One way firms can influence public policy is by setting expectations with government. For example, utility companies know that disasters can damage or destroy their infrastructure. Electrical transformers short out. Gas mains blow up. Water lines crack. When disasters happen, they disrupt service to utility customers. And customers must wait for utility companies to restore service of electricity, gas, or water. This sets up a three-way tension between utility companies, the public, and government. Companies want to restore service quickly, but also want to do so at low cost. The public wants the services restored as quickly as possible, regardless of the cost to the firm. Government officials pressure utility companies to work faster if citizens complain about slow service restoration.

To avoid the possibility of an ugly public confrontation between government and utility companies, the public and private sectors can collaborate to shape emergency management policy. Utility companies can share their own emergency management plans with government counterparts, and government can exchange its plans with firms. This permits greater coordination of emergency management activities between utility companies and government. Over time, this coordination can "crystallize" and help to shape public policy. This process is being increasingly implemented nationally. For example, in the Portland, Oregon metropolitan area, close coordination between utility companies and local government officials has been formalized and codified in emergency plans.[52] This type of coordination also helps government officials to set expectations with the public about restoration of utilities. It can be very helpful for elected officials at press conferences to make statements like the following: "Utility companies are working hard to restore service to affected areas. At the same time, however, residents should be aware that this is a very challenging environment, and power may not be restored for over a week." When government officials can set expectations in this manner, it eases public pressure on utility companies and can help to assure the public that service is going to be restored quickly.

Additionally, this coordination reduces the likelihood of citizen complaints to utility companies about service not being restored after a disaster. Since the general public's expectations are set up front, then residents should expect that it will actually take a week to restore service—there is no guesswork involved about the timeframe for service restoration. But if the government were to *not* set expectations with the public, then the public perception of both government and utility companies would be affected. If there are delays in restoring service, then the public may think that government officials are not looking out for its interests. Moreover, the public may believe that utility companies are unresponsive or incompetent. But public-private sector collaboration leads to clearer public expectations, which can help to produce better outcomes for government, businesses, and the general public.

A second way that firms can influence public policy is by acting as team members with government during disasters. Government often looks to businesses to provide certain products or services during disasters like food, building supplies, and shelter equipment. When firms play this kind of role during disasters, they naturally influence public policy because of their proximity to government activities during disasters. By partnering in this way, government gains a sense of what is feasible—and what is not feasible—based upon what businesses say that they can and cannot deliver, and what the businesses actually do or do not deliver.

For example, a local government may wonder how long it will take for a given neighborhood to have access to emergency repair supplies after a disaster. The local government may turn to Home Depot, which has a store in the neighborhood. Home Depot informs the local government that it will take three days to re-stock and re-open the store. This information then shapes government actions. It may mean that government dips into its own building supplies to help select homeowners in dire need in the affected neighborhood. It also means that government will *not* supply certain homeowners with emergency repair materials, since it knows that the homeowners will be able to independently purchase those same goods from Home Depot in three days' time. In this case, public-private partnerships provide government greater flexibility in deciding how to divide up relief supplies among residents.

Today, public-private partnerships can continue to shape public policy related to emergency management. We are not suggesting that government should abdicate its role in making public policy, nor are we suggesting that policymaking itself be somehow outsourced to the private sector. But we do believe that public policy is ultimately better when firms have a seat at the table.[53] Businesses can provide government officials with input on their own needs and aspirations. This leads to more thoughtfully crafted policy that includes a wider variety of stakeholder viewpoints. By including businesses in public policymaking, government, the private sector, and the general public all benefit.

Government and businesses now have a wide range of opportunities to deepen and strengthen their public-private partnerships for emergency management. Whether in defining expectations for public-private partnerships, bolstering partnerships forged during emergencies, or shaping public policy, public-private partnerships in emergency management are well positioned to enhance resilience in the coming years.

III. Challenges for Public-Private Partnerships in Emergency Management

Although numerous opportunities exist for public-private partnerships in emergency management, businesses and government will still need to navigate multiple challenges in order for these partnerships to prove successful over the long run. Below we address three of these challenges: ill-defined expectations, free-riders, and prisoners' dilemmas; problems with accountability, and the "hollowing out" effect. This is not a comprehensive list of all the challenges that public-private partnerships in emergency management face, but it does illustrate the diverse types and degrees of challenges that businesses and government will have to work through over time.

Ill-Defined Expectations, Free-Riders, and Prisoners' Dilemmas

As discussed above, the public and private sector actors need to define more fully what they each want to achieve from partnerships in emergency management. Unless the expectations and responsibilities are clearly established ahead of time, the partnership can encounter "free-rider" and "prisoners' dilemma" scenarios that can undermine the partnership or even scuttle it altogether.

In a "free-rider" scenario, one partner may exert less effort in the knowledge that the other partner will exert more effort to achieve the goals of the partnership.[54] Although this may be in the interest of the "free-rider," the other partner may come to resent the free-rider's lack of effort. Over time this free-riding can erode the effectiveness of the partnership and even cause both partners to abandon the partnership.

The prospect of both partners abandoning the partnership becomes a potential prisoners' dilemma. In a classic prisoners' dilemma, where two suspects are interrogated by the police, each suspect could be tempted to "defect" from the partnership by blaming the other for the crime. However, if both suspects defect, they both receive a larger sentence than they otherwise would. Ill-defined expectations in a public-private partnership could lead to a similar result, where both partners "defect" from the partnership. This scenario would end the partnership by default.

Thus, the public and private sector may have various incentives to leave their responsibilities ambiguous. But in order for public-private partnerships to be effective, public and private sector partners must agree to specific responsibilities in the context of the partnership. If they do not agree to specific responsibilities, then it is not reasonable to expect the partnership to achieve meaningful objectives.

Problems with Accountability

When businesses and government partners collaborate in emergency management, it can provide benefits for both sectors and the general public. Yet one clear challenge for these partnerships is maintaining a sense of accountability.[55] There is a question of direction and authority—that is, to what extent (if any) can a business employee influence a government employee to perform a certain action? During an oil spill emergency, for example, can an oil company employee direct a Coast Guard officer to deploy spill containment boom in a given area? Using the Incident Command System (ICS), which is DHS's flexible, scalable, modular approach to coordinating emergency response nationwide, the answer is: yes, to some extent. But conditions are murkier in normal emergency management operations—that is, during non-emergency situations that are related to emergency management. After all, in a non-emergency situation, under what circumstances could an oil company employee direct a Coast Guard officer to perform *any* action?

There is also a question of management and oversight—how can government ensure that it remains "in charge" of emergency management if substantial responsibilities are handed to the private sector? And what does that management and oversight look like? The specific nature of public-private partnership management and oversight can vary considerably. For example, the management and oversight required in an information sharing partnership will differ from that required for a service contract.[56] Yet in order to work properly, these management and oversight functions must be built-in to public-private partnerships, regardless of the type of partnership under consideration. There is also a question of employee loyalty in public-private partnerships—how do private sector employees remain good stewards of public funds, and at the same time continue to report to private sector supervisors? There are not clear or obvious answers to any of these questions. Yet public and private sector partners will need to face these questions head-on if public-private partnerships are to continue to grow and thrive in the future.

The Politics of Public-Private Partnerships
for Emergency Management

Public-private partnerships can be tremendously helpful in emergency management. But there are limits to what public-private partnerships can achieve, particularly when politics enter into the equation. The Deepwater Horizon oil rig explosion and spill of 2010 demonstrates what can happen when disaster responses become politicized. As the disaster dragged on, representatives from the oil industry and the federal government publically criticized one another's handling of the spill.[57] Yet at the same time, BP and the federal government had to continue to work together to contain the spill. Their public criticisms of one another did not help them to collaborate more effectively. If anything, these public criticisms eroded trust between BP and the federal government—trust which is essential to fostering effective outcomes in disaster response.

So while BP and the federal government had to work together to contain the spill, political realities created tensions inside the partnership. The oil industry had to appear to "push back" against the government, because not to do so would infuriate oil industry investors. The government had to create the appearance that it was pushing BP to contain the spill quickly, because not doing so would anger the public. Both the private and the public sectors had to continue to collaborate in responding to the Deepwater Horizon disaster while also appealing to their respective constituencies.

Future disasters will require close public-private sector cooperation. But political realities may mean that government and businesses need to occasionally call one another out, or cast blame entirely on one another. At the same time, businesses and government can continue to work productively together by communicating effectively with one another privately and away from public scrutiny. For example, if a disaster occurs that affects a business, and government is to blame for the disaster's effects on that business, then the firm's leader can telephone his counterpart in government before issuing a public statement criticizing the government.

By doing this, the business leader can accomplish many goals: he can calmly convey his concerns to his government counterpart; he can proactively ease tension between his business and the government by notifying his government counterpart of the forthcoming public statement that will criticize the government; and he can reassure his government counterpart that while his criticisms remain legitimate, publically criticizing the government is something that he must do in order to reassure his investors and other stakeholders. This type of effective, nuanced communication between private and public sector representatives can strengthen public-private partnerships, because it balances the need for excellent cooperation with the need to appeal to political constituencies.

The "Hollowing Out" Effect

Many scholars study the "hollowing out" effect that can occur when government functions become privatized.[58] This effect refers to a diminishment in governmental capacity to perform in certain ways as more and more functions are moved out of government. For example, a government agency that completely outsources its food service operations becomes "hollow" in food service—that is, the agency is no longer able to independently offer food service without some kind of outside assistance from a firm. Emergency management agencies face a similar challenge in public-private partnerships.

For example, if a government agency turns over its emergency planning functions to outside consultants, this can slowly degrade the agency's capacity to perform emergency planning over time. As emergency plans go through multiple iterations over several years, organizational knowledge of how the plans were drafted, who was involved in consultations to create the drafts, and what templates or standards were used for the drafts can erode. After all, it is not an emergency management agency employee doing the emergency planning—it is outside consultants. Moreover, the consultants who work on specific emergency planning projects can be transferred, resign, or retire prior to an emergency plan's completion. These kinds of losses of organizational knowledge further disrupt a government agency's ability to perform emergency planning over time.

If the agency does not retain some capacity for emergency planning then outsourcing emergency planning may become the agency's "new normal." Having effectively lost the ability to draft emergency plans, the agency is beholden to the private sector to do its own emergency planning. In this sense, the agency's ability to create emergency plans has been "hollowed out." This poses a problem for the emergency management agency, because it is has effectively lost control of one of its most important functions. This puts the agency in an awkward position vis-à-vis its private sector partner, and it also raises an important question of accountability for the agency: who, precisely, is controlling the emergency planning process?

IV. The Road Ahead

In recent years firms that provide valuable products and services in disasters have become the target of severe criticism. The most pointed of these critiques accuse businesses of engaging in predatory practices such as price gouging or performing services for government without a transparent bid process and at exorbitant cost to taxpayers.[59] One such critic even goes so far as to describe these companies as "disaster capitalists."[60] Although we do not deny that these kinds of unfortunate practices can occur from time to time, we contend that these criticisms are overstated at best and misguided at worst. When such violations of law or regulations occur, we agree that they should be swiftly investigated and, if appropriate, severely punished. But these criticisms of the private sector's role can also overshadow the tremendous good that public-private partnerships do for communities affected by disasters. As this chapter has demonstrated, these partnerships can have positive strategic, operational, and tactical impacts in emergency management. These impacts strengthen community resilience. And the increasing presence of public-private partnerships in emergency management suggests that these partnerships will be around for the foreseeable future. To maximize the long-term potential of public-private partnerships in emergency management, we offer a few suggestions below to improve their efficiency and effectiveness:

- **Government and businesses must clearly define what they want from public-private partnerships.** Both government and businesses must resist the temptation to leave their relationships in an ambiguous state so as to minimize their contributions to the partnership while maximizing potential net gains from the partnership. Instead, they should clearly spell out what they each expect from one another in a public-private partnership. Although clearly defining expectations for public-private partnerships may reduce the potential individual net gains from a partnership, it has clear benefits, too. Well-defined expectations help to ensure that both the public and the private sector actually deliver what they are supposed to deliver, rather than putting minimal efforts into partnerships. This means that the value of the partnership as a whole is strengthened, providing mutually beneficial effects for firms and government alike.

- **Government and businesses should further develop relationships that were forged in crisis.** Government and businesses would be remiss to not cultivate new relationships with one another that are formed during shared responses to emergencies. Shared experience during crisis can help both sectors to collaborate better in the future. And while there may not be an obvious near-term payoff for this collaboration, these relationships might become valuable in the future. In this sense, there is value in building public-private sector relationships that were born of immediate necessity, because they may offer unforeseen payoffs at a later date. This is a wise investment of time and energy for the public and private sector alike.

- **Government and businesses should directly address concerns about accountability.** When businesses and government work closely together under non-emergency circumstances, the lines of organizational authority and accountability can become blurry. There are not simple solutions to the problem of accountability in public-private partnerships for emergency management, yet directly confronting the issue of accountability itself is a positive first step in tackling this challenge. The fact remains that firms are profit-driven and have a vested interest in developing business with government. The public sector, for its part, strives to keep costs down and deliver high-value services for the public. As a first step toward better addressing accountability concerns, it is sensible for government managers to directly ask business leaders how the public sector can continue to drive down costs and deliver services while also engaging more fully with businesses. Similarly, it is reasonable for business leaders to directly ask public sector managers how they can continue to develop business with government. FEMA Administrator Craig Fugate recently noted that often government asks the private sector to support its mission during disasters, when in fact government should ask businesses how it can help businesses to re-open after a disaster. This direct engagement provides benefits for both government and businesses:

> You know for every grocery store, for every pharmacy, for every hardware store that opens up, in a disaster area, [this] means there's [sic] fewer demands for the government to provide those resources. And since the private sector already has a much more efficient mechanism for providing those services, it only makes sense to work as partners.[61]

This sort of direct dialogue between public and private sector leaders will not lead to quick solutions, but it will help public-private partnerships to develop more fully, while also ensuring that the individual needs of businesses and government are being met.

- **Contracts should contain clear terms and deliverables.** Contracts between the public and private sectors need to contain concrete expectations, and they should be open to transparent public oversight. Measurable deliverables in contracts hold its signatories accountable for their actions. These measurable deliverables reduce ambiguities about product and service delivery, reducing the potential for confusion and frustration in public-private partnerships. Although clear contractual terms can limit individual opportunities to free ride, they ultimately help public-private partnerships as a whole to be more beneficial for both the public and private sector.

- **Government should consider business input when creating policy.** When businesses have a seat at the table alongside government policymakers, their input can provide policymakers with new insights and awareness of issues that they may not have been privy to previously. To be clear, we are not recommending that government delegate public policymaking to the private sector, or otherwise make businesses the authors of public policy. On the contrary, to do so would clearly violate numerous legal and ethical provisions. But consulting businesses in this process can help government to craft better public policies that benefit from an additional range of private sector perspectives. Including firms in policymaking not only results in smarter policies, which benefit the general public, but it also helps to build relationships between government and businesses generally. These relationships are valuable for emergency management during non-emergency situations, and they are also helpful during active emergency response.

- **Government agencies should hire partnership-oriented managers.** How can public sector entities involved in emergency management also ensure that they maintain some degree of capacity and control over certain functions that are outsourced? To avoid the "hollowing out" effect, government agencies should recruit managers who are able to coordinate the actions of a wide range of public, private, and non-profit sector resources. Managers that can synchronize the actions of disparate actors introduce new skills, values, and practices into their organizations. Their influence can permeate the agency in which they work, which can change the agency itself from within.[62] Hiring managers with these abilities means that an emergency management agency will never be completely dependent upon firms for knowledge and expertise; they will always have an "in-house" resource with capacity to effectively supervise private sector activities. And while this does not completely eliminate the risk of the "hollowing out" effect, it does mean that government agencies involved in emergency management will be better able to maintain control of their operations over time.

V. Conclusions

When businesses and government collaborate it can change the strategic trajectory of emergency management as a whole. Government no longer has to view emergency management as a purely public sector responsibility. Instead, businesses and government work together in partnerships, and this cooperation changes the strategic orientation of emergency management itself, from a solely public sector activity to a shared cross-sector activity. Public-private partnerships also change the day-to-day operations of emergency management agencies and businesses, for when businesses and government work together, this alters recurring tasks like creating emergency plans, mapping out training exercises, and preparing the public for disasters. Government is able to do more with less in completing these tasks, because it can rely on businesses for information and resources. The private sector can make smarter business decisions related to emergency management because it is better informed by government representatives. Both sectors benefit operationally from working with one another.

Government and businesses repeatedly show that public-private partnerships are also beneficial for tactical decisions in emergency management. Cross-sector cooperation in response to Hurricane Katrina, the Deepwater Horizon oil rig explosion and spill, and the 2011 Joplin, Missouri tornado demonstrates that businesses can accelerate and improve response to and recovery from disasters. This underscores that when businesses and government work together in emergency management, it can deliver immediate and sometimes dramatic benefits for disaster survivors.

As disaster relief operations become more complex, there is also an increasing need for societies to become resilient in the face of disasters. And while in recent years there has been excellent progress toward this objective, we remain a far stretch from fully achieving societal resilience.[63] But public-private partnerships, if properly defined, implemented, and regulated, adapt emergency management practices to the increasing complexity of today's large-scale emergencies. In this way, public-private partnerships bolster societal resilience. These partnerships are already helping to save lives and property and are poised to continue doing so for years to come.

Notes

1. Richard Esposito, Leezel Tanglao, Kevin Dolak, and Michael Murray, "Joplin Death Toll at 116 Making It Deadliest Tornado in Nearly 60 Years," abcnews.com, May 23, 2011, accessed May 21, 2013, http://abcnews.go.com/US/joplin-tornado-death-toll-116-makes-deadliest-single/story?id=13662193#.UOcBzpgVoro.

2. National Weather Service Weather Forecast Office (Springfield, MO), "Joplin Tornado Event Summary," noaa.gov, May 21, 2012, accessed May 21, 2013, http://www.crh.noaa.gov/sgf/?n=event_2011may22_ summary; "Joplin Tornado: Death and Destruction by the Numbers," abcnews.com, May 25, 2011, accessed May 21, 2013, http://abcnews. go.com/US/joplin-tornado-death-destruction-numbers/story?id=13685464#. UOcFTZgVorp.

3. Esposito et al., "Joplin Death Toll."

4. Ibid.

5. Portions of this chapter appeared in Nathan E. Busch and Austen D. Givens, "Achieving Resilience in Disaster Management: The Role of Public-Private Partnerships," *Journal of Strategic Security* 6, no. 2 (Summer 2013): 1–19.

6. North American Retail Hardware Association, "Home Depot, Walmart to Give $1 Million to Joplin Relief Efforts," May 26, 2011, accessed May 21, 2013, http://ace.nrha.org/v2/Hardware_Retailing/Emergencymanagement. aspx?slug=home-depot-walmart-to-give-1-million-to-joplin-relief-efforts.

7. Craig Allen, "As Joplin, Missouri Rebuilds, a Home Depot Store Reopens," homedepot.com, January 11, 2012, accessed May 21, 2013, http://ext. homedepot.com/community/blog/tag/joplin/.

8. Ibid.

9. Federal Emergency Management Agency, *The Response to the 2011 Joplin, Missouri, Tornado: Lessons Learned Study*, December 20, 2011, accessed May 21, 2013, http://kyem.ky.gov/teams/documents/joplin%20tornado% 20response,%20lessons%20learned%20report,%20fema,%20december%202 0,%202011.pdf, 19.

10. Ibid., 19–20.

11. EOCs are facilities where decision-makers gather to coordinate responses to large-scale emergencies, and are physically located away from an emergency scene itself. See also Federal Emergency Management Agency, *The Response to the 2011 Joplin, Missouri, Tornado*, 20.

12. Debby Woodin, "Texas firm could guide Joplin's tornado recovery," *The Joplin Globe*, March 27, 2012, accessed May 21, 2013, http://www.joplin globe.com/tornadomay2011/x1940320988/Texas-firm-could-guide-Joplin-s-tornado-recovery.

13. U.S. Department of Homeland Security, *Quadrennial Homeland Security Review Report: A Strategic Framework for a Secure Homeland*, February 2010, 31–33.

14. The U.S. federal government considers emergency management a subfield of homeland security. For examples of homeland security perspectives on public-private partnerships, see U.S. Department of Homeland Security, *National Response Framework*, 2008, 18–20; U.S. Department of Homeland Security, *National Incident Management System*, 2008, 15–16; U.S. Department of Homeland Security, *National Infrastructure Protection Plan*, 2009; U.S. Department of Homeland Security, *National Cyber Incident Re-*

sponse Plan [Interim Version], September 2010; U.S. Department of Homeland Security, *National Disaster Recovery Framework,* September 2011; U.S. Department of Homeland Security, *Quadrennial Homeland Security Review Report: A Strategic Framework for a Secure Homeland,* February 2010; Thomas A. Cellucci, *Partnership Program Benefits Taxpayers as Well as Public and Private Sectors,* U.S. Department of Homeland Security, September 2008; Douglas A. Smith and Thomas A. Cellucci, eds., *Harnessing the Valuable Experience and Resources of the Private Sector for the Public Good: Innovative Public-Private Partnerships,* U.S. Department of Homeland Security, June 2010. For examples of the efficiencies of public-private partnerships, see Emanuel S. Savas, "Privatization and the New Public Management," *Fordham Urban Law Journal* 28, no. 5 (June 2001): 1731–1737; Darrin Grimsey and Mervyn K. Lewis, "Are Public Private Partnerships value for money? Evaluating alternative approaches and comparing academic and practitioner views," *Accounting Forum* 29, no. 4 (December 2005): 345–378.

15. Dan Stoneking, "Public Private Partnership Conference," FEMA Blog, Federal Emergency Management Agency, August 8, 2011, accessed May 21, 2013, http://blog.fema.gov/2011/08/public-private-partnership-conference.html.

16. Federal Emergency Management Agency, "FEMA Administrator: Business Community is Critical Partner in Disaster Response and Recovery," November 4, 2011, accessed May 21, 2013, http://www.fema.gov/news-release/2011/11/04/fema-administrator-business-community-critical-partner-disaster-response-and. Fugate is FEMA's top official.

17. Stephen Goldsmith and William D. Eggers, *Governing By Network: The New Shape of the Public Sector* (Washington, DC: Brookings Institution Press, 2004), 69–70.

18. Asia Pacific Economic Cooperation, *Public-Private Partnerships and Disaster Resilience,* report from APEC Workshop on Public-Private Partnerships and Disaster Resilience, Bangkok, Thailand, August 24–29, 2010, 2011; Michelle Brown and Judy Joffee, "The All-County Disaster Preparedness Team," *Risk Management Magazine,* June 2007, 8–9; State of New York, "New York State Responds: Hurricane Irene and Tropical Storm Lee: One Year Later," August 2012; Robert McCreight, "Critical Challenge: Assessing Critical Infrastructure," *Homeland Defense Journal* 6, no. 5 (June 2008): 44–45; S. Shane Stovall, "Public-Private Partnerships in the 21st Century," iaem.com, n.d., available at: http://www.iaem.com/committees/

publicprivate/.../PPPinthe21stCentury.pdf; David Raths, "Working Together," *Emergency Management* magazine, May/June 2010, 29–34.

19. Yossi Sheffi, "Supply Chain Management Under the Threat of International Terrorism," *International Journal of Logistics Management* 12, no. 2 (January 2001): 1–11; David J. Closs and Edmund F. McGarrell, "Enhancing Security Throughout the Supply Chain," Special Report Series, IBM Center for the Business of Government, 2004; Goldsmith and Eggers, *Governing By Network*; Beauregard, "Public-Private Partnerships as Historical Chameleons," 52–70.

20. Crystal Franco, Eric Toner, Richard Waldhorn, Thomas Inglesby, and Tara O'Toole, "The National Disaster Medical System: Past, Present, and Suggestions for the Future," *Biosecurity and Bioterrorism: Biodefense Strategy, Practice, and Science* 5, no. 4 (December 2007): 319–325; Mary C. Comerio, "Public policy for reducing earthquake risks: a US perspective," *Building Research and Information* 32, no. 5 (September/October 2004): 403–413.

21. The most comprehensive study of public-private partnerships in U.S. emergency management to date is Abou-bakr, *Managing Disasters*; see also Bonnie L. Regan, *Enhancing Emergency Preparedness and Response: Partnering with the Private Business Sector*, December 2009, Naval Postgraduate School Thesis, Homeland Security Digital Library, accessed March 4, 2012, 14–15. For studies of public-non-profit partnerships in emergency management, see Naim Kapucu, "Public-Nonprofit Partnerships for Collective Action in Dynamic Contexts of Emergencies," *Public Administration* 84, no. 1 (March 2006): 205–220; Naim Kapucu and Montgomery Van Wart, "The Evolving Role of the Public Sector in Managing Catastrophic Disasters: Lessons Learned," *Administration & Society* 38, no. 3 (July 2006): 279–308; Naim Kapucu, "Non-profit response to catastrophic disasters"; Naim Kapucu, "Collaborative emergency management: Better community organising, better public preparedness and response," *Disasters* 32, no. 2 (June 2008): 239–262; Naim Kapucu, Maria-Elena Augustin, and Vener Garayev, "Interstate Partnerships in Emergency Management: Emergency Management Assistance Compact in Response to Catastrophic Disasters," *Public Administration Review* 69, no. 2 (March/April 2009): 297–313; Naim Kapucu, Tolga Arslan, and Fatih Demiroz, "Collaborative emergency management and national emergency management network," *Disaster Prevention and Management* 19, no. 4 (August 2010): 452–468.

22. U.S. Department of Homeland Security, *The Integrated Planning System*, January 2009, accessed May 21, 2013, http://www.hlswatch.com/wp-

content/uploads/2009/01/dhs-integrated-planning-system-january-2009.pdf, 2–9.

23. Ibid.

24. Ibid., 2–10.

25. For discussions of how the private sector can operate faster than the public sector, see George Boyne, "Public and Private Management: What's the Difference?" *Journal of Management Studies* 39, no. 1 (January 2002): 97–122; Mary K. Feeney and Hal G. Rainey, "Personnel Flexibility and Red Tape in Public and Nonprofit Organizations: Distinctions Due to Institutional and Political Accountability," *Journal of Public Administration Research & Theory* 20, no. 4 (October 2010): 801–826. For a discussion of how public-private partnerships can improve efficiency, see David Parker and Keith Hartley, "Transaction costs, relational contracting and public private partnerships: A case study of UK defence," *Journal of Purchasing and Supply Management* 9, no. 3 (May 2003): 103.

26. Boyne, "Public and Private Management"; Feeney and Rainey, "Personnel Flexibility."

27. Ibid.

28. Ben Worthen, "How Wal-Mart Beat Feds to New Orleans," cio.com, November 1, 2005, accessed May 21, 2013, http://www.cio.com/emergency management/13532/How_Wal_Mart_Beat_Feds_to_New_Orleans; "Media Information: Wal-Mart's Response to Hurricane Katrina," walmart.com, n.d., accessed May 21, 2013, http://news.walmart.com/news-archive/2005/09/04/media-information-wal-marts-response-to-hurricane-katrina; Parija Bhatnagar, "Wal-Mart redeems itself, but what's next," cnn.com, September 9, 2005, accessed May 21, 2013, http://money.cnn.com/2005/09/09/news/fortune500/walmart_image/index.htm.

29. National Commission on the BP Deepwater Horizon Oil Spill and Offshore Drilling, *Deep Water: The Gulf Oil Disaster and The Future of Offshore Drilling – Report to the President*, January 2011, accessed May 21, 2013, http://www.oilspillcommission.gov/sites/default/files/documents/DEEPWAT ER_ReporttothePresident_FINAL.pdf, 140, 145.

30. Marianne Lavell, "Can Hurricane Sandy Shed Light on Curbing Power Outages?" nationalgeographic.com, November 2, 2012, accessed May 21, 2013, http://news.nationalgeographic.com/news/energy/2012/11/121102-hurricane-sandy-power-outages/; Jonathan Lemire, "Feds' secretary to oversee response to Hurricane Sandy vows not to let New York down," *New York Daily News*, December 2, 2012, accessed May 21, 2013, http://www.

nydailynews.com/new-york/feds-secretary-oversee-response-hurricane-sandy-vows-new-york-emergency management-1.1211585; "Time for National Catastrophe Fund," Herald-Tribune Media Group, November 1, 2012, accessed May 21, 2013, http://www.heraldtribune.com/emergency management/20121101/OPINION/311019996.

31. For a classic treatment of how poorly defined expectations can contribute to inter-organizational conflict, see Louis R. Pondy, "Organizational Conflict: Concepts and Models," *Administrative Science Quarterly* 12, no. 12 (September 1967): 300, 314; see also Abou-bakr, *Managing Disasters*, 188–193.

32. Abou-bakr, *Managing Disasters*, 188–193.

33. Ann Marie Thomson, James L. Perry, and Theodore K. Miller, "Conceptualizing and Measuring Collaboration," *Journal of Public Administration Research and Theory* 19, no. 1 (January 2009): 23–56.

34. Keith G. Provan and Patrick Kenis, "Modes of Network Governance: Structure, Management, and Effectiveness," *Journal of Public Administration Research and Theory* 18, no. 2 (April 2008): 229–252.

35. Scott E. Robinson and Benjamin S. Gaddis, "Seeing Past Parallel Play: Survey Measures of Collaboration in Disaster Situations," *The Policy Studies Journal* 40, no. 2 (May 2012): 256–273.

36. Ibid., 260, emphasis ours.

37. New York Police Department, "NYPD Shield," 2006, accessed May 21, 2013, http://www.nypdshield.org/public/about.aspx.

38. Ibid.

39. Ibid.

40. Ibid.

41. Oksana Farber, "NYPD SHIELD—An Outstanding Achievement in Public / Private Cooperation for Public Safety," ASIS International, New York City Chapter, April 2, 2007, accessed May 21, 2013, http://www.asisnyc.org/emergency managements/2007_04_02.htm.

42. "ASIS Awards NYPD Shield for Excellence in Public Private Partnership at Orlando Convention," security-today.com, July 28, 2011, accessed May 21, 2013, http://security-today.com/emergencymanagements/2011/07/28/asis-awards-nypd-shield-for-excellence-in-public-private-partnership-at-orlando-convention.aspx.

43. Peter J. Denning, "Hastily Formed Networks," *Communications of the ACM* 49, no. 4 (April 2006): 15–16.

44. National Commission on Terrorist Attacks Upon the United States, *The 9/11 Commission Report* (Executive Summary), 2004, accessed May 21, 2013, http://govinfo.library.unt.edu/911/report/911Report_Exec.pdf.

45. Ibid.

46. National Commission on Terrorist Attacks Upon the United States, *The 9/11 Commission Report* (Full Report), 2004, accessed May 21, 2013, http://govinfo.library.unt.edu/911/report/911Report.pdf, 416–419.

47. The White House, *National Strategy for Information Sharing,* October 2007, accessed May 21, 2013, http://www.fas.org/sgp/library/infoshare.pdf, 10.

48. U.S. Department of Homeland Security, *Department of Homeland Security Information Sharing Strategy*, April 18, 2008, accessed May 21, 2013, http://www.dhs.gov/xlibrary/assets/dhs_information_sharing_strategy.pdf, 2.

49. Tom R. Tyler, *Why People Cooperate: The Role of Social Motivations* (Princeton, NJ: Princeton University Press, 2011).

50. Ibid., 157–166.

51. "Store Wars: When Wal-Mart Comes to Town," pbs.org, n.d., accessed May 21, 2013, http://www.pbs.org/itvs/storewars/stores3.html.

52. Office of Consolidated Emergency Management, Washington County, Oregon, "Regional Utility Coordination Plan," February 14, 2005, accessed May 21, 2013, http://www.ocem.org/Plans/Regional_Utility_Coord_Plan_no_ Tab_A.pdf.

53. For examples of how firms can influence government homeland security policy, see Nathan E. Busch and Austen D. Givens, "Public-Private Partnerships in Homeland Security: Opportunities and Challenges," *Homeland Security Affairs* 8, Art. 18 (October 2012): 8–9; Jon D. Michaels, "Deputizing Homeland Security," *Texas Law Review* 88, no. 7 (June 2010): 1435–1473; Cooper J. Strickland, "Regulation Without Agency: A Practical Response to Private Policing in United States v. Day," *North Carolina Law Review* 89, no. 4 (May 2011): 1338–1363.

54. Notable studies of the free rider effect include R. Marc Isaac, James M. Walker, and Susan H. Thomas, "Divergent evidence on free riding: An experimental examination of possible explanations," *Public Choice* 43, no. 2 (May 1984): 113–149; James Andreoni, "Why Free Ride? Strategies and Learning in Public Goods Experiments," *Journal of Public Economics* 37, no. 3 (December 1988): 291–304.

55. Busch and Givens, "Public-Private Partnerships in Homeland Security," 10.

56. Management and oversight of public-private partnerships is one form of network governance. See Ismael Blanco, Vivien Lowndes, and Lawrence Pranchett, "Policy Networks and Governance Networks: Towards Greater Conceptual Clarity," *Political Studies Review* 9, no. 3 (September 2011): 301.

57. Campbell Robertson and Eric Lipton, "BP Is Criticized Over Oil Spill, but U.S. Missed Chances to Act," *The New York Times*, April 30, 2010, accessed May 21, 2013, http://www.nytimes.com/2010/05/01/us/01gulf.html; Jane Wardell and Jennifer Quinn, "Big Oil Criticizes Obama's Drilling Ban," chem.info, June 22, 2010, accessed May 21, 2013, http://www.chem.info/News/2010/06/Plant-Operations-Big-Oil-Criticizes-Obamas-Drilling-Ban/.

58. For example, see R.A.W. Rhodes, "The Hollowing Out of the State: The Changing Nature of the Public Service in Great Britain," *The Political Quarterly* 65, no. 2 (April/June 1994): 138–151.

59. For example, see Bill Briggs, "New Jersey investigating reports of price gouging," nbcnews.com, n.d., accessed May 21, 2013, http://www.nbcnews.com/business/new-jersey-investigating-reports-price-gouging-1C6791587.

60. Naomi Klein, "Hurricane Sandy: Beware of America's disaster capitalists," *The Guardian*, November 6, 2012, accessed May 21, 2013, http://www.guardian.co.uk/commentisfree/2012/nov/06/hurricane-sandy-americas-disaster-capitalists.

61. Federal Emergency Management Agency, "The Private Sector in Disasters: An Introduction (Transcript)," n.d., accessed May 21, 2013, http://www.fema.gov/medialibrary/media_records/1161/transcripts/1121; "The Private Sector in Disasters: An Introduction," YouTube video, 1:24–1:54, posted by "FEMA," September 23, 2009, accessed May 21, 2013, http://www.youtube.com/watch?v=PxvyZcgIYog.

62. Busch and Givens, "Public-Private Partnerships in Homeland Security," 10.

63. Stephen Flynn, "Recalibrating Homeland Security," *Foreign Affairs* 90, no. 3 (May/June 2011): 130–140.

Conclusion

Taking Care of Business: The Future of Public-Private Partnerships in Homeland Security

This book shows how public-private partnerships have a significant and far-reaching impact across the many disciplines that comprise homeland security today. This trend strengthens homeland security and helps to reduce the impact of natural and man-made disasters on society. Yet at the same time, these partnerships face a number of current and emerging challenges. In order for public-private partnerships to continue benefitting homeland security, and ultimately protect the American public as a whole, businesses and government will have to navigate these challenges effectively.

In this final chapter we take stock of the changing landscape of homeland security: how public-private partnerships affect homeland security today, and what this might mean for the future. In the first part of the chapter we draw together the strategic, operational, and tactical implications of public-private partnerships for homeland security as a whole. The second part of the chapter synthesizes the many opportunities facing public-private partnerships in homeland security, while the third part of the chapter explores the challenges that these partnerships must confront in the coming years. The fourth part of the chapter explores a number of theoretical questions about how to maximize the effectiveness of public-private partnerships in homeland security. The final part of the chapter offers a set of policy recommendations to further develop public-private partnerships for homeland security.

I. The Changing Landscape of Homeland Security

Partnerships between businesses and government affect homeland security in strategic, operational, and tactical ways. These effects illustrate the far-reaching impact of public-private partnerships on homeland security. And they also underline that, on balance, public-private partnerships in homeland security are worth preserving and expanding, for they help to achieve the homeland security mission in ways that would not be possible if government or businesses acted independent of one another. While the examples below are not comprehensive, they do outline the extent to which public-private partnerships touch virtually every facet of homeland security today.

Strategic Effects of Public-Private Partnerships in Homeland Security

Public-private partnerships impact the strategic direction of their participants. This means that something fundamental changes when a public or private sector entity decides to enter into a partnership. Over the long run, it assumes new responsibilities and also gives up certain obligations. For example, in critical infrastructure protection, businesses and government routinely partner to share information and exchange goods and services. The Department of Homeland Security's (DHS) Office of Infrastructure Protection (OIP), as well as its Critical Infrastructure Partnership Advisory Council (CIPAC), institutionalize these partnerships. [1] Firms that coordinate with OIP and the CIPAC tacitly (and sometimes explicitly) agree to share information with DHS, and DHS shares information with them. Over time, firms begin to count upon this information flow, and DHS begins to expect that firms will share information with it. Moreover, some of these firms provide DHS with technology and consulting services to augment its protection capabilities. In effect, part of DHS's operations rests on the shoulders of these businesses, because they provide resources that DHS cannot produce on its own.

This synergy between DHS and the private sector helps both parties to achieve individual and shared strategic objectives. DHS is able to access information, technology, and specialized workers in an efficient manner. And in doing so, DHS is better able to fulfill its mission of protecting critical infrastructure. Firms also gain from government information flows, which can provide them with intelligence that they would not have access to otherwise. Sales of goods and services to the government increase businesses' bottom lines. Collectively DHS and private sector entities are better able to protect critical infrastructure. And this arrangement has staying power, because over the long run, DHS and firms rely on each other's "value-added" traits to achieve their goals.[2]

Operational Effects of Public-Private Partnerships in Homeland Security

Public-private partnerships alter the day-to-day operations of businesses and government entities. This operational assistance can come in numerous forms. For example, in Virginia, CRA, Inc. partners with the Virginia Department of Emergency Management (VDEM) to design and facilitate emergency training exercises.[3] The U.S. Secret Service worked closely with JC Penney and Target to support the prosecution of Albert Gonzalez, a notorious cybercriminal who pilfered millions of dollars using stolen credit card numbers.[4] Through InfraGard, a Federal Bureau of Investigation (FBI)-

led initiative, industry leaders and government officials meet nationwide to discuss critical infrastructure protection-related issues.[5] Microsoft built an electronic tool for the U.S. Coast Guard to use in processing private shipping manifests as part of a broader maritime port security initiative.[6]

These examples show that public-private partnerships have far-reaching impacts upon homeland security operations. When businesses and government work together in homeland security, it can affect countless functions, including training, information sharing, networking, and innovation. Not only do these partnerships help to improve operational efficiency and effectiveness, but they help to achieve the homeland security mission as a whole. In this sense, public-private partnerships benefit the government, businesses, and the general public.

Tactical Effects of Public-Private Partnerships in Homeland Security

Public-private partnerships can deliver where it counts most in homeland security—during the heat of an incident. Since the September 11th terrorist attacks, history is full of examples illustrating how these partnerships help to save lives and property in dire circumstances. After 9/11, Verizon's efforts to rebuild communications infrastructure in lower Manhattan helped the New York Stock Exchange (NYSE) to re-open quickly and forestall global financial panic.[7] In August 2007, the I-35 West bridge collapsed into the Mississippi River in Minneapolis, tragically killing over a dozen people and injuring more than a hundred. Carl Bolander & Sons—a local waste management company—swiftly began delicate recovery operations to pull cars and debris from the riverbed.[8] Their around-the-clock operations accelerated the process of rebuilding and re-opening this critical piece of transportation infrastructure 13 months after the initial bridge collapse.[9]

When businesses and government work together during natural or man-made incidents, they help to preserve life and property. There are certain functions that government is incapable of performing due to lack of specialized equipment, expertise, or related reasons. And there are other functions that only government can perform as an agent of the public it serves. Businesses are generally more flexible, adaptable, and streamlined than government entities. These characteristics mean firms can contribute to incident management activities and add value to government functions. Business-government collaboration helps to achieve the homeland security mission by protecting people and things that are in immediate danger.

Achieving Resilience through Public-Private Partnerships

In recent years homeland security officials emphasize the importance of resilience. Many definitions exist for "resilience," but one of those offered by DHS is:

> [T]he ability to reduce the magnitude and/or duration of disruptive events. The effectiveness of a resilient infrastructure or enterprise depends upon its ability to anticipate, absorb, adapt to, and/or rapidly recover from a potentially disruptive event.[10]

At the same time, critics dismiss resilience as merely "another government buzzword," devoid of concrete meaning and operational clarity.[11] There is a grain of truth in these criticisms. It is not clear if resilience represents a qualitative or quantitative leap forward in homeland security activities, or if it is simply a change in philosophy and organizational mindset. Yet using the definition above, public-private partnerships can also demonstrably contribute to societal resilience:

- Public-private partnerships can reduce the magnitude or duration of disruptive events, such as when government agencies partner with firms to develop disaster-resistant building materials.

- Public-private partnerships can help to anticipate potentially disruptive events, such as when firms and homeland security agencies collaborate to produce intelligence analysis technologies.[12]

- Public-private partnerships can help communities to recover from disruptive events, exemplified by Home Depot in helping to rebuild Joplin, Missouri after a tornado there in 2011, and the efforts of Wal-Mart, which delivered relief supplies to the Gulf after Hurricane Katrina in 2005.[13]

Moreover, in considering the strategic, operational, and tactical effects of public-private partnerships on homeland security today, it is clear that public-private partnerships help to achieve societal resilience.

II. Opportunities for Public-Private Partnerships in Homeland Security

Business-government partnerships can deliver a host of benefits for homeland security operations. These can range from personnel-related processes to the use of technology and relationship building. The examples below demonstrate many of the ways that public-private partnerships can have a positive impact upon homeland security. Although this list does not include every possible benefit that public-private partnerships can have for homeland security, the list does address some of the most common benefits of public-private partnerships for homeland security.

Public-Private Partnerships Improve Efficiency

Research demonstrates that public-private partnerships improve operational efficiency.[14] The principal reasons for this improved efficiency are competitive forces, better management, and increased sensitivity to costs.[15] Competition prompts firms to streamline operations to reduce overhead costs and increase profit margins. And when firms have to bid for government homeland security contracts, they are forced to develop efficiencies that keep their overhead costs down, maximize their profits, and make their bids appear enticing to government. These factors benefit homeland security, for they can converge to reduce the total cost of a contract for government.

Better management also bolsters efficiency. Both public and private sector leaders scrutinize government contracts, because they are both stakeholders in the contract. In theory, this extra scrutiny leads to more engaged and effective public and private sector management. It also encourages a continual search for improvements within the scope of a contract, because these improvements can maximize a firm's profits and increase its chances of future government business. Thus better management adds value to both the public and private sectors in the context of a contract.

Public-private partnerships can increase government and the private sector's sensitivity to costs, which enhances efficiency. Savas notes that normally the cost of government services is masked inside government budgets, rather than being explicitly spelled out in invoices.[16] By contrast, when firms perform those services for government, they print up invoices that show *precisely* how much their services cost. This "unmasking" of costs makes government more sensitive to costs in general, because government wishes to limit its out-of-pocket expenses, and it is government that must pay firms for their work. Firms also wish to limit out-of-pocket expenses and are likely to seek their own efficiencies to maximize their profits. In this way, via public-private partnerships, both businesses and government enhance efficiencies through greater awareness of costs.

Flexible Hiring

Public-private partnerships can make hiring easier for government homeland security agencies. It generally takes longer to hire a government employee than a private sector employee. The primary reason for this is that government agencies must address more bureaucratic hurdles in their hiring process, whereas businesses tend to be more streamlined in their hiring practices. But government can benefit from the private sector's hiring flexibility when augmenting its own staff. In recent years homeland security agencies pair up private sector consultants with government employees. These teams work shoulder-to-shoulder in government homeland security offices. If government needs to augment its own workforce rapidly, then it can do so by retaining these consultants. And after a project is complete, government can quickly re-assign these consultants to work on other projects, or discharge them as it sees fit. Were this same work to be performed by government employees, transferring them laterally within a government agency, or getting rid of them altogether, the process would be far more complex. Through public-private partnerships government homeland security agencies can rapidly scale their own workforces without facing the many administrative obstacles that typically come with hiring public sector employees.

Specialization

Public-private partnerships can swiftly identify and integrate subject matter experts into homeland security operations. For example, at the time of this writing in 2013, there is a critical government need for speakers of "hard target" languages like Arabic, Mandarin Chinese, Tagalog, and Urdu. But very few homeland security analysts speak these languages. And the process of hiring government linguists can be drawn out. Private firms like SAIC and Booz Allen Hamilton routinely hire linguists and assign them to government homeland security agencies. As noted above, this private sector hiring can happen faster than if a government agency was doing the hiring. These private sector linguists can then be assigned to government projects requiring their specialized skills. In this way, public-private partnerships not only take advantage of hiring speed but also the ability to rapidly bring in specialists with desirable skills.

Resource Utilization

Public-private partnerships can make more effective use of limited government money and personnel. For example, programs like SECURE and FutureTECH show how private sector involvement can save government money in research and development.[17] These programs actively pair public and private sector officials to collaborate on research and development projects. Moreover, when firms try to anticipate coming homeland security needs, then they can offer innovative products and services to government when those needs actually materialize. This makes better use of limited government money, which instead of being spent on research and development, can be re-routed to other important homeland security priorities. At the same time, the private sector assumes greater financial risk for these research and development projects, and it also absorbs greater costs. Yet the potential pay-off to firms is also great, because they know that the products and services they develop are more likely to be purchased by government homeland security agencies.

Building Trust

Public-private partnerships build trust, and trust increases effectiveness. Trust is essential for successful homeland security operations, for without it, communication can break down and actors can end up working at cross-purposes. But whether in the midst of a crisis like the Deepwater Horizon oil spill, or something longer-term, like analyzing the vulnerabilities of a nuclear power plant, trust between public and private sector officials develops slowly. When a government agency and a private firm work together, this provides repeated opportunities for public and private sector representatives to get to know one another. This repeated contact increases the likelihood of trust developing between them. While public-private partnerships are not a sure path to strong trust between government and businesses, their existence increases the chance of trust developing. This trust is indispensable for achieving effective outcomes in homeland security.

III. Challenges for Public-Private Partnerships in Homeland Security

While public-private partnerships offer numerous benefits, they also introduce a set of new challenges into homeland security operations. Among these are issues with regulation and management; politics, budgets, and long-term planning; the "hollowing out" effect; avoiding "war profiteering;" and outright failure of public-private partnerships. These are not all of the challenges facing public-private partnerships in homeland security, but they do provide a clear sense of how these partnerships must evolve in order to endure.

Regulation and Management Challenges

Public-private partnerships are sometimes difficult to regulate. For example, owner/operators of critical infrastructure and government regulators may find themselves at odds with one another. If a private sector official wants to provide the government with information on her facility's vulnerabilities, she may also run the risk of disclosing compromising information that she otherwise would not want to disclose. This compromising information could open up her facility to regulatory enforcement action—which owner/operators of critical infrastructure do not want. This places both the facility owner and the government in an awkward position. On one hand, sharing vulnerability information can benefit the private sector official, but at the same time, she does not want to open her facility to regulatory action. On the other hand, government homeland security officials want the private sector official to share vulnerability information but cannot turn a blind eye to regulatory violations.

Management challenges can also complicate public-private partnerships. Earlier in the book Thomas S. Winkowski, Acting Deputy Administrator for U.S. Customs and Border Protection, provided an excellent example of this. According to Winkowski, CBP's Virtual Fence project suffered from a number of oversight problems, but one of the most significant of these was CBP's lack of technical expertise to effectively supervise the project. This lack of in-house expertise meant that, in a sense, CBP was beholden to Boeing—the prime contractor for the Virtual Fence project. In part, CBP's inability to manage Boeing doomed the project.

Politics, Budgets, and Long-Term Planning

Politics can change homeland security budgets, and changing budgets affect long-term planning. This means that politics can indirectly affect contracts between businesses and government. At the federal level, if a presidential administration wants to reduce homeland security spending, then that reduction will also reduce the pool of money available for private sector contracts. This reduced pool of money can translate into scaled-back, or fewer, public-private partnerships in homeland security. Moreover, if reduced funding levels become entrenched, then over the long run public-private partnerships will likely shrink in number and scope. Although it is impossible to forecast how politics will affect homeland security budgets in the years ahead, the fact that politics will affect homeland security budgets is certain.

Avoiding the "Hollowing-Out" Effect

Public-private partnerships run the risk of "hollowing out" certain government homeland security capabilities. As more functions in homeland security are performed by businesses, homeland security agencies can inadvertently erode their own capacity to perform these functions. Over time this can degrade homeland security agencies' ability to work effectively with these private firms. And in the extreme, this can compromise otherwise thoughtful, well-designed projects. For example, an emergency management agency may decide to outsource certain functions, like emergency sheltering or emergency planning. In principle there is nothing wrong with this idea. On the contrary, it may save the agency money and improve efficiency. But over time agency personnel may resign, transfer, or retire. And the agency may then lose the historical in-house knowledge of how to perform these tasks. This leaves the agency in a difficult position. It is forced to rely on private sector partners to perform emergency sheltering and emergency planning activities. The agency's ability to do these things is "hollowed out" since it can no longer perform these tasks on its own.

Avoiding "War Profiteering"

Businesses can provide valuable products and services during crises. But at the same time, they must also carefully manage how their efforts are perceived. Earlier in the book we described how Wal-Mart delivered tons of relief supplies to the Gulf region after Hurricane Katrina, earning it significant praise in national media outlets. Firms rushed to assist first responders and survivors following the collapse of the I-35 west bridge in Minneapolis, Minnesota in 2007. After a powerful tornado in 2011, businesses in Joplin, Missouri scrambled to help the community begin to rebuild. These incidents demonstrate that firms can deliver needed products and services to communities affected by disasters.

Yet businesses must be mindful of how they are perceived. It is important for them to avoid the perception that they are "war profiteering"—that is, exploiting communities laid helpless by disasters. The testimonials above are counter-balanced by media accounts describing firms gouging customers or performing shoddy work in the wake of disasters.[18] Even if these events are isolated, their dissemination in the media magnifies the perception that firms can take advantage of community vulnerability after disasters. In communities affected by disasters, even well-intentioned firms need to be aware of how others interpret their actions.

The Potential Failure of Public-Private Partnerships

Public and private sector leaders that enter into partnerships always face the prospect of the partnership failing. These partnerships can fail for numerous reasons. Expectations between public and private sector partners can go unmet. Costs can blow through budget estimates. And for legal and regulatory reasons, firms may not be able to perform certain functions that have to be reserved for government employees. Public-private partnerships hold great promise for homeland security, but that does not mean that they are always desirable, or that they will always succeed.

Today public-private partnerships in homeland security confront many opportunities and challenges. This fundamental tension illustrates their great potential, as well as the extent to which they must continue to adapt over the long run. It also points toward new potential theories of public-private partnerships in homeland security.

IV. Toward a Theory of Public-Private Partnerships for Homeland Security

What are public-private partnerships for homeland security? Why do they come about? And how can we make them better? This section offers four preliminary theories about public-private partnerships in homeland security. Our intent here is to draw together the lessons of the preceding chapters and to advance theory about public-private partnerships in homeland security. To be clear, these theories cannot answer every question about public-private partnerships in homeland security. Nor can they fully explain the increasing popularity and importance of public-private partnerships in homeland security. But these theories are rooted in the empirical evidence developed in this book, and the empirical evidence suggests that this is the theoretical direction that public-private partnerships are taking.

- **Public-private partnerships in homeland security exist because they add value.** Public-private partnerships in homeland security take many forms, including information sharing agreements, in which one or more parties shares data with the other; service contracts, in which one party pays another to provide a service; and civic switchboard partnerships, in which one partner "connects" the other partner to an additional third partner—much like telephone operators once used wires and plugs to connect callers to one another. At the root of these diverse types of partnerships is a central concept: added value.[19] One or more parties gain "something" from the public-private partnership, whether that something is information, money, political capital, operational effectiveness, or some other factor. When businesspeople and law enforcement officials show up at InfraGard meetings, they acquire information and develop professional relationships. The FBI, which facilitates InfraGard, gains from its own relationships with InfraGard members. When firms like SAIC and Booz Allen Hamilton consult for DHS, they make money, and DHS benefits from their expertise. When Home Depot delivers relief supplies to a disaster area, they gain from marketing appeal and increased name recognition—which can earn the firm political capital. And the affected community benefits from the supplies that Home Depot delivers. Public-private partnerships will not form unless they add value for all parties in the partnership.

The specific nature of that added value will vary considerably. But there *is always* added value.

- **There is no "best" framework for public-private partnerships in homeland security.** Needs dictate the architecture of public-private partnerships in homeland security. If information is needed, then an information sharing partnership forms. If products are needed, then a business contract emerges. If both information and products are needed, then a "hybrid" partnership develops. There is no "best" framework for public-private partnerships, because they cannot and should not be one-size-fits-all. Abou-bakr shows that, at least in emergency management, ill-defined partnerships increase the possibility of a partnership running into conflicts, and potentially failing altogether.[20] It is imperative that public and private sector partners clearly define the nature of their partnership early in the life of the partnership itself. They must also develop concrete, measurable, mutually agreed upon goals and expectations. Doing these things increases the chances of a public-private partnership succeeding over the long run.

- **Tomorrow's homeland security leaders will be partnership-oriented.** Government budgets are almost always strained. This means that future government managers must develop efficiencies where they can. Public-private partnerships offer one way to increase the efficiency and effectiveness of homeland security operations. Moreover, given that businesses own or operate about 85% of all critical infrastructure, government homeland security leaders will have little choice but to continue to partner with the private sector. Future managers will be partnership-oriented as a result.

- **Public-private partnerships change government agencies and businesses from within.** When businesses and government agencies partner together, this can change businesses and government from within. From the private sector's perspective, partnering with government can generate a certain level of dependence on government information, revenue, and other factors. From a government agency's perspective, partnering with businesses can make government come to rely on private sector technology, information, and personnel. Public and private sector officials need to recognize that entering into partnerships can fundamentally shift the way that they do business. Moreover, public-private partnerships can change organizational cultures. Over time, government agencies and businesses can begin to internalize the notion that they *are* partners. This means that they begin to think of one another as a kind of first, rather than last, resort. Importantly, this change occurs from within. Just as human relationships can change individuals, public-private partnerships can change organizations.

The above theories help to explain what it is happening in homeland security today and they also help to inform specific policy recommendations that can improve the prospects of public-private partnerships enduring over the long run. In the next section we outline five specific policy recommendations that can help to increase the efficiency and effectiveness of public-private partnerships in homeland security. Although this list of policy recommendations is not exhaustive, it is informed by the theories we outline above—and these theories flow from the evidence in the preceding chapters of this book.

V. Policy Recommendations to Improve Public-Private Partnerships in Homeland Security

Public-private partnerships in homeland security require diligent attention and maintenance over time in order to achieve all that they should. Yet if businesses and government agencies get the fundamental building blocks of these partnerships wrong, it can doom public-private partnerships, regardless of how attentive they are to these partnerships or how well they maintain these partnerships. The policy recommendations below therefore target the basic building blocks of public-private partnerships in homeland security. They are oriented toward creating strong foundations for future success and fixing deeply rooted institutional challenges. They are not designed to paper over problems, differences, or conflicts between public and private sector partners, and they do not lend themselves to quick fixes or easy solutions. If anything, they are designed to quickly surface those problems, differences, or conflicts so that businesses and government agencies can address and resolve them. By getting the basics right, public and private sector partners will have to worry less about fixing their partnerships. Less worry means partners can focus more on achieving successful outcomes, which ultimately benefits homeland security as a whole.

- **Define the relationship.** Businesses and government agencies that partner together must figure out exactly what they need from one another and explicitly define their relationship according to those needs. If they do not do this, it opens the door to misaligned expectations and leaves each partner's role ambiguous. Over time this ambiguity can lead to conflict, frustration, and failure. By contrast, the faster two organizations can figure out what their relationship is, and what they each hope to achieve from it, the better off they both will be. It is not necessary for each partner to define in meticulous detail what they each want and need for a partnership. Going too far in this direction can actually deny a public-private partnership the flexibility needed for future growth and development. But at a minimum, public and private sector partners should know clearly what they are expected to do in the context of a partnership, and what the ultimate goal of the partnership is.

- **Measure progress.** How do we know if a public-private partnership is successful? Do we count the number of terrorist attacks averted, or explain how successfully we managed certain natural disasters? Or is the right metric money saved, or efficiencies gained? Measuring the success of public-private partnerships in homeland security defies easy solutions. Yet in order for these partnerships to be successful over the long run, their effects must somehow be measured. Evaluating success provides a number of clear benefits. First, it creates a yardstick against which public and private sector partners can measure their success and progress. Second, it can give leaders in each organization a clear sense of how they are benefitting (or not benefitting) from a partnership. Third, measurement provides the data necessary to make informed tactical and strategic decisions for the partnership itself. Fourth, measuring the effects of public-private partnerships invites future comparative studies of public-private partnerships. While we do not think that perfect apples-to-apples studies of public-private partnerships may be realistic or feasible, measurement data can provide a kind of benchmark against which to compare and contrast different types of public-private partnerships. And these comparative studies would be valuable for both homeland security scholars and practitioners.

- **Hire partnership-oriented leaders.** To make the most of public-private partnerships, government agencies and businesses that work in homeland security should seek leaders who can skillfully coordinate the actions of a diverse range of public and private sector partners. In the long run, we believe that these partnerships will improve the overall effectiveness and efficiency of homeland security as a whole. But only government and private sector leaders can make this a reality, and they must be able to translate rhetoric about the benefits of public-private partnerships into reality. This translational skill requires a new kind of manager who is adept at building and maintaining professional relationships with people in many different organizations.

- **Make accountability and transparency a priority.** Fuzzy lines of accountability and authority are a challenge for public-private partnerships in homeland security. To keep the confidence of citizens, government agencies and businesses must determine where their own lines of authority and accountability are, how to operate within those lines, and how to describe what they are doing to the general public. Not doing this can jeopardize public-private partnerships, because it invites accusations of opacity and can lead to damaging finger-pointing when things go wrong. By making transparency and openness a priority, government agencies and businesses can diffuse charges that they are "war-profiteering" or "disaster capitalists," and this can increase public confidence in public-private partnerships. This may sometimes require the public and private sectors to disclose embarrassing information about the inner workings of their partnerships—information which government and business leaders would prefer not to release publically. But on balance, tilting toward transparency and openness will help to increase the chances of public-private partnerships succeeding over the long run, because it can reduce public suspicion of public-private partnerships and lay bare both the advantages and disadvantages of public-private partnerships.

- **Plan for the future.** The best way to determine the future direction of public-private partnerships in homeland security is to plan. Yet too often government agencies find themselves in an endless reactionary mode, responding constantly to the latest crisis and pushing aside important-but-less-urgent priorities in favor of immediate needs. Similarly, firms must keep up with current trends and their competitors while also developing strategic plans for the future. So businesses also react to what is in front of them, and at the same time, must revise and adapt their strategic plans according to immediate circumstances. While some of this priority shuffling is inevitable in the public and private sector, business and government officials need to take a different approach when planning for the future of their partnerships for homeland security.

    Much like a marriage can take on a life of its own, existing alongside the individual lives of the partners in that marriage, public-private partnerships take on a life of their own, existing alongside the public and private sector organizations that partner together. Public and private sector partners must plan effectively for the future of this third entity—the partnership itself. It is important for representatives from both sectors to ask critical questions about the partnership as part of this planning. For example, should the partnership grow? Should it shrink? Should the partnership morph into a different form, such as an information sharing agreement instead of a service contract? What is the timeline for that change? And how will we know when we get there?

Planning in this way has a number of tangible benefits. It maintains public and private sector engagement in the partnership, because the act of planning means that business and government officials are investing resources in discussing the future of the partnership, and are therefore more likely to stick with the partnership, since they have a stake in the outcome of the planning. This planning can also help both partners to re-evaluate what they want from a partnership. And planning can give public and private sector partners the opportunity to take stock of how the partnership has performed to date, and what can be improved upon in the partnership.

Since September 11, 2001, homeland security has constantly been evolving. Critical infrastructure is better protected now than ever before. Cybersecurity threats, a "back burner" issue in public discourse just ten years ago, are now routinely top fold headlines. Information on homeland security threats is being shared more broadly and more effectively within the organizations and individuals that need to know about it. America's sea, land, and airports are guarded and monitored more closely. And nationwide, emergency management practices are sharper and more effective. Public-private partnerships are deeply connected to each of these changes. These partnerships offer numerous benefits for businesses, government, and the general public. Yet they also face an imposing set of challenges to overcome. Understanding public-private partnerships in homeland security can aid understanding of homeland security as a whole. And with this understanding, government agencies and businesses can implement policy changes to ensure that their partnerships thrive today and tomorrow. Although the future of homeland security is unclear, the business of counterterrorism will continue to be a significant part of homeland security operations, regardless of the specific direction that homeland security takes. For the citizens of that future, we hope that this book can contribute, in a modest way, to a greater sense of peace and security.

Notes

1. "More About the Office of Infrastructure Protection," U.S. Department of Homeland Security, 2010, accessed January 26, 2012, http://www.dhs.gov/xabout/structure/gc_1189775491423.shtm; "Critical Infrastructure Sector Partnerships," U.S. Department of Homeland Security, 2011, accessed February 8, 2013, http://www.dhs.gov/files/partnerships/editorial_0206.shtm; "Council Members, Critical Infrastructure Partnership Advisory Council," U.S. Department of Homeland Security, 2012, accessed January 26, 2012, http://www.dhs.gov/files/committees/editorial _0848.shtm.

2. Erik Hans Klijn and Geert R. Teisman, "Governing public-private partnerships: Analysing and managing the processes and institutional characteristics of public-private partnerships," in *Public-Private Partnerships: Theory and practice in international perspective*, ed. Stephen P. Osborne (London, UK: Routledge, 2000), 91.

3. CRA, "Virginia Department of Emergency Management," 2011, accessed June 26, 2013, http://www.cra-usa.net/clients_case_studies/case_studies/vdem/.

4. The Associated Press, "20-Year Sentence In Theft of Card Numbers," *The New York Times*, March 25, 2010, accessed June 26, 2013, http://www.nytimes.com/2010/03/26/technology/26hacker.html.

5. Federal Bureau of Investigation, infragard.net, 2012, accessed February 8, 2013, http://www.infragard.net/.

6. Microsoft, "U.S. Coast Guard Expects to Save $1 Million Annually With Data Transmission Solution," n.d., accessed December 6, 2012 from http://www.judyb.com/coastguardcs.doc, 1–5.

7. Ami J. Abou-bakr, *Managing Disasters through Public-Private Partnerships* (Washington, DC: Georgetown University Press, 2013), 18–19.

8. National Solid Wastes Management Association, "Solid Waste Industry There At Time Of National Crisis," n.d., accessed June 26, 2013, http://www.environmentalisteveryday.org/solid-waste-management/green-waste-industry-professionals/i-35-bridge-demolition.php.

9. Minnesota Department of Transportation, "Interstate 35W Bridge in Minneapolis," 2012, accessed June 26, 2013, http://projects.dot.state.mn.us/35wbridge/.

10. National Infrastructure Advisory Council, *Critical Infrastructure Resilience: Final Report and Recommendations*, September 8, 2009, accessed June 26, 2013, http://www.dhs.gov/xlibrary/assets/niac/niac_critical_infrastructure_resilience.pdf, 2.

11. For example, see Federal News Radio, "Resilience becomes new buzzword for homeland security committee," January 12, 2010, accessed June 26, 2013, http://www.federalnewsradio.com/88/1861889/Resilience-becomes-new-buzzword-for-homeland-security-committee.

12. Darryl Plecas, Amanda V. McCormick, Jason Levine, Patrick Neal, and Irwin M. Cohen, "Evidence-based information sharing solution between law enforcement agencies," *Policing: An International Journal of Police Strategies and Management* 34, no. 1 (2011): 120–134.

13. Craig Allen, "As Joplin, Missouri Rebuilds, a Home Depot Store Reopens," homedepot.com, January 11, 2012, accessed June 26, 2013, http://ext.homedepot.com/community/blog/tag/joplin/; Ben Worthen, "How Wal-Mart Beat Feds to New Orleans," cio.com, November 1, 2005, accessed June 26, 2013, http://www.cio.com/article/13532/How_Wal_Mart_Beat_Feds_to_New_Orleans.

14. Emanuel S. Savas, *Privatization and Public-Private Partnerships* (New York, NY: Chatham House Publishers, 2000), 76–77.

15. Ibid.

16. Ibid.

17. See Chapter 1.

18. For example, see Bill Briggs, "New Jersey investigating reports of price gouging," nbcnews.com, n.d., available at: http://www.nbcnews.com/business/new-jersey-investigating-reports-price-gouging-1C6791587.

19. Klijn and Teisman identify added value as a key factor in public-private partnerships in general. The evidence from our study affirms their observation. See Erik-Hans Klijn and Geert R. Teisman, "Governing public-private partnerships: Analysing and managing the processes and institutional characteristics of public-private partnerships," in *Public-Private Partnerships: Theory and practice in international perspective*, ed. Stephen P. Osborne (London, United Kingdom: Routledge, 2000), 91.

20. Abou-bakr, *Managing Disasters*, 171–200.

Bibliography

Government Documents, Primary Sources

Best Jr., Richard A. "Intelligence Information: Need-to-Know vs. Need-to-Share." Congressional Research Service, Report No. R41848, June 6, 2011, http://www.fas.org/ sgp/crs/intel/R41848.pdf.

BP. *Deepwater Horizon: Accident Investigation Report*. September 8, 2010.

Buccella, Donna. "Border Security Threats to the Homeland: DHS' Response to Innovative Tactics and Techniques." Written testimony by the Assistant Commissioner of the U.S. Customs and Border Protection Office of Intelligence and Investigative Liaison before the House Committee on Homeland Security, Subcommittee on Border and Maritime Security, 112th Cong., 2nd Sess., June 15, 2012, http://www.dhs.gov/ news/2012/06/15/written-testimony-us-customs-border-protection-house-homeland-security-subcommittee.

California Emergency Management Agency. *Golden Guardian 2010: After Action Report Executive Summary*. N.d., http://bit.ly/13uUxkg.

Cellucci, Thomas A. "Innovative Public-Private Partnerships: Pathway to Effectively Solving Problems." U.S. Department of Homeland Security. July 2010.

———. "FutureTECH: Concept of Operations." U.S. Department of Homeland Security. N.d., http://www.dhs.gov/xlibrary/assets/st_commercialization_ office_futuretech_conops.pdf.

———. *Partnership Program Benefits Taxpayers as Well as Public and Private Sectors*. U.S. Department of Homeland Security. 2008.

Cellucci, Thomas A. and James W. Grove. *Leveraging Public-Private Partnership Models and the Free Market System to Increase Speed-of-Execution of High-Impact Solutions Throughout State and Local Governments*. U.S. Department of Homeland Security. August 2011.

Dingell, John D. "Protecting the Electrical Grid from Cybersecurity Threats." Testimony before the U.S. House of Representatives Committee on Energy and Commerce, Subcommittee on Energy and Air Quality, 110th Cong., 2nd Sess., September 11, 2008.

Diop, Adboulaye and David Hartman. "Customs-Trade Partnership against Terrorism Cost-Benefit Survey." U.S. Customs and Border Protection. August 2007, http://www.cbp.gov/linkhandler/cgov/trade/cargo_security/ctpat/what_ ctpat/ctpat_cost_survey.ctt/ctpat_cost_survey.pdf.

Dixon, Nancy M. and Laura A. McNamara. "Our Experience with Intellipedia: An Ethnographic Study at the Defense Intelligence Agency." Defense Intelligence Agency Laboratory Project, February 5, 2008, http://www.au.af.mil/au/awc/awcgate/sandia/dixon_mcnamara_intellipedia.pdf.

Fanguy, Maurine. Testimony of the Program Director, Transportation Security Administration, before the U.S. House of Representatives Committee on Homeland Security, Subcommittee on Border, Maritime, and Global Counterterrorism, Transportation Security Administration, September 27, 2008, http://www.tsa.gov/press/speeches/091708_fanguy_twic_depolyment_complete.shtm.

Farrell, Brenda S. Letter from the Director of Defense Capabilities and Management, U.S. Government Accountability Office, to U.S. Senators Daniel Akaka and George Voinovich. July 14, 2008, http://www.gao.gov/new.items/d08965r.pdf.

———. "Personnel Clearances: Key Factors for Reforming the Security Clearance Process." Statement for the U.S. Government Accountability Office. May 22, 2008, http://www.gao.gov/assets/130/120165.pdf.

Gates, Robert. "A Statement on Department Budget and Efficiencies." U.S. Department of Defense. January 6, 2011, http://www.defense.gov/speeches/speech.aspx?speechid=1527.

Grewe, Barbara A. "Legal Barriers to Information Sharing: The Erection of a Wall Between Intelligence and Law Enforcement Organizations." National Commission on Terrorist Attacks Upon the United States: Staff Monograph, August 20, 2004, http://www.fas.org/ irp/eprint/wall.pdf.

Homeland Security National Preparedness Task Force. "Civil Defense and Homeland Security: A Short History of National Preparedness Efforts." September 2006, http://training.fema.gov/EMIWeb/edu/docs/DHS%20Civil%20Defense-HS%20-%20Short%20History.pdf.

Hampton Roads Planning District Commission. "Committees." 2012, http://www.hrpdc.org/page/committees.

Martinez, Pablo A. "Cybercrime: Updating the Computer Fraud and Abuse Act to Protect Cyberspace and Combat Emerging Threats." Statement for the record of the Deputy Special Agent in Charge, Criminal Investigative Division, U.S. Secret Service, before the Senate Committee on the Judiciary, 112th Cong., 1st Sess., September 7, 2011, http://www.dhs.gov/news/2011/09/06/statement-record-usss-senate-committee-judiciary-hearing-titled-cybercrime-updating.

Massachusetts. Standards for the Protection of Personal Information of Residents of the Commonwealth. 201 CMR 17.00, 2010, http://www.mass.gov/ocabr/docs/idtheft/ 201cmr1700reg.pdf.

Minnesota Department of Transportation. "Interstate 35W Bridge in Minneapolis." 2012, http://projects.dot.state.mn.us/35wbridge/.

————. Interstate 35W Mississippi River Bridge, Minneapolis, Fact Sheet. October 16, 2007, http://www.dot.state.mn.us/i35wbridge/pdfs/factsheet.pdf.

————. "Interstate 35W Rebuild Plans." N.d., http://www.dot.state.mn.us/ i35wbridge/ rebuild/designbuild.html.

————. "The New I-35W Bridge." 2008, http://projects.dot.state.mn.us/ 35wbridge/.

Monke, Jim. *Agroterrorism: Threats and Preparedness*. Congressional Research Service, March 12, 2007, http://www.fas.org/sgp/crs/terror/RL32521.pdf.

National Commission on Terrorist Attacks Upon the United States, *The 9/11 Commission Report* (Full Report), 2004, http://govinfo.library.unt.edu/ 911/report/911Report.pdf.

National Commission on the BP Deepwater Horizon Oil Spill and Offshore Drilling. *Deep Water: The Gulf Oil Disaster and The Future of Offshore Drilling—Report to the President*, January 2011, http://www.oilspillcommission. gov/sites/default/files/documents/DEEPWATER_ReporttothePresident_ FINAL.pdf.

National Counterterrorism Center. "About the National Counterterrorism Center." N.d., http://www.nctc.gov/about_us/about_nctc.html.

National Institute of Standards and Technology. "The United States Government Configuration Baseline (USGCB)–Windows 7 Firewall Content." June 21, 2012, http://usgcb.nist.gov/usgcb/microsoft/download_win7firewall.html.

National Transportation Safety Board. *Collapse of I-35W Highway Bridge— Minneapolis, Minnesota, August 1, 2007*. November 14, 2008.

National Weather Service Weather Forecast Office (Springfield, MO). "Joplin Tornado Event Summary." May 21, 2012, http://www.crh.noaa.gov/ sgf/?n=event_2011may22_summary.

New York City Metropolitan Transportation Authority. "If You See Something, Say Something." N.d., http://web.mta.info/ mta/security.html.

New York Police Department. "NYPD Shield: About." 2006, http://www. nypdshield.org/ public/about.aspx.

New York (State). "Governor Cuomo Signs Law to Approve $50 Million in Additional Relief for Areas Devastated by Flooding." Press release, December 9, 2011, http://www.governor.ny.gov/press/120911_flooding_relief.

————. "New York State Responds: Hurricane Irene and Tropical Storm Lee: One Year Later." August 2012, http://www.governor.ny.gov/assets/documents/ Irene-Lee-One-Year-Report.pdf.

Office of Consolidated Emergency Management (Washington County, Oregon). "Regional Utility Coordination Plan." February 14, 2005, http://www.ocem. org/Plans/Regional_ Utility_Coord_Plan_ no_Tab_A.pdf.

Orszag, Peter R. "Homeland Security: The Problems With Providing Tax Incentives to Private Firms." Testimony before the House Committee on Small

Business, Subcommittee on Rural Enterprise, Agriculture, and Technology, 108th Cong., 2nd Sess., July 21, 2004.

Port of Los Angeles. "Homeland Security." 2012, http://www.portoflosangeles. org/security/homeland_security.asp.

Port of New Orleans. "History of the Harbor Police Department." March 11, 2005, http://www.portno.com/hpdhistory.htm.

Port Authority of New York and New Jersey. "LaGuardia Airport Facts and Information." 2012, http://www.panynj.gov/airports/lga-facts-info.html.

Port of Yokohama. "Port Security Officer of the Port of Oakland Visit (sic) the Port of Yokohama." 2012, http://www.city.yokohama.lg.jp/kowan/english/ interexchange/2012/20120604.html.

President's Commission on Critical Infrastructure Protection. *Critical Foundations: Protecting America's Infrastructures, Report of the President's Commission on Critical Infrastructure Protection.* 1997.

Smith, Douglas A. and Thomas A. Cellucci, eds. *Harnessing the Valuable Experience and Resources of the Private Sector for the Public Good: Innovative Public-Private Partnerships.* U.S. Department of Homeland Security, June 2010.

Stoneking, Dan. "Public Private Partnership Conference." FEMA Blog, Federal Emergency Management Agency. August 8, 2011, http://blog.fema.gov/2011/ 08/public-private-partnership-conference.html.

Travers, Russell. "Information Sharing, Dot Connecting and Intelligence Failures: Revisiting Conventional Wisdom." National Counterterrorism Center, August 2009, http://www.nctc.gov/docs/2009_Galileo_Award.pdf.

Upton, Harold F. *The Deepwater Horizon Oil Spill and the Gulf of Mexico Fishing Industry.* Congressional Research Service, 2011.

U.S. Central Intelligence Agency. "Intellipedia Celebrates Third Anniversary with a Successful Challenge." April 29, 2009, http://1.usa.gov/17c6xs.

U.S. Coast Guard. "National Maritime Security Advisory Committee." 2012, http://bit.ly/11ZiUce.

U.S. Congress. *Aviation and Transportation Security Act of 2001.* Public Law 107-71, http://www.gpo.gov/fdsys/pkg/PLAW-107publ71/html/PLAW-107publ71. htm.

———. *Federal Information Security Act (FISMA) of 2002.* Public Law 107-347, http://www.gpo.gov/fdsys/pkg/PLAW-107publ347/pdf/PLAW-107publ347.pdf.

———. *Fraud and Related Activity in Connection with Computers.* 18 U.S.C. § 1830, http://www.law.cornell.edu/uscode/text/18/1030.

———. *Passenger Manifests.* 49 U.S.C. § 44909, http://www.law.cornell.edu/ uscode/text/49/44909.

U.S. Customs and Border Protection. "C-TPAT Overview." December 13, 2007, http://www.cbp.gov/xp/cgov/trade/cargo_security/ctpat/what_ctpat/ctpat_ overview.xml.

———. "Things Commercial Carriers (i.e. Truckers) Should Know Before Transporting Cargo from Canada or Mexico into the United States." November 1, 2012, http://1.usa.gov/18phQiM.

U.S. Department of Agriculture. "Homeland Security-Overview." N.d., http://www.usda.gov/wps/portal/usda/usdahome?navid=HOMELANDSECU&navtype=CO.

U.S. Department of Defense. "Active Denial System Frequently Asked Questions." N.d., http://jnlwp.defense.gov/pressroom/faq_p2.html.

———. *Annual Report to Congress: Military and Security Developments Involving the People's Republic of China.* 2013, http://www.defense.gov/pubs/2013_china_report_final.pdf.

———. "DoD Antivirus PEO-MA/IA Tools." Defense Information Systems Agency, N.d., http://www.disa.mil/Services/Information-Assurance/HBS/Antivirus/Downloads-and-Resources.

U.S. Department of Energy. "Ronald William Pelton." N.d., http://www.hanford.gov/c.cfm/oci/ci_spy.cfm?dossier=118.

U.S. Department of Homeland Security. "CIPAC Working Groups by CIKR Sector." 2012, http://www.dhs.gov/cipac-working-groups-cikr-sector.

———. *Configuring and Managing Remote Access for Industrial Control Systems.* November 2010, http://www.hsdl.org/?view&did=7974.

———. "Council Members, Critical Infrastructure Partnership Advisory Council." 2012, http://www.dhs.gov/files/committees/editorial_0848.shtm.

———. "Critical Infrastructure." 2010, http://www.dhs.gov/files/programs/gc_1189168948944.shtm.

———. "Critical Infrastructure Partnership Advisory Council." 2012, http://www.dhs.gov/critical-infrastructure-partnership-advisory-council.

———. "Critical Infrastructure Sectors." N.d., http://www.dhs.gov/critical-infrastructure.

———. "Critical Infrastructure Sector Partnerships." 2011, http://www.dhs.gov/critical-infrastructure-sector-partnerships.

———. *Department of Homeland Security Information Sharing Strategy.* April 18, 2008, http://www.dhs.gov/xlibrary/assets/dhs_information_sharing_strategy.pdf.

———. "DHS Announces New Information-Sharing Tool to Help Fusion Centers Combat Terrorism." Press release, September 14, 2009, http://www.dhs.gov/news/2009/09/14/new-information-sharing-tool-fusion-centers-announced.

———. "DHS Highlights Two Cybersecurity Initiatives to Enhance Coordination with State and Local Governments and Private Sector Partners." November 18, 2010, http://www.dhs.gov/news/2010/11/18/dhs-highlights-two-cybersecurity-initiatives-enhance-coordination-state-and-local.

———. "Food, Agriculture, and Veterinary Defense Division." N.d., http://www. dhs.gov/xabout/structure/gc_1234195670177.shtm.

———. "FutureTECH." N.d., http://www.dhs.gov/ futuretech.

———. *FY 2012: Budget In Brief.* N.d., http://www.dhs.gov/xlibrary/assets/budget-bib-fy2012.pdf.

———. "Homeland Security Act of 2002." 2011, http://www.dhs.gov/xabout/laws/law_regulation_rule_0011.shtm.

———. "Homeland Security Information Network." N.d., http://www.dhs.gov/ homeland-security-information-network.

———. "Homeland Security Presidential Directive 7: Critical Infrastructure Identification, Prioritization, and Protection." 2008, http://www.dhs.gov/ xabout/laws/gc_ 1214597989952.shtm.

———. *Implementing 9/11 Commission Recommendations: Progress Report 2011.* 2011, http://www.dhs.gov/xlibrary/assets/implementing-9-11-commission-report-progress-2011.pdf.

———. *Information Sharing on Foreign Nationals: Border Security (Redacted).* Office of the Inspector General, OIG-12-39, February 2012.

———. *The Integrated Planning System.* January 2009, http://www.hlswatch.com/ wp-content/uploads/2009/01/dhs-integrated-planning-system-january-2009. pdf.

———. "Maritime Security in the Port of Houston." June 16, 2010, http://www. asishouston.org/ChapterNews/Speakers/061610_USCG_Speaker_Peresentati on.pdf

———. "Mature and Strengthen the Homeland Security Enterprise." March 14, 2011, http://www.dhs.gov/xabout/gc_1240838201772.shtm.

———. "Memorandum of Agreement Between the Department of Homeland Security and the Department of Defense Regarding Cybersecurity." September 2010, http://www.dhs.gov/xlibrary/assets/20101013-dod-dhs-cyber-moa. pdf.

———. "More About the Office of Infrastructure Protection." 2010, http://www.dhs. gov/xabout/structure/gc_1189775491423.shtm.

———. *National Infrastructure Advisory Council, Critical Infrastructure Resilience: Final Report and Recommendations.* September 8, 2009, http://www.dhs. gov/xlibrary/assets/niac/niac_critical_infrastructure_resilience.pdf.

———. "National Infrastructure Protection Plan: Maritime Transportation Mode." 2011, http://www.dhs.gov/xlibrary/assets/nppd/nppd-ip-maritime-snapshot-2011.pdf.

———. *National Response Framework.* Washington, DC, 2008.

———. *Quadrennial Homeland Security Review Report: A Strategic Framework for a Secure Homeland.* February 2010.

———. "SECURE (System Efficacy through Commercialization, Utilization, Relevance, and Evaluation) Program." N.d., http://www.dhs.gov/secure-system-efficacy-through-commercialization-utilization-relevance-and-evaluation-program.

———. "State and Urban Area Fusion Centers." N.d., http://www.dhs.gov/state-and-major-urban-area-fusion-centers.

———. "Transportation Systems Sector: Critical Infrastructure." N.d., http://www.dhs.gov/transportation-systems-sector.

U.S. Federal Bureau of Investigation. "2011 Request for Information on Tamerlan Tsarnaev from Foreign Government." April 19, 2013, http://www.fbi.gov/news/pressrel/press-releases/2011-request-for-information-on-tamerlan-tsarnaev-from-foreign-government.

———. "About InfraGard." 2012, http://www.infragard.net/about.php?mn=1&sm=1-0.

———. "Aldrich Hazen Ames." N.d., http://www.fbi.gov/about-us/history/famous-cases/aldrich-hazen-ames.

———. "The FBI's Business Alliance Initiative." N.d., http://www.fbi.gov/about-us/investigate/counterintelligence/us-business-1.

———. InfraGard Portal. 2012, http://www.infragard.net/.

———. Law Enforcement Online Portal. N.d., http://www.leo.gov/.

———. "New E-Scams and Warnings." N.d., http://www.fbi.gov/scams-safety/e-scams/.

———. "Robert Phillip Hannsen Espionage Case." February 20, 2001, http://www.fbi.gov/ about-us/history/famous-cases/robert-hanssen.

———. "Safety and Security for the Business Professional Traveling Abroad." N.d., http://www.fbi.gov/about-us/investigate/counterintelligence/business-brochure.

U.S. Federal Emergency Management Agency. "About Industry Liaison Program." 2010, http://www.fema.gov/privatesector/industry/about.shtm.

———. "FEMA Administrator: Business Community is Critical Partner in Disaster Response and Recovery." November 4, 2011, http://www.fema.gov/news/newsrelease.fema? id=59308.

———. "FEMA History." August 11, 2010, http://www.fema.gov/about/history.shtm.

———. Lessons Learned Information Sharing Portal. N.d., https://www.llis.dhs.gov/.

———. Louisiana Katrina/Rita Recovery." http://www.fema.gov/pdf/hazard/hurricane/2005katrina/la_progress_ report_0810.pdf.

———. *I-35W Bridge Collapse and Response: Minneapolis, Minnesota.* U.S. Fire Administration/Technical Report Series, August 2007.

———. "Make A Plan." June 11, 2013, http://www.ready.gov/make-a-plan.

———. *The Response to the 2011 Joplin, Missouri, Tornado: Lessons Learned Study*. December 20, 2011, http://1.usa.gov/143ey1r.

———. "The Private Sector in Disasters: An Introduction." Video, September 23, 2009, http://www.youtube.com/watch?v=PxvyZcgIYog.

———. "The Private Sector in Disasters: An Introduction." Transcript, N.d., http://www.fema.gov/medialibrary/media_records/1161/transcripts/1121.

U.S. Government Accountability Office. "Critical Infrastructure Critical Protection: Current Cyber Sector-Specific Planning Approach Needs Re-Assessment." September 2009.

———. "Critical Infrastructure Protection: Key Private and Public Cyber Expectations Need to Be Consistently Addressed." GAO-10-628, July 2010.

———. "Homeland Security: Actions Needed to Improve Response to Potential Terrorist Attacks and Natural Disasters Affecting Food and Agriculture." Report to the Chairman of the U.S. Senate Committee on Homeland Security and Governmental Affairs, Subcommittee on Oversight of Government Management, the Federal Workforce, and the District of Columbia, August 2011.

———. "Personnel Security Clearances: An Outcome-Focused Strategy Is Needed to Guide Implementation of the Reformed Clearance Process." May 2009, http://www.gao.gov/ new. items/d09488.pdf.

———. "Secure Border Initiative: DHS Needs to Strengthen Management and Oversight of Its Prime Contractor." GAO-11-6, October 2010, http://www.gao.gov/new.items/d116.pdf.

U.S. House Committee on Homeland Security, Subcommittee on Transportation Security. *Screening Partnership: Why Is A Job Creating, Public-Private Partnership Meeting Resistance at TSA?* 112th Cong., 1st sess., February 16, 2012.

U.S. Immigration and Customs Enforcement. "Underwear Bomber Umar Farouk Abdulmutallab Sentenced to Life." Press release, February 16, 2012, accessed October 5, 2012, http://www.ice.gov/news/releases/1202/120216detroit.htm.

U.S. Intelligence Community. "Our Strength Lies In Who We Are." N.d., http://www.intelligence.gov/about-the-intelligence-community/member-agencies.html.

U.S. Office of Management and Budget. "Fiscal Year 2012: Mid-Session Review – Budget of the U.S. Government." September 1, 2011, http://www.whitehouse.gov/sites/default/files/omb/budget/fy2012/assets/12msr.pdf.

———. Letter (with attachment) from Dionne Hardy, FOIA Officer to Steven Aftergood, Federation of American Scientists. May 20, 2011, http://www.fas.org/irp/dni/irtpa-2011.pdf.

U.S. Senate. Department of Homeland Security Appropriations Bill. Committee Reports, 112th Congress, Senate Report 112-074, 2012, http://thomas.loc.gov/cgi-bin/cpquery/?&sid=cp112YCOmu&r_n= sr074.112&dbname=cp112&&sel= TOC_56275&.

———. Senate Select Committee on Intelligence. "Attempted Terrorist Attack on Northwest Airlines Flight 253." May 24, 2010, http://www.intelligence.senate.gov/pdfs/111199.pdf.

U.S. Transportation Security Administration. "'Checkpoint Friendly' Laptop Bag Procedures." August 15, 2008, http://www.tsa.gov/press/happenings/simplifying_laptop_bag_procedures.shtm.

———. "Federal Port Security Credential Now Available Nationwide." September 17, 2008, http://www.tsa.gov/press/releases/2008/0917.shtm.

———. "Frequently Asked Questions: Transportation Worker Identification Credential." November 20, 2012, http://www.tsa.gov/stakeholders/frequently-asked-questions-0.

———. "Laptop Bags: Industry Process and Guidelines." July 29, 2008, http://www.tsa.gov/press/happenings/innovative_laptop_bag_designs.shtm.

———. "Program Information: Transportation Worker Identification Credential." October 15, 2012, http://www.tsa.gov/stakeholders/program-information.

———. "Screening Partnership Program." November 21, 2012, http://www.tsa.gov/stakeholders/screening-partnership-program.

———. "Transportation Worker Identification Credential." November 20, 2012, http://www.tsa.gov/stakeholders/transportation-worker-identification-credential-twic%C2%AE.

Van Wagenen, James S. "A Review of Congressional Oversight." Central Intelligence Agency, April 14, 2007, http://1.usa.gov/1boSseP.

Virginia Fusion Center. "7 Signs of Terrorism." 2007, http://www.vsp.state.va.us/FusionCenter/7-Signs.shtm.

White House. "Executive Order Establishing the Office of Homeland Security." October 8, 2001, http://georgewbush-whitehouse.archives.gov/news/releases/2001/10/20011008-2.html.

———. *National Cyber Incident Response Plan [Interim Version]*. Washington, DC, September 2010.

———. *National Disaster Recovery Framework*. Washington, DC, September 2011.

———. *National Incident Management System*. Washington, DC, 2008.

———. *National Infrastructure Protection Plan*. Washington, DC, 2009.

———. *National Security Strategy*. May 2010, http://www.whitehouse.gov/sites/default/files/rss_viewer/national_security_strategy.pdf.

———. *National Strategy for Information Sharing*. October 2007, http://www.fas.org/sgp/library/infoshare.pdf.

———. "Presidential Policy Directive—Critical Infrastructure Protection and Resilience." February 12, 2013, http://1.usa.gov/Wk7hbC.

News Sources

ABC News
Associated Press
BBC News
CBS News
Christian Science Monitor
CNN
The Denver Post
The Detroit News
The Guardian
The Huffington Post
Los Angeles Times
MSNBC
NBC News
The New York Times
NPR
Reuters
The Sydney Morning Herald
The Telegraph
Time
USA Today
The Wall Street Journal
The Washington Post

Journals, Books, Internet Resources

Abou-bakr, Ami Jihan. *Managing Disasters Through Public-Private Partnerships.* Washington, D.C.: Georgetown University Press, 2013.

Abou-Bakr, Ami Jihan. "Managing Disaster: Public-Private Partnerships as A Tool For Mitigation, Preparedness, Response & Resiliency in the United States." Ph.D. diss., King's College London, February 2011.

Aerovation. "Aerovation Products." N.d., http://aerovation.com/.

Alden, Edwin and Bryan Roberts. "Are U.S. Borders Secure?" *Foreign Affairs* 90, no. 4 (July 2011): 19–26.

Allen, Albert J., Albert E. Myles, Porfirio A. Fuentes, and Safdar Muhammad. "Agricultural Terrorism: Potential Economic Effects on the Poultry Industry in Mississippi." Paper presented at the Southern Agricultural Economics Association Annual Meeting, February 14–18, 2004, Tulsa, Oklahoma.

Allen, Craig. "As Joplin, Missouri Rebuilds, a Home Depot Store Reopens." *The Apron*, January 11, 2012, http://ext.homedepot.com/community/blog/tag/joplin.

All Hazards Consortium. "Critical Infrastructure Protection." 2012, http://www.ahcusa.org/criticalInfra.htm.

American Association of Port Authorities. "U.S. Waterborne Foreign Trade 2010: Ranking of U.S. Customs Districts by Volume of Cargo." November 23, 2011, http://bit.ly/1eEk3bM.

American Civil Liberties Union. "ACLU Backgrounder on Body Scanners and Virtual Strip Searches." January 8, 2012, http://www.aclu.org/technology-and-liberty/aclu-backgrounder-body-scanners-and-virtual-strip-searches.

American Red Cross. "Gulf Coast Beach Safety." June 21, 2010, http://rdcrss.org/cGyCoQ.

Andreoni, James. "Why Free Ride? Strategies and Learning in Public Goods Experiments." *Journal of Public Economics* 37, no. 3 (December 1988): 291–304.

Anti Phishing Working Group. "Anti Phishing Working Group (APWG) Public Education Initiative." N.d., http://education.apwg.org/index.html.

APPDS Maritime Security Ltd. "Anti-piracy Training Courses." N.d., 2012, http://www.appds-maritime-security.com/en/appds-maritime-services/anti-piracy-training-courses-en.

Apptis, Inc. "About Us." 2012, http://www.apptis.com/about/default.aspx.

Arehart, Mark. "Indexing Methods for Faster and More Effective Person Name Search." Proceedings of the 2010 Language Resources Evaluation Conference, 2010, http://www.lrec-conf.org/proceedings/lrec2010/pdf/166_Paper.pdf.

AS&E. Home Page. 2012, http://as-e.com/.

Asia Pacific Economic Cooperation. *Public-Private Partnerships and Disaster Resilience*. Report from the APEC Workshop on Public-Private Partnerships and Disaster Resilience, August 24–29, 2010, 2011, Bangkok, Thailand.

ASIS International Permanent Select Committee on Intelligence, Subcommittee on Intelligence Community Management. "Security Clearance Reform: Upgrading the Gateway to the National Security Community." September 25, 2008, http://www.asisonline.org/councils/documents/govt_secclearance.pdf.

Assaf, Dan. "Conceptualizing the Use of Public-private Partnerships as a Regulatory Arrangement in Critical Information Infrastructure Protection." In *Non-State Actors as Standard Setters,* edited by Anne Peters, Lucy Koechlin, Till Forster, and Greta Fenner Zinkernagel. New York, NY: Cambridge University Press, 2009.

Auerswald, Phillip, Lewis Branscomb, Todd La Porte, and Erwann Michel-Kerjan, eds. *Seeds of Disaster, Roots of Response: How Private Action Can Reduce Public Vulnerability*. New York, NY: Cambridge University Press, 2006.

Bain, Ben. "Information-sharing Platform Hacked." *Federal Computer Week*, May 13, 2009, http://fcw.com/articles/2009/05/13/web-dhs-hsin-intrusion-hack.aspx.

Bakir, Niyazi and Detlof Von Winterfeldt. "Is Better Nuclear Weapon Detection Capability Justified?" *Journal of Homeland Security and Emergency Management* 8, no. 1 (2011): Article 16.

Bakshi, Nitin, Stephen E. Flynn, and Noah Gans, "Estimating the Operational Impact of Container Inspections at International Ports." *Management Science* 57, no. 1 (January 2011): 1–20.

Bardach, Eugene. *Getting Agencies to Work Together: The Practice and Theory of Managerial Craftsmanship*. Washington, DC: Brookings Institution Press, 1998.

Bean, Hamilton. "Exploring the Relationship Between Homeland Security Information Sharing & Local Emergency Preparedness." *Homeland Security Affairs* 5, no. 2 (September 2009): 1–18.

Bean, Hamilton and Lisa Keränen. "The Role of Homeland Security Information Bulletins Within Emergency Management Organizations: A Case Study of Enactment." *Journal of Homeland Security and Emergency Management* 4, no. 2 (June 2007): Article 6.

Beauregard, Robert A. "Public-Private Partnerships as Historical Chameleons." In *Partnerships in Urban Governance: European and American Experience*, edited by Jon Pierre, 52–70. London: MacMillan Press, 1997.

Biesecker, Calvin. "Lockheed Martin Snares $70 Million TWIC Contract." *Security Info Watch*, February 5, 2007, http://www.securityinfowatch.com/news/10558983/lockheed-martin-snares-70-million-twic-contract.

Blanco, Ismael, Vivien Lowndes, and Lawrence Pranchett. "Policy Networks and Governance Networks: Towards Greater Conceptual Clarity." *Political Studies Review* 9, no. 3 (September 2011): 297–308.

Bonabeau, Eric and W. David Stephenson. "Expecting the Unexpected: The Need for a Networked Terrorism and Disaster Response Strategy." *Homeland Security Affairs* 3, no. 2 (February 2007): Article 3, 1–9.

Booz Allen Hamilton. "Homeland Security." 2012, http://www.boozallen.com/consultants/civilian-government/homeland-security-consulting.

Boyne, George. "Public and Private Management: What's the Difference?" *Journal of Management Studies* 39, no. 1 (2002): 97–122.

Brelsford, James F. "California Raises the Bar on Data Security and Privacy." *Findlaw*, March 26, 2008, http://corporate.findlaw.com/law-library/california-raises-the-bar-on-data-security-and-privacy.html.

Brown, Michelle and Judy Joffe. "The All-County Disaster Preparedness Team." *Risk Management Magazine* 54, no. 6 (June 2007): 8–9.

Bruijne, Mark de and Michel Van Eeten. "Systems That Should Have Failed: Critical Infrastructure Protection in an Institutionally Fragmented Environment." *Journal of Contingencies and Crisis Management* 15, no. 1 (March 2007): 18–29.

Busch, Nathan E. and Austen D. Givens. "Achieving Resilience in Disaster Management: The Role of Public-Private Partnerships." *Journal of Strategic Security*. 6, no. 2 (Summer 2013): 1–19.

———. "Public-Private Partnerships in Homeland Security: Opportunities and Challenges." *Homeland Security Affairs* 8, Art. 18 (October 2012): 1–24.

Butler Jr., John K. "Toward Understanding and Measuring Conditions of Trust: Evolution of a Conditions of Trust Inventory." *Journal of Management* 17, no. 3 (September 1991): 643–663.

Carlstrom, Gregg. "Senator: DHS Budget Begins 'Turnaround' Away from Contracting." *Federal Times*, February 24, 2010, http://www.federaltimes.com/article/20100224/CONGRESS03/2240304/1055/AGENCY.

Carter, Ashton B. "The Architecture of Government in the Face of Terrorism." *International Security* 26, no. 3 (Winter 2001–2002): 5–23.

Carucci, Dominic, David Overhuls, and Nicolas Soares. "Computer Crimes." *American Criminal Law Review* 48, no. 2 (Spring 2011): 375–419.

Cavelty, Myriam Dunn. "Cyber-Terror—Looming Threat or Phantom Menace? The Framing of the US Cyber-Threat Debate." *Journal of Information Technology & Politics* 4, no. 1 (2007): 19–36.

Cavelty, Myriam Dunn and Manuel Suter. Chamber of Commerce, Business Software Alliance, TechAmerica, Internet Security Alliance (ISA), and the Center for Democracy and Technology. "Improving Our Nation's Cybersecurity through the Public-Private Partnership: A White Paper." March 2011, https://www.cdt.org/files/pdfs/ 20110308_cbyersec_paper.pdf.

———. "Public-Private Partnerships Are No Silver Bullet: An Expanded Governance Model for Critical Infrastructure Protection." *International Journal of Critical Infrastructure Protection* 2, no. 4 (December 2009): 179–187.

CBS. "Face the Nation Transcripts April 28, 2013: Syria and Boston, Graham, McCaskill, and Chambliss." Transcript. April 28, 2013, http://cbsn.ws/12lzAXu.

Charette, Robert N. "Napolitano Cancels the US $1 billion SBINet Virtual Fence Project." *IEEE Spectrum*. March 2011, http://bit.ly/1ctDR5U.

Chase. "Fraudulent E-mail Examples." 2012, https://www.chase.com/index.jsp?pg_name=ccpmapp/privacy_security/fraud/page/fraud_examples.

ChicagoFIRST. "About Us." 2012, https://www.chicagofirst.org/about/ about_us.jsp.

Cisco. "US Department of Defense (DoD) Unified Capabilities (UC) Approved Products List (APL)." N.d., http://www.cisco.com/web/strategy/government/security_certification/net_business_benefit_secvpn_dod.html.

Claburn, Thomas. "Google's Gmail Blocks Phishers Sending Forged eBay, PayPal E-Mail." *Information Week Security*, July 8, 2008, http://www.informationweek.com/news/ security/client/208803181.

Clarke, Richard A. and Robert A. Knake. *Cyber War: The Next Threat to National Security and What To Do About It*. New York, NY: HarperCollins Publishers, 2010.

Closs, David J. and Edmund F. McGarrell. "Enhancing Security Throughout the Supply Chain." Special Report Series, IBM Center for the Business of Government, 2004.

Coles-Kemp, Lizzie and Marianthi Haridou. "Insider Threat and Information Security Management." In Christian Probst, Jeffrey Hunker, Dieter Gollman, Matt Bishop, eds., *Insider Threats in Cyber Security*. New York: Springer, 2010.

Comerio, Mary C. "Public Policy for Reducing Earthquake Risks: A US Perspective." *Building Research and Information* 32, no. 5 (Sept./Oct. 2005): 403–413.

Cone, Edward. "Crash Landing Ahead?" *Information Week*, January 12, 1998, http://www.informationweek.com/664/64iufaa.htm.

CRA. "Virginia Department of Emergency Management." 2011, http://www.cra-usa.net/ clients_case_studies/case_studies/vdem/.

Curry, Colleen. "6.4 Million Passwords Reportedly Stolen From LinkedIn Website." *ABC*, June 6, 2012, http://abcnews.go.com/US/linkedin-hacked-64-million-user-passwords-reportedly-leaked/story?id=16508728.

Dell. "How to Avoid Phishing Scams Through Fraudulent E-mails." October 20, 2010, http://dell.to/17J2PWR.

———. "Transforming the Federal Government for the Future." 2012, http://content.dell.com/us/en/fedgov/fed.aspx?c=us&l=en&s=fed&cs=RC974327&~ck=bt&redirect=1.

Denning, Peter J. "Hastily Formed Networks." *Communications of the ACM* 49, no. 4 (April 2006): 15–20.

Eckert, Sue E. "Protecting Critical Infrastructure: The Role of the Private Sector." In *Guns and Butter: The Political Economy of International Security*, edited by Peter Dombrowski. Boulder, CO: Lynne Rienner Publishers, Inc., 2005.

Facebook. "Active Facebook Phishing Warning! – Friends Posting Links to Your Wall Which Urge You to Watch a Video." February 26, 2011, http://www.facebook.com/note.php?note_id=191956910837067.

Farber, Oksana. "NYPD SHIELD—An Outstanding Achievement in Public/Private Cooperation for Public Safety." ASIS International, New York City Chapter, April 2, 2007, http://www.asisnyc.org/emergencymanagements/2007_04_02.htm.

Federal News Radio. "Resilience Becomes New Buzzword for Homeland Security Committee." January 12, 2010, http://www.federalnewsradio.com/88/1861889/Resilience-becomes-new-buzzword-for-homeland-security-committee.

Federation of American Scientists. "Intelligence Budget Data." N.d., http://www.fas.org/irp/budget/index.html.

FedEx. "Defending Against Fraud." 2012, http://www.fedex.com/us/security/prevent-fraud/index.html.

Feeney, Mary K. and Hal G. Rainey. "Personnel Flexibility and Red Tape in Public and Nonprofit Organizations: Distinctions Due to Institutional and Political Accountability." *Journal of Public Administration Research & Theory* 20, no. 4 (October 2010): 801–826.

Felson, Marcus and Rachel A. Boba. *Crime and Everyday Life: Fourth Edition.* Thousand Oaks, CA: Sage Publications, Inc., 2010.

Flynn, Stephen E. "The Brittle Superpower." In *Seeds of Disaster Roots of Response: How Private Action Can Reduce Public Vulnerability*, edited by Phillip Auerswald et al. New York, NY: Cambridge University Press, 2006.

———. *The Edge of Disaster.* New York, NY: Random House, Inc., 2007.

———. "Recalibrating Homeland Security." *Foreign Affairs* 90, no. 3 (May/June 2011): 130–140.

Flynn, Stephen E. and Daniel B. Prieto. "Neglected Defense: Mobilizing the Private Sector to Support Homeland Security." Council Special Report No. 13, Council on Foreign Relations, March 2006.

Foley, John. "FAA's New Flight Control System Has Security Holes: Researcher." *Information Week*, July 26, 2012, http://www.informationweek.com/security/government/faas-new-flight-control-system-has-secur/240004424.

Franco, Crystal, Eric Toner, Richard Waldhorn, Thomas Inglesby, and Tara O'Toole. "The National Disaster Medical System: Past, Present, and Suggestions for the Future." *Biosecurity and Bioterrorism: Biodefense Strategy, Practice, and Science* 5, no. 4 (December 2007): 319–326.

Frost, Thomas. M. "Border Related Corruption." *Trends in Organized Crime* 13 (September 2010): 179–183.

General Dynamics C4 Systems. "Homeland Security." 2012, http://www.gdc4s.com/content/detail.cfm?item=a96ae1cb-eb74-47d6-bffc-bc7ada51469a.

Gerencser, Marc, Jim Weinberg, and Don Vincent. *Port Security War Game: Implications for U.S. Supply Chains.* Booz Allen Hamilton. 2002, http://www.boozallen.com/media/file/Port_Security_War_Game.pdf.

Givens, Austen. "Deepwater Horizon Oil Spill Is An Ominous Sign for Critical Infrastructure's Future." *Emergency Management*, May 27, 2011, http://www.emergencymgmt.com/disaster/Deepwater-Horizon-Oil-Spill-Critical-Infrastructure-052711.html?page=1&.

Givens, Austen D. and Nathan E. Busch., "Information Sharing and Public-Private Partnerships: The Impact on Homeland Security." *Homeland Security Review.* 7, no. 2 (Summer 2013): 1–28.

——. "Integrating Federal Approaches to Post-Cyber Incident Mitigation." *Journal of Homeland Security and Emergency Management.* 10, no. 1 (July 2013): 1–28.

——. "Realizing the Promise of Public-Private Partnerships in Critical Infrastructure Protection." *International Journal of Critical Infrastructure Protection.* 6, no. 1 (March 2013): 39–50.

Glennon, Michael J. "State-level Cybersecurity." *Policy Review* 171 (February/March 2012): 85–102.

Goldsmith, Stephen and William D. Eggers. *Governing By Network: The New Shape of the Public Sector.* Washington, DC: Brookings Institution, 2004.

Gomez, Peter L. "Enhancing FBI Terrorism and Homeland Security Information Sharing with State, Local, and Tribal Agencies." Master's thesis, Naval Postgraduate School, September 2010.

Grillot, Suzette R., Rebecca J. Cruise, and Valerie J. D'Erman. "National and Global Efforts to Enhance Containerized Freight Security." *Journal of Homeland Security and Emergency Management* 6, no. 1 (July 2009): Article 51, 1–31.

Grimsey, Darrin and Mervyn K. Lewis. "Are Public Private Partnerships Value for Money? Evaluating Alternative Approaches and Comparing Academic and Practitioner Views." *Accounting Forum* 29, no. 4 (December 2005): 345–378.

Gross, Grant. "Sixth State Dept. Worker Pleads Guilty to Passport Snooping." *PC World*, August 26, 2009, http://www.pcworld.com/article/170864/sixth_state_dept_worker_pleads_guilty_to_passport_snooping.html.

——. "State Department Worker Sentenced for Passport Snooping." *Network World*, July 8, 2009, http://www.networkworld.com/news/2009/ 070809-state-department-worker-sentenced-for.html?page=1.

Guillermopuerto, Alma. "Mexico: Risking Life for Truth." *The New York Review of Books*, November 22, 2012, http://www.nybooks.com/articles/archives/2012/nov/22/mexico-risking-life-truth/?pagination=false.

Hardy, Keiran. "WWWMDs: Cyber-attacks Against Infrastructure in Domestic Anti-terror Laws." *Computer Law & Science Review* 27, no. 2 (April 2011): 152–161.

Haveman, Jon D., Ethan M. Jennings, Howard J. Shatz, and Greg C. Wright. "The Container Security Initiative and Ocean Container Threats." *Journal of Homeland Security and Emergency Management* 4, no. 1 (2007): 1–19.

Henderson, William. "How Much Does It Really Cost to Get a Security Clearance?" *Clearance Jobs*, August 7, 2011, http://bit.ly/1eEnZcv.

Herald-Tribune Media Group. "Time for National Catastrophe Fund." November 1, 2012, http://www.heraldtribune.com/emergencymanagement/20121101/OPINION/311019996.

Hill, Kashmir. "The Department of Homeland Security Wants All The Information It Has On You Accessible From One Place." *Forbes*, November 29, 2011, http://onforb.es/twWgpn.

Holmes, David, Samsun Kashfi, and Syed Uzair Aqeel. "Transliterated Arabic Name Search." Proceedings of the Third IASTED International Conference: Communications, Internet, and Information Technology, November 2004, http://uzair.nairang.org/wp-content/uploads/2006/10/433-175.pdf.

Homeland Security Institute. *Financing Recovery from Catastrophic Events: Final Report.* Homeland Security and Analysis Institute, March 30, 2007, http://recoverydiva.files.wordpress.com/2013/06/financing_recovery_hsi-2007.pdf.

Homeland Security Television. "Public-Private Partnerships for Homeland Security." Video, August 3, 2011, http://www.youtube.com/watch?v=ka6dgMxLrJI.

Hosenball, Mark. "What the CIA Did and Didn't Know About Alleged Underpants Bomber." *The Daily Beast*, December 30, 2009, http://www.thedailybeast.com/newsweek/blogs/declassified/2009/12/30/what-the-cia-did-and-didn-t-know-about-alleged-underpants-bomber.html.

Info Security. "DoD Works with Industry on Automated Network Intrusion Detection System." *Info Security*, March 21, 2011, http://www.infosecurity-magazine.com/view/16745/dod-works-with-industry-on-automated-network-intrusion-defense-system-/.

International Association of Chiefs of Police. *National Policy Summit: Building Private/Public Policing Partnerships to Prevent and Respond to Terrorism and Public Disorder—Vital Issues and Policy Recommendations.* 2004, https://www.theiacp.org/LinkClick.aspx?fileticket=UVc2ImxcWpQ%3D&tabid=938.

International Association of Emergency Managers. *Principles of Emergency Management Supplement.* September 11, 2007, http://www.iaem.com/documents/EMPrinciples 091107.pdf.

International Maritime Security Network LLC. Home Page. 2011, http://www.imsn.us/.

Isaac, R. Marc, James M. Walker, and Susan H. Thomas. "Divergent Evidence on Free Riding: An Experimental Examination of Possible Explanations." *Public Choice* 43, no. 2 (May 1984): 113–149.

Jackson, Joab. "A-Space Melds Social Media and Intelligence Gathering." *Government Computer News*, November 20, 2009, http://gcn.com/articles/2009/11/30/a-space-dia-intell-sharing-wiki.aspx.

Jaeger, Kai and Edward P. Stringham. "Private Policing Options for the Poor." National Center for Policy Analysis. December 15, 2011, http://www.ncpa.org/pub/ba763.

Johnsen, Stig and Mona Veen. "Risk Assessment and Resilience of Critical Communication Infrastructure in Railways." *Cognition, Technology & Work* 15, no. 1 (March 2013): 95–107.

Jones, Dale and Austen Givens. "Public Administration: The Central Discipline in Homeland Security." In *The Future of Public Administration, Public Management, and Public Service Around the World: The Minnowbrook Perspective*, edited by Rosemary O'Leary, David Van Slyke, and Soonhee Kim, 67–78. Washington, DC: Georgetown University Press, 2011.

Kapucu, Naim. "Collaborative Emergency Management: Better Community Organising, Better Public Preparedness and Response." *Disasters* 32, no. 2 (June 2008): 239–262.

———. "Interorganizational Coordination in Dynamic Context: Networks in Emergency Response Management." *Connections* 26, no. 2 (2005): 33–48.

———. "Non-Profit Response to Catastrophic Disasters." *Disaster Prevention and Management* 16, no. 4 (September 2007): 551–561.

———. "Public-Nonprofit Partnerships For Collective Action in Dynamic Contexts of Emergencies." *Public Administration* 84, no. 1 (March 2006): 205–220.

Kapucu, Naim, Maria-Elena Augustin, and Vener Garayev. "Interstate Partnerships in Emergency Management: Emergency Management Assistance Compact in Response to Catastrophic Disasters." *Public Administration Review* 69, no. 2 (March/April 2009): 297–313.

Kapucu, Naim and Montgomery Van Wart. "The Evolving Role of the Public Sector in Managing Catastrophic Disasters: Lessons Learned." *Administration & Society* 38, no. 3 (July 2006): 279–308.

Kapucu, Naim, Tolga Arslan, and Fatih Demiroz. "Collaborative Emergency Management and National Emergency Management Network." *Disaster Prevention and Management* 19, no. 4 (August 2010): 452–468.

Kemp, Tom. "Buckle Up With Cybersecurity...It's the Law." *Forbes*, February 1, 2012, http://www.forbes.com/sites/tomkemp/2012/02/01/buckle-up-with-cybersecurity-its-the-law/.

Keren, Michael and David Levhari. "The Optimum Span of Control in a Pure Hierarchy." *Management Science* 25, no. 11 (November 1979): 1162–1172.

Kettl, Donald F. "Managing Indirect Government." In *The Tools of Government: A Guide to the New Governance*, edited by Lester M. Salamon, 490–510. New York, NY: Oxford University Press, 2002.

Kilroy Jr., Richard J., Abelardo Rodriguez Sumano, and Todd S. Hataley. "Toward a New Trilateral Strategic Security Relationship: United States, Canada, and Mexico." *Journal of Strategic Security* 3, no. 1 (March 2010): 51–64.

Klijn, Erik Hans and Geert R. Teisman. "Governing Public-private Partnerships: Analysing and Managing the Processes and Institutional Characteristics of Public-private Partnerships." in *Public-Private Partnerships: Theory and Practice in International Perspective*, Stephen P. Osborne, ed. London, UK: Routledge, 2000.

Kowalski-Trakofler, Kathleen M., Charles Vaught, Michael R. Brinch Jr., and Jacqueline H. Jansky. "A Study of First Moments In Underground Mine Emergency Response." *Journal of Homeland Security and Emergency Management* 7, no. 1 (2010): Article 39, 1–28.

Laing, Keith. "TSA Approves Private Screeners for Orlando Airport." *The Hill*, June 11, 2012, http://thehill.com/blogs/transportation-report/tsa/232093-tsa-approves-private-screeners-for-orlando-airport.

Lavell, Marianne. "Can Hurricane Sandy Shed Light on Curbing Power Outages?" *National Geographic*, November 2, 2012, http://news.nationalgeographic.com/news/energy/2012/11/121102-hurricane-sandy-power-outages/.

Lawson, Sean. "Just How Big Is The Cyber Threat To The Department of Defense?" *Forbes*, June 4, 2010, http://www.forbes.com/sites/firewall/2010/06/04/just-how-big-is-the-cyber-threat-to-dod/.

Lee, Jolie. "Agencies Get Better at 'Whole of Government' Info Sharing." *Federal News Radio*, August 30, 2012, http://www.federalnewsradio.com/490/3014484/Agencies-get-better-at-whole-of-government-info-sharing.

Lemire, Jonathan. "Feds' Secretary to Oversee Response to Hurricane Sandy Vows Not to Let New York Down." *New York Daily News*, December 2, 2012, http://nydn.us/1cZJFlt.

Lennon, Mike. "Threat From Cyber Attacks Nearing Statistical Certainty." *SecurityWeek*, June 22, 2011, http://www.securityweek.com/threat-cyber-attacks-nearing-statistical-certainty/.

Le Toquin, Jean-Christophe. "Public-private Partnerships against Cybercrime." Organisation for Economic Co-Operation and Development, N.d., http://www.oecd.org/internet/consumerpolicy/42534994.pdf.

Lewis, James A. "Aux Armes, Citoyens: Cyber Security and Regulation in the United States." *Telecommunications Policy* 29, no. 11 (December 2005): 821–830.

Lewis, Ted G. and Rudy Darken. "Potholes and Detours in the Road to Critical Infrastructure Protection Policy." *Homeland Security Affairs* 1, no. 2 (Fall 2005): Art. 1, 1–11.

Lipowicz, Alice. "Boeing's SBINet Contract Gets the Axe." *Washington Technology*, January 14, 2011, http://bit.ly/143i1wP.

———. "New Border Strategy to Incorporate SBINet-like Capabilities." *Government Computer News*, March 18, 2011, http://bit.ly/13ewPxX.

Logisuite Corporation. "Automated Manifest System." 2012, http://www.logisuite. com/automated-manifest-system/.

Lohrmann, Dan. "5 Reasons Cybersecurity Should Be a Top Priority." *Governing.* December 2010, http://www.governing.com/topics/technology/five-reasons-why-cybersecurity-should-be-priority-public-officials.html.

Lopez, Brian. "Critical Infrastructure Protection in the United States since 1993." In *Seeds of Disaster, Roots of Response: How Private Action Can Reduce Public Vulnerability,* edited by Phillip Auerswald, 37–50. New York, NY: Cambridge University Press, 2006.

Losey, Stephen. "TSA Awards Contract for Information Technology Infrastructure." *Federal Times.* September 28, 2009, http://www.federaltimes.com/article/20110131/DEPARTMENTS03/101310303/1050/PERSONNEL04.

———."TSA Halts Expansion of Privatized Airport Screening." *Federal Times.* January 31, 2011, http://www.federaltimes.com/article/20110131/DEPARTMENTS03/101310303/1050/PERSONNEL04.

Loten, Angus. "Most Business Owners Unprepared for Natural Disasters." *Inc. Magazine,* April 24, 2006, http://www.inc.com/news/articles/200604/disaster.html.

Loveday, Eric. "Pentagon Deploys T3 Series Electric Three-wheeler for Perimeter Security." *Autoblog Green.* January 12, 2011, http://green.autoblog.com/2011/01/12/pentagon-t3-series-electric-three-wheeler-security/.

LRAD Corporation. "LRAD Product Overview." N.d., http://www.lradx.com/site/content/ view/15/110/.

Lynn III, William J. "Defending a New Domain." *Foreign Affairs* 89, no. 5 (September/October 2010): 97–108.

Madison, James. Federalist No. 45: "The Alleged Danger from the Powers of the Union to State Governments Considered for the Independent Fournal." Yale Law School: The Avalon Project, 2008. http://avalon.law.yale.edu/18th_century/fed45.asp.

Mandiant. *APT1: Exposing One of China's Cyber Espionage Units.* 2013, http://intelreport.mandiant.com/Mandiant _APT1_Report.pdf.

Maritime Security Council. Home Page. 2011, http://www.maritimesecurity.org/.

———. "MSC Leaders Speak at Global Futures Forum." September 2012, http://www.maritimesecurity.org/Press%20Releases/Global%20Futures%20Forum%20Release.10.3.2012.pdf.

———. "MSC Programs." 2009, http://www.maritimesecurity.org/program. html.

Matison, Katie Smith. "What's in the Box? An Overview of Domestic and International Developments in Port Security and Safe Carriage of Containerized Cargo." *Journal of Transportation Law, Logistics & Policy* 76, no. 3 (Third Quarter, 2009): 329–349.

McCreight, Robert. "Critical Challenge: Assessing Critical Infrastructure." *Homeland Defense Journal* 6, no. 5 (June 2008): 44–45.

McIntyre, Dave. "What Is Homeland Security? A Short Story." N.d., http://www.homelandsecurity.org/bulletin/ActionPlan_WhatIsHLS.htm.

McKinney, Roger. "Resource: FEMA Specialists on Hand at Home Depot." *The Joplin Globe*, July 1, 2011, http://www.joplinglobe.com/tornadoresources/x652255506/FEMA-specialists-on-hand-at-Home-Depot.

McManus, Susan A. and Kiki Caruson. "Emergency Management: Gauging the Extensiveness and Quality of Public and Private-Sector Collaboration at the Local Level." *Urban Affairs Review* 47, no. 2 (March 2011): 280–299.

McNicholas, Michael. *Maritime Security*. Burlington, MA: Elsevier, Inc., 2008.

McNiff, Jean and Jack Whitehead. *Action Research in Organisations*. London: Routledge, 2001.

Michaels, Jon D. "Deputizing Homeland Security." *Texas Law Review* 88, no. 7 (June 2010): 1435–1473.

Microsoft. "Microsoft in Government." 2012, http://www.microsoft.com/government/en-us/dod/pages/default.aspx.

———. "U.S. Coast Guard Expects to Save $1 Million Annually With Data Transmission Solution." N.d., http://www.judyb.com/coastguardcs.doc.

Naftali, Timothy. "Intelligence and National Security." Lecture given at the University of Virginia, Spring 2004, Charlottesville, VA.

Napolitano, Janet. Interviewed in "State of the Union with John King: Interview with Janet Napolitano." Transcript. *CNN*, December 27, 2009, http://transcripts.cnn.com/TRANSCRIPTS/0912/27/sotu.01.html.

National Council of ISACs. "About Us." 2012, http://www.isaccouncil.org/aboutus.html.

National Cyber Security Alliance. "Board Members." N.d., http://www.staysafeonline.org/about-us/board-members.

———. "National Cyber Security Awareness Month 2010 Results in Brief." January 14, 2011, http://www.staysafeonline.org/sites/default/files/resource_documents/NCSAM% 202010%20Short%20 Report 011411.docx.

National Solid Wastes Management Association and Waste Equipment Technology Association. "Solid Waste Industry There at Time of National Crisis." 2011, http://bit.ly/1eEoROl.

North American Retail Hardware Association. "Home Depot, Walmart to Give $1 Million to Joplin Relief Efforts." May 26, 2011, http://ace.nrha.org/v2/Hardware_Retailing/Emergencymanagement.aspx?slug=home-depot-walmart-to-give-1-million-to-joplin-relief-efforts.

Northrop Grumman. "Homeland Security." 2012, http://www.is.northropgrumman.com/by_solution/homeland_security/index.html.

Omer, Mayada, Roshanak Milchiani, and Ali Mostashari. "Measuring the Resilience of the Global Internet Infrastructure System." *IEEE International Systems Conference Proceedings*, 2009, 156-162.

Organisation for Economic Co-Operation and Development. *Security in Maritime Transport: Risk Factors and Economic Impact.* July 2003, http://www.oecd.org/sti/transport/maritimetransport/18521672.pdf.

Overby, Stephanie. "Comair's Christmas Disaster: Bound to Fail." *CIO*, May 1, 2005, http://www.cio.com/article/112103/Comair_s_Christmas_Disaster_Bound_To_Fail?page=1&taxonomyId=3206.

Oxford Analytica. "Drone Aircraft Market Surges in U.S." *Forbes*, July 30, 2009, http://www.forbes.com/2009/07/29/aircraft-drone-market-business-oxford-analytica.html.

Panasci, Robert. "New York State's Competitive Market for Electricity Generation: An Overview." *Albany Law Environmental Outlook Journal* 6 (2001): 25–32.

Pape, Robert A. *Dying to Win: The Strategic Logic of Suicide Terrorism.* New York, NY: Random House, 2005.

Park, Ji Young. "The Economic Impacts of Dirty Bomb Attacks on the Los Angeles and Long Beach Ports: Applying the Supply-Driven National Interstate Economic Model." *Journal of Homeland Security and Emergency Management* 5, no. 1 (May 2008): Art. 21, 1–20.

Parker, David and Keith Hartley. "Transaction Costs, Relational Contracting and Public Private Partnerships: A Case Study of UK Defence." *Journal of Purchasing and Supply Management* 9, no. 3 (May 2003): 97–108.

Pate, Antony, Bruce Taylor, and Bruce Kubu. *Protecting America's Ports: Promising Practices.* Police Executive Research Forum, November 20, 2007.

Pattak, Paul Byron. Comments in a panel on "Public-Private Sector Information Sharing." Symposium on Homeland Security, July 19–20, 2012, Christopher Newport University, Newport News, VA, http://www.symposiumonhomelandsecurity.com/Panel3.html.

PBS. "Store Wars: When Wal-Mart Comes to Town." N.d., http://www.pbs.org/itvs/storewars/stores3.html.

Permann, May, Jon Hammer, Kathy Lee, and Ken Rohde. "Mitigations for Security Vulnerabilities Found in Control System Networks." Presentation at the 16th Annual Joint Instrumentation, Systems, and Automation Society POWID/EPRI Controls and Instrumentation Conference, 2006.

Peterson, Danny and Richard Besserman. "Analysis of Informal Networking in Emergency Management." *Journal of Homeland Security and Emergency Management* 7, no. 1 (2010): Article 62, 1–14.

Pfeifer, Joseph W. "Network Fusion: Information and Intelligence Sharing for a Networked World." *Homeland Security Affairs* 8 (October 2012): Art. 17, 1–19.

Pittman, Elaine. "What Big-Box Retailers Can Teach Government About Disaster Recovery." *Government Technology*. November 28, 2011, http://www.govtech.com/policy-management/Big-Box-Retailers-Teach-Disaster-Recovery.html.

Plecas, Darryl, Amanda V. McCormick, Jason Levine, Patrick Neal, and Irwin M. Cohen. "Evidence-based Information Sharing Solution Between Law Enforcement Agencies." *Policing: An International Journal of Police Strategies and Management* 34, no. 1 (2011): 120–134.

Pondy, Louis R. "Organizational Conflict: Concepts and Models." *Administrative Science Quarterly* 12, no. 12 (September 1967): 296–320.

Popkin, Jim. "Robert Soloway Exits Prison, Disavows 'Spam King' Ways." *Wired*, March 3, 2011, http://www.wired.com/business/2011/03/spam-king-robert-soloway/.

Poulsen, Kevin. "Former Teen Hacker's Suicide Linked to TJX Probe." *Wired*, July 9, 2009, http://www.wired.com/threatlevel/2009/07/hacker/.

Pound, Edward T. "Security Clearance Challenges Defy Easy Fixes." *Government Executive*, August 14, 2007, http://bit.ly/1cZKWJe.

Prichard, Janet J. and Laurie E. MacDonald. "Cyber Terrorism: A Study of the Extent of Coverage in Computer Security Textbooks." *Journal of Information Technology Education* 3 (2004): 279–289.

Priest, Dana and William M. Arkin. *Top Secret America: The Rise of the New American Security State*. New York, NY: Little, Brown and Company, 2011.

Prieto, Daniel. "Information Sharing With the Private Sector." In *Seeds of Disaster, Roots of Response: How Private Action Can Reduce Public Vulnerability*, edited by Phillip Auerswald, 404–428. New York, NY: Cambridge University Press, 2006.

Prizzia, Ross. "Coordinating Disaster Prevention and Management in Hawaii." *Disaster Prevention and Management* 15, no. 2 (March 2006): 275–285.

Proctor, Edward. "Spelling and Searching the Internet: An Overlooked Problem." *Journal of Academic Librarianship* 28, no. 5 (September 2002): 297–305.

Provan, Keith G. and Patrick Kenis. "Modes of Network Governance: Structure, Management, and Effectiveness." *Journal of Public Administration Research and Theory* 18, no. 2 (April 2008): 229–252.

Radio Free Europe. "What Is 'Anonymous' And How Does It Operate?" February 29, 2012, http://www.rferl.org/content/explainer_what_is_anonymous_and_how_does_it_operate/24500381.html.

Ramasastry, Anita. "Lost in Translation – Data Mining, National Security and the Adverse Inference Problem." *Santa Clara Computer & High Technology Law Journal* 22, no. 4 (January 2006): 757–796.

Raths, David. "Working Together." *Emergency Management*. May/June 2010, 29–34.

Raytheon. "Raytheon Homeland Security." 2011, http://www.raytheon.com/capabilities/homeland/.

———. "Raytheon Produces Active Denial and Other Directed Energy Solutions." 2008, http://www.raytheon.com/newsroom/feature/ads_03-08/.

Regan, Bonnie L. *Enhancing Emergency Preparedness and Response: Partnering with the Private Business Sector.* Thesis, Naval Postgraduate School, December 2009.

Restorethegulf.gov. "Technical Assistance: Guide to Private/Non-profit Programs." 2012, http://www.restorethegulf.gov/node/4621#redcross.

Rhodes, R.A.W. "The Hollowing Out of the State: The Changing Nature of the Public Service in Britain." *The Political Quarterly* 65, no. 2 (April/June 1994): 138–151.

Rid, Thomas. "Cyber War Will Not Take Place." *Journal of Strategic Studies* 35, no. 1 (February 2012): 5–32.

Rittel, Horst W.J. and Melvin Webber. "Dilemmas in a General Theory of Planning." *Policy Sciences* 4, no. 2 (June 1973): 155–169.

Robinson, Scott E. and Benjamin S. Gaddis. "Seeing Past Parallel Play: Measures of Collaboration in Disaster Situations." *The Policy Studies Journal* 40, no. 2 (May 2012): 256–273.

Rosenau, Pauline V., ed. *Public-Private Policy Partnerships.* Cambridge, MA: MIT Press, 2000.

Rubin, Courtney. "Why You Should Stop Reading This and Go Get A Data Backup Plan." *Inc. Magazine*, September 15, 2011, http://www.inc.com/news/articles/201109/small-businesses-unprepared-for-data-disaster.html.

Rundle, Elaine. "Port Security Improves with Nonintrusive Cargo Inspection and Secure Port Access." *Emergency Management*, July 28, 2009, http://www.emergencymgmt.com/infrastructure/Port-Security-Improves-With.html.

Safety4Sea. "Cargo Ship Hijacked at Port." *Safety4Sea*, November 1, 2012, http://www.safety4sea.com/page/13783/4/cargo-ship-hijacked-at-port.

SAIC. "Borders and Transportation Security." 2012, http://www.saic.com/natsec/homeland-security/border-security.html.

———. "Homeland Security." 2012, http://www.saic.com/natsec/homeland-security/.

Sales, Nathan Alexander. "Mending Walls: Information Sharing After the USA PATRIOT Act." *Texas Law Review* 88, no. 7 (June 2010): 1795–1854.

Sasso, Brendan. "After Defeat of Senate Cybersecurity Bill, Obama Weighs Executive-order Option." *The Hill*, August 4, 2012, http://thehill.com/blogs/hillicon-valley/technology/242227-with-defeat-of-cybersecurity-bill-obama-weighs-executive-order-option.

Savas, Emanuel S. *Privatization and Public-Private Partnerships.* New York, NY: Chatham House Publishers, 2000.

——. "Privatization and the New Public Management." *Fordham Urban Law Journal* 28, no. 5 (June 2001): 1731–1737.

Schaeffer, Peter V. and Scott Loveridge. "Toward an Understanding of Types of Public-Private Cooperation." *Public Performance & Management Review* 26, no. 2 (December 2002): 169–189.

Schneier, Bruce. *Beyond Fear: Thinking Sensibly About Security In an Uncertain World.* New York, NY: Copernicus Books, 2003.

Security Magazine. "Most Americans Unprepared for Disasters." *Security Magazine,* March 1, 2012, http://www.securitymagazine.com/articles/82813-most-americans-unprepared-for-disasters-.

Security Today. "ASIS Awards NYPD Shield for Excellence in Public Private Partnership at Orlando Convention." July 28, 2011, http://bit.ly/13SNIgb.

Sequiera, Sandra and Simeon Djankov. "Trade Costs and Corruption in Ports." *Port Technology International,* March 8, 2012, http://www.porttechnology.org/images/uploads/technical_papers/PTI-12.pdf.

Sheffi, Yossi. "Supply Chain Management Under the Threat of International Terrorism." *International Journal of Logistics Management* 12, no. 2 (January 2001): 1–11.

Singer, P.W. *Corporate Warriors: The Rise of the Privatized Military Industry.* Ithaca, NY: Cornell University Press, 2003.

Smith, Tony. "Hacker Jailed for Revenge Sewage Attacks." *The Register,* October 31, 2001, http://www.theregister.co.uk/2001/10/31/hacker_jailed_for_revenge_sewage/.

Someren, Marten van, Niels Netten, Vanessa Evers, Henriette Cramer, Robert de Hoog, and Guido Bruinsma. "A Trainable Information Distribution System to Support Crisis Management." *Proceedings of the Second International IS-CRAM Conference,* April 2005, Brussels, Belgium.

Steinmetz, Todd. "Mitigating the Exploitation of U.S. Borders by Jihadists and Criminal Organizations." *Journal of Strategic Security* 4, no. 3 (Fall 2011): 29–48.

Stewart, Geoffrey T., Ramesh Kolluru, and Mark Smith. "Leveraging Public-Private Partnerships to Improve Resilience in Times of Disaster." *International Journal of Physical Distribution and Logistics Management* 39, no. 5 (2009): 343–364.

Stewart, Mark G. and John Mueller. "Cost-Benefit Analysis of Advanced Imaging Technology Full Body Scanners for Airline Passenger Security Screening." *Journal of Homeland Security and Emergency Management* 8, no. 1 (2011): Art. 30, 1–18.

Stivers, Camilla. "'So Poor and So Black': Hurricane Katrina, Public Administration, and the Issue of Race." *Public Administration Review* 67, no. 1 (Special Issue, December 2007): 48–56.

Stockton, Peter. "Nuclear Power Plant Security: Voices From Inside the Fences." *Project on Government Oversight*. September 12, 2002, http://www.pogo.org/our-work/reports/2002/nss-npp-20020912.html.

Stone, Charles A. and Anne Zissu. "Registered Traveler Program: The Financial Value of Registering the Good Guys." *Review of Policy Research* 24, no. 5 (September 2007): 443–462.

Stovall, S. Shane. "Public-Private Partnerships in the 21st Century." IAEM. N.d., http://www.iaem.com/committees/publicprivate/.../PPPinthe21st Century.pdf.

Straw, Joseph. "Intelligence Sharing Improves." *Security Management*, N.d., http://www.securitymanagement.com/article/intelligence-sharing-improves.

———. "New Views On Airport Screening." N.d., *Security Management*, http://www.securitymanagement.com/article/new-views-airport-screening-004586?page=0%2C1.

Strickland, Cooper J. "Regulation Without Agency: A Practical Response to Private Policing in United States v. Day." *North Carolina Law Review* 89 (2011): 1338–1363.

Suburban Emergency Management Project. "History of Federal Domestic Disaster Aid Before the Civil War." July 24, 2006, http://www.semp.us/publications/biot_reader.php?BiotID=379.

Szyliowicz, Joseph S. "Aviation Security: Promise or Reality?" *Studies in Conflict and Terrorism* 27 (June 2004): 47–63.

Tactical Intelligence International. "Maritime Security." N.d., http://www.tacticalintel.com/maritime-security.html.

Tanase, Matthew. "IP Spoofing: An Introduction." *Symantec*, November 2, 2010, http://www.symantec.com/connect/articles/ip-spoofing-introduction.

Taser. "About Taser." 2012, http://www.taser.com/about-taser.

Tek84 Engineering Group. "Body Scanner." N.d., http://www.tek84.com/bodyscanner.html.

Terry, Sue Mi. "How to Prevent the Next Edward Snowden." *Foreign Affairs*. June 17, 2013, http://www.foreignaffairs.com/articles/139516/sue-mi-terry/how-to-prevent-the-next-edward-snowden.

Thibault, Marc, Mary R. Brooks, and Kenneth J. Button. "The Response of the U.S. Maritime Industry to the New Container Security Initiatives." *Transportation Journal* 45, no. 1 (Winter 2006): 5–15.

Thomas, Rachel Nyswander. "Securing Cyberspace Through Public Private Partnership: A Comparative Analysis of Partnership Models." Master's thesis, Georgetown University, 2012.

Thomson, Ann Marie, James L. Perry, and Theodore K. Miller. "Conceptualizing and Measuring Collaboration." *Journal of Public Administration Research and Theory* 19, no. 1 (January 2009): 23–56.

Thurber, Matt. "Hackers, FAA Disagree Over ADS-B Vulnerability." *AIN Online*, August 21, 2012, http://www.ainonline.com/aviation-news/ainalerts/2012-08-21/hackers-faa-disagree-over-ads-b-vulnerability.

Trojan Securities. "Maritime Security." 2012, http://www.trojansecurities.com/trojan-maritime-security.html.

Tyler, Tom R. *Why People Cooperate: The Role of Social Motivations*. Princeton, NJ: Princeton University Press, 2011.

Verizon. "World Trade Center—A Year Later." 2012, http://newscenter.verizon.com/kit/ wtc2/.

Viana, Liza Porteus. "Best Practices Half a World Away." *HSToday*, March 2009.

Walmart. "Media Information: Wal-Mart's Response to Hurricane Katrina." N.d., http://news.walmart.com/news-archive/2005/09/04/media-information-wal-marts-response-to-hurricane-katrina.

Wardell, Jane and Jennifer Quinn. "Big Oil Criticizes Obama's Drilling Ban." *Chem.Info*, June 22, 2010, http://www.chem.info/News/2010/06/Plant-Operations-Big-Oil-Criticizes-Obamas-Drilling-Ban/.

Waugh, Jr., William L. "Terrorism, Homeland Security, and the National Emergency Management Network." *Public Organization Review* 3 (December 2003): 373–385.

Waugh, William L. and Gregory Streib. "Collaboration and Leadership for Effective Emergency Management." *Public Administration Review* 66, no. S1 (2006): 131–140.

Whitehead, Jack and Jean McNiff. *Action Research: Living Theory*. Thousand Oaks, CA: Sage Publications, Inc., 2006.

Wigginton, Michael P. and Carl J. Jensen. "The Texas Border Sheriff's Coalition: An Analysis of Policing Along the U.S.-Mexican Border." *Homeland Security Review* 6, no. 1 (Winter 2012): 35–59.

Wildavsky, Aaron. "Riskless Society." *The Concise Encyclopedia of Economics*. 2002, http://www.econlib.org/library/Enc1/RisklessSociety.html.

Willis, Henry H., Genevieve Lester, and Gregory F. Treverton. "Information Sharing for Infrastructure Risk Management: Barriers and Solutions." *Intelligence and Security* 24, no. 3 (June 2009): 339–365.

Winkowski, Thomas S. "Day Two Keynote Speech." Speech given at the Symposium on Homeland Security, July 19–20, 2012, Christopher Newport University, Newport News, VA, http://www.symposiumonhomelandsecurity.com/Day2PostLunchKeynote.html.

Woodin, Debby. "Texas Firm Could Guide Joplin's Tornado Recovery." *The Joplin Globe*, March 27, 2012, http://bit.ly/14DJ98Y.

Worboys, Katherine J. "Recent Research from *Lessons Learned Information Sharing*: The Importance of Partnerships in the Rural Water Response to

Hurricane Katrina." *Journal of Environmental Health* 69, no. 2 (September 2006): 31–33.

Worthen, Ben. "How Wal-Mart Beat Feds to New Orleans." *CIO*, November 1, 2005, http://www.cio.com/emergencymanagement/13532/How_Wal_Mart_Beat_Feds_to_New_Orleans.

Wright, Candice L. "Bridging the Gap in Port Security: Network-Centric Theory Applied to Public/Private Collaboration." Master's thesis, Naval Postgraduate School, 2007.

WZZM 13. "Montcalm County Gets Homeland Security Snow Cone Machine." *WZZM 13*, December 5, 2011, http://www.wzzm13.com/news/article/188877/14/Montcalm-County-gets-homeland-security-snow-cone-machine.

Zetter, Kim. "$74 Million Scareware Ring Raided." *Wired*, June 23, 2011, http://www.wired.com/threatlevel/2011/06/scareware-raid/.

Index

TERRORISM STUDIES

Lori J. Underwood
General Editor

The Terrorism Studies series is intended to promote a deeper understanding of the root causes of and potential solutions to the global issues related to terrorism. The series welcomes publications of scholars who specialize in social and political philosophy, ethics, religious studies, political theory, and political science. Those scholars with other disciplinary expertise are welcome to submit proposals as well. Contributions to the series may deal with particular, narrow-range problems and/or synthetic, interdisciplinary issues related to the issue of terrorism. Likewise, the publications may refer to both systematic problems and more practical considerations. Especially welcome are scholarly works that deal with the subject of terrorism in new and innovative ways. This series welcomes both individually authored and collaboratively authored books and monographs as well as conference proceedings and edited collections of essays.

For additional information about the series or for the submission of manuscripts, please contact:

Peter Lang Publishing, Inc.
Acquisitions Department
29 Broadway, 18th floor
New York, NY 10006

To order other books in this series, please contact our Customer Service Department at:

(800) 770-LANG (within the U.S.)
(212) 647-7706 (outside the U.S.)
(212) 647-7707 FAX

Or browse online by series at:

WWW.PETERLANG.COM